JULIA MORGAN

JULIA MORGAN

THE ROAD TO SAN SIMEON

Visionary Architect
of the California Renaissance

LAGUNA ART MUSEUM   *Rizzoli* Electa

PREFACE

You might be surprised to learn how many exhibitions and art history books got their start from unlikely—even unpromising—personal experiences. In the early 1960s, my parents took our family on a vacation up the California coast, motoring from L.A. to San Francisco. Hearst Castle was the halfway point. Open to the public since 1958, it still had fresh novelty, and that put it on our itinerary. As a junior high schooler with timid "artistic interests," I experienced William Randolph Hearst's hilltop architectural ensemble as a visual and spatial avalanche. It didn't help matters that the tour guides' gossipy patter told us nothing about the Castle's architect, the historical styles of the complex, or the circumstances contributing to its design and construction. Worse, I got carsick from the vertiginous journey back to the parking lot below.

Years later, when I was a graduate student in UCLA's art history program and the deadline for submitting my master's thesis drew nigh, I found myself forced to reckon with architecture as an art form. In order to demonstrate my argument about the cultural significance of Late Roman villas (ca. 250–450 C.E.), I had to examine the social position of their builders—the aristocratic *domini* of vast tracts of lands (*latifundia*) their rural mansions surveyed. In short, I needed to convince my thesis committee that these grand pleasure domes with their expanses of pictorial mosaic floorings, colorful murals, marble statuary, fountains, garden courts, columned reception halls, heated bath complexes, and lavish furnishings employed an array of aesthetic means to convey their owners' high position in Roman society. This meant I had to say something new about the famous Villa Romana del Casale near Piazza Armerina, Sicily.[1]

While analyzing this sprawling villa complex room by room, I found that my memories of Hearst Castle vividly returned. With sudden clarity, it became obvious that the palatial Sicilian villa purported to have belonged to the fourth-century imperial consul and urban prefect of Rome, Lucius Aradius Valerius Proculus, had an awful lot in common with media mogul William Randolph Hearst's architectural ensemble, which he called La Cuesta Encantada (The Enchanted Ridge). Further driving home the link to antiquity at this time was my year as a student intern at the Getty Villa Museum in Malibu. This provided me a daily physical encounter with a re-created Roman villa—walking along its outer peristyle and gardens, traversing the length of its statuary-adorned pool, and convening tour groups in its two-story colonnaded court.[2]

Years later, as an art historian, teacher, and exhibition and collections curator, I relocated from the Midwest to Atascadero, California, a semi-rural town of some 25,000 in northern San Luis Obispo County founded as a planned community in 1913. Exploring our town's historic core, I had a startling déjà vu moment when I first saw our majestic 1918 classicist city hall (FIG. 1 and FIG. 2). Who was the architect channeling the High Renaissance Vicenza/Venice designer Andrea Palladio (1508–1580) and why (FIG. 3)?

It was Walter Danforth Bliss (1874–1956) of San Francisco's Bliss and Faville, who I learned was one of the most highly regarded "artistic architects" in early twentieth-century California. After first drafting for Boston's McKim, Mead & White, America's foremost designers of Beaux-Arts, or classicist, buildings, Bliss and William Baker Faville (1866–1946) relocated to California in 1898. (In addition to the Atascadero city hall, Bliss and Faville designed numerous civic and commercial buildings in the Bay Area, as well as for the Panama-Pacific International Exposition.) Marked by French architectural principles applied with a nod to historical precedent, eclectic classicism is the hallmark of America's Beaux-Arts era, which lasted from circa 1870 to circa 1930 and coincided with the overarching cultural aspirations of the American Renaissance (1876 to 1919). Surely, I thought, there were more California architects from this era who were trained in and worked in historicist styles. My search led me to, among others, Albert Pissis, A. Page Brown, Bernard Maybeck, John Galen Howard, Arthur Brown Jr.—and Julia Morgan, the designer of Hearst Castle. All had been trained in academic classicism at the École des Beaux-Arts, Paris.

Residing in Atascadero also meant that Hearst Castle was a convenient thirty-seven miles up the coast. I made my first visit in forty-five years, whereupon I learned from former director Hoyt Fields that among its holdings were some 9,000 drawings by Morgan and her studio for Hearst Castle executed during various phases of its design. A mere handful had been exhibited—and those infrequently, and never in an art museum survey.

My curiosity led me to other important Morgan holdings. Even more conveniently, Cal Poly San Luis Obispo's Kennedy Library—just twenty miles south—possessed a significant trove of Morgan drawings and materials. I completed my trifecta with a visit to the University of California, Berkeley's Environmental Design Archives within the College of Environmental Design, another major repository of Morgan's work. (The archives also contain drawings by Maybeck and Howard.)

As my research progressed, I realized that much remains to be known about the art and architecture of the American Renaissance. Julia Morgan professionally came of age during its heyday, spanning from America's centennial to the onset of the Jazz Age. Even after Morgan received belated recognition for her singular role in California architecture in the 1980s, her legacy was confined under the honorific rubric of "pioneering woman architect," minimizing her contributions among her contemporaries—the Bay Area's community of Beaux-Arts trained architects. Further, she is often overshadowed by her larger-than-life patron, William Randolph Hearst, who was actually her collaborator on a number of projects.

And then there is Hearst Castle itself. Reimagined as the fictional Xanadu in Orson Welles's classic but disapproving film *Citizen Kane*, the state monument tends to be perceived by the public as a sensational roadside attraction instead of what it really is: an eclectic twentieth-century expression of the Spanish Mediterranean Renaissance combining indoor and outdoor neoclassical pools. Viewed historically, Hearst Castle easily compares to its near contemporary cousins—the art-filled Gilded Age mansions of the Fricks, Astors, Bostwicks, and Vanderbilts.

This publication advances our understanding of Julia Morgan's role in designing Hearst Castle while examining its meaning for its patron and his era. It also treats for the first time Morgan's earlier designs of the Italian Renaissance–style Oakland YWCA and the Mission Revival/Spanish Colonial Los Angeles Herald Examiner Building. Deepening the viewer and reader's understanding of late nineteenth- and early twentieth-century California architecture, this project surveys the changing cultural environment in the Bay Area that aided the ascendance of Beaux-Arts trained architects and encouraged the commissioning of their buildings. Further, to understand Beaux-Arts training in theory and practice, the reader will be taken through the École curriculum (methods, theories, competitions, and ateliers), which American students like Morgan had to complete in order to be awarded the coveted *diplôme*. In addition, employing gender studies analyses, we learn of Morgan's network of personal alliances, tactics, and strategies as a woman shaping a successful career in a discipline largely ruled by male exclusivity. For too long, both Morgan and her times have been given short shrift by modernist partisans—relegated to a way station in art history preceding the inevitable triumph of a "more enlightened" art and architecture that followed. With *Julia Morgan, The Road to San Simeon*, a diminutive and self-effacing artist and the vibrant, aspirational culture of California's Progressive Era are at last given the attention they fully deserve.

GORDON L. FUGLIE
Editor and Project Organizer

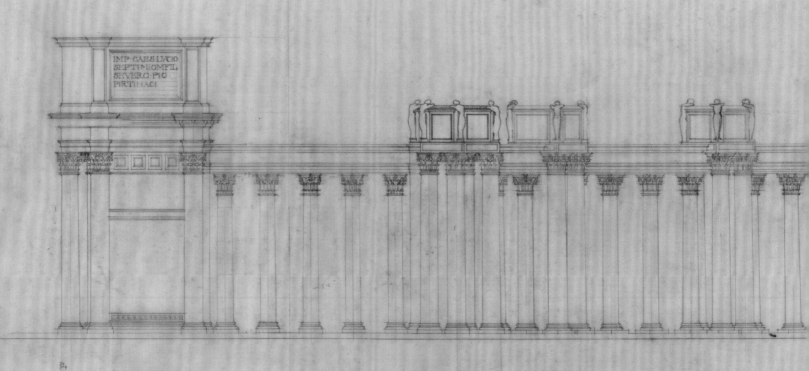

INP·CAES·LVCIO
SEPTIMIO·MPFIL
SEVERO·PIO
PERTINACI

Elevation of the Entrance towards West · Front Elevation of Colonade ·

Introduction

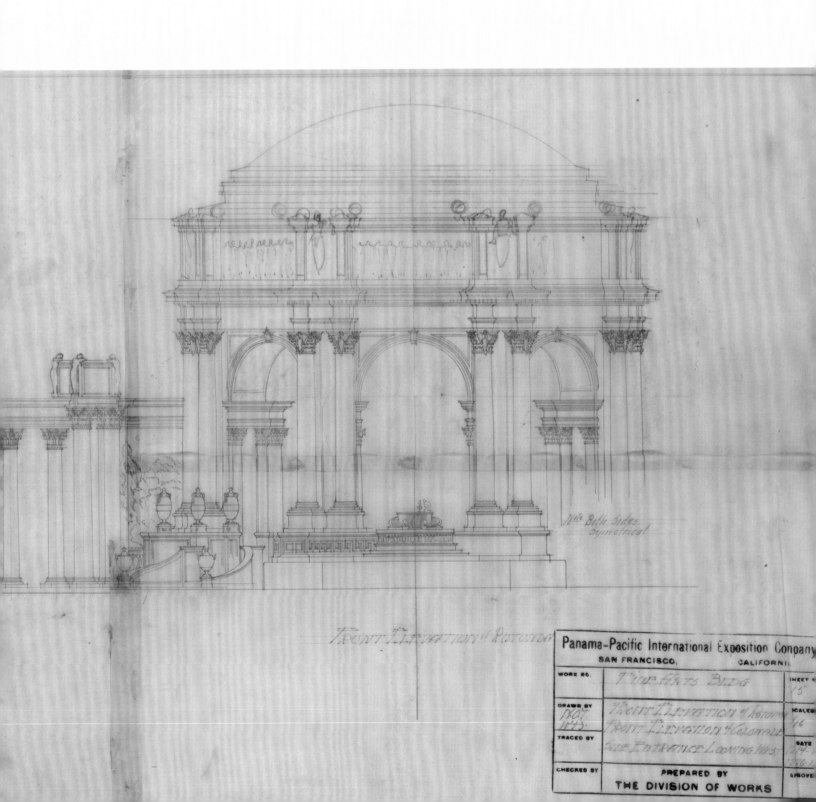

BEAUX-ARTS ARCHITECTURE AND THE AMERICAN RENAISSANCE IN CALIFORNIA

BY GORDON L. FUGLIE

Like all styles in art history, the Beaux-Arts movement had its rise and fall. A Parisian import, it ascended to prominence during the American Renaissance (from 1876 to 1919), a period of westward and imperial expansion, industrial growth, scientific advances, modernization of cities, social upheaval, and an eclectic cultural renewal. Academic neoclassicism—as Beaux-Arts architecture was sometimes called—gained traction in the United States around 1880, soared to prominence in the 1890s, spread nationwide through World War I, and fell off in the years leading up to 1929 and the start of the Great Depression. Classical traces could still be discerned in art moderne and art deco buildings from 1930 up to the end of World War II. After that, skyscrapers designed in the international style—sheer, towering slabs of glass and steel—filled the urban landscape.

Beaux-Arts architecture as theory, movement, and practice originated in France and was spurred by Georges-Eugène Haussmann's (1809–1891) bold, controversial, modernizing redesign of Paris—a massive public works program that was most active from 1853 to 1870 and continued for another fifty years. Haussmann's renovation demolished entire Parisian neighborhoods in the cramped and squalid medieval city, replacing them with wide and straight boulevards, parks, fountains, and squares. The latter served as focal points and were articulated with stately monuments and dramatic sculptural ensembles that define the cityscape to this day.

Haussmann's civic overhaul corresponded with the evolution of architectural teaching at the École des Beaux-Arts (School of the Fine Arts). Since the early nineteenth century, the school's pedagogy was grounded in the architecture of classical Greece and Rome, with attention to its revival in the Italian Renaissance and baroque eras. Through the influence of Romanticism, the École considered medieval models, thanks to the advocacy of the designer and avid restorationist Eugène Emmanuel Viollet-le-Duc (1814–1879).[1] In the second half of the nineteenth century, there were struggles over who administered the school and what was taught and how. These topics were hotly debated, a situation that continued into the 1890s. By the fin de siècle, the theories and teachings of École professor Julien Guadet (1834–1908) predominated. He codified and published them in four volumes between 1901 and 1904.[2] Known in the profession simply as "the Guadet" or "Elements," his lavishly illustrated texts served as the basic reference for a generation of academic European and American architects (FIG. 1).

While Guadet required mastery of Greco-Roman models, he encouraged his students to be eclectic in deploying these elements in contemporary buildings, an approach he called "free classicism." In addition, École students were told to visit historic architectural sites and make pen-and-ink and watercolor studies to hone their observational skills. The American Julia Morgan (1872–1957), the first female student admitted to the École des Beaux-Arts in 1898, traveled throughout France sketching buildings and villages, imprinting a wide stylistic vocabulary in her memory (FIG. 2). In Paris she frequented the École's library of illustrated books and portfolios, as well as its halls of plaster casts of classical and Renaissance architectural elements and sculpture. But in the classroom, once students received assignments from their professors, they were expected to translate classical and historical sources into original designs—that is, buildings with artistic *caractère*. Drawings overly derivative of historical masterworks were rejected. Further, students were expected to stay current with new construction technologies like ferroconcrete, ironwork, and steel framing.

Once American students completed their coursework at the École, how did they ply their skills in the United States? Let me illustrate with an example of classicist Beaux-Arts architecture in my central California home town, the Atascadero Administration Building. It was designed by San Francisco architects Walter Danforth Bliss and William Baker Faville in a High Renaissance style and completed in 1918 (FIG. 3). Bliss (1874–1956), the principal designer of the city hall, was trained at the Massachusetts Institute of Technology—the first professional architectural school in the United States. During the 1890s, he was a draftsman at New York's McKim, Mead & White, the nation's foremost designers of Beaux-Arts projects. Bliss came west in 1898 and formed a practice with Faville, a fellow MIT graduate. Both men were Bay Area contemporaries of Julia Morgan.

The Atascadero building has a massing typical of American Beaux-Arts structures, a tightly symmetrical classical facade—its flat roof rimmed with balustrades. Rising from the center of the main block is an eight-sided drum upon which rests a shallow saucer dome roofed with clay tiles. At ground level the entrance is preceded by wide stairs ascending to a protruding porch supported by six Ionic columns of the ancient Greek order. The tall, framed doorway is capped with a triangular gable (pediment). The walls of the building were articulated by bas-relief decorations and brick patterning. Also composing the exterior ornamentation are orderly classicist appointments of egg-and-dart bands, rosettes, cartouches, laurel garlands, decorative swags, medallions, and ancient Roman fasces. Passing into the interior, one encounters a high central dome patterned with coffers that ascend to an apex that is decorated by a large medallion from which hangs a large chandelier (FIG. 4).

Bliss's design demonstrates the free classicism that Guadet advocated at the École while also responding to its Renaissance source: Andrea Palladio's masterpiece, the Villa Rotonda in Vicenza (FIG. 5). American architects trained in Beaux-Arts methods kept extensive reference libraries that they consulted for inspiration and classical standards of design. Palladio (1508–1580) himself learned of classical theory and canons through studying the first century B.C.E. Roman architect Vitruvius's text *De Architectura*. With the spread of printing technologies in the sixteenth century, numerous editions of Vitruvius were published: first in Latin; later in translations into European languages. The text was available with richly detailed illustrations by the 1520s. Regarding himself as the Vitruvius of his era, Palladio published his *I Quattro libri dell'architettura* (The Four Books of Architecture) that became an essential source for Beaux-Arts students and architects three centuries later.[3]

Palladio's Villa Rotonda and Bliss's re-working of it for the Atascadero city hall were designed from a centralizing plan out of which the other elements extend, projecting identical facades on its four aspects. For the California building, Bliss and his patron, E. G. Lewis, decided upon a plain, single-arched architrave over the porch columns instead of Palladio's Roman temple facade with its ancient religious associations. Lewis wanted Atascadero, the first planned community in California, to be associated with the Renaissance and American civic renewal, reflecting the era's reformist City Beautiful movement.

THE EXPANSION OF BEAUX-ARTS IN THE UNITED STATES

The academic movement, as the Parisian method was called in the United States, gained widespread adherence as a de facto official civic style in the late

Previous spread and opposite

FIG. 3 AND FIG. 4
Walter D. Bliss (Bliss & Faville), Atascadero Administration Building, 1914–18

Following spread

FIG. 5
Andrea Palladio, Villa Rotonda, Vicenza, Italy, 1567–1592

nineteenth century. At the same time, Beaux-Arts pedagogy informed the curricula of American universities and accelerated the professionalization of American architectural practice, especially on the East Coast but also in rising industrial and transit centers of Chicago, Kansas City, and Saint Louis. By contrast, booming San Francisco, barely forty years old in 1890, presented a cityscape of undulating, tightly packed rows of Victorian structures sheathed in wood planking. More picturesque structures sported machine-engraved boards or jig-sawed trim with decorative patterns; some went further, adding painted color accents in the Queen Anne style. Commercial buildings and domestic residences alike sported jutting bay windows and bulbous corner towers. Dissatisfaction with this monotonous, superficial, and pretentious cityscape was pronounced among a younger generation of professionally trained artists and architects who began arriving on the scene in the mid-1880s. One was the artist Ernest Peixotto (1869–1940), who, after absorbing the refined aesthetics of the Académie Julian, a private painting and sculpture school in Paris, returned to his hometown and cast a baleful gaze on its "absurdities . . . piled up without rhyme and reason—restless, turreted, gabled, loaded with meaningless detail, defaced with fantastic and hideous chimneys."[4]

ALBERT PISSIS IN SAN FRANCISCO
A Beaux-Arts Beachhead on Market Street

It is easy to sympathize with the impatience of Peixotto and other Young Turks with the aesthetic failures of the San Francisco cityscape. They had been to Paris or seen the new architecture going up in Boston, New York, or Chicago. While they were anxious to mold their callow city into a modern metropolis with rational and serious styles, they were better advised to take notice of recent architectural progress. Indeed, the inspiring example they hoped for had been dedicated the year preceding Peixotto's critique.

Born in Sonora to a French father and Mexican mother, Albert Pissis (1852–1914) emigrated to the city with his family in 1858 at age five. As he matured, his creative abilities were recognized and encouraged by San Francisco's French immigrant community. Fluent

in Spanish, French, and English, Pissis had educational aspirations beyond what frontier California offered in the 1870s. After journeying to Paris, he applied to and passed the entry examinations for admission to the École des Beaux-Arts. Pissis studied under a then-young Julien Guadet and earned a *certificat de capacité* in 1876.[5] He was the first Californian to attend the French architectural academy. Returning to San Francisco in 1880, he set up a practice with William P. Moore, and they bided their time designing Victorian homes with Beaux-Arts details.

An opportunity to apply their fullest talents arose in 1890 when a competition was announced to design a new bank building for the Hibernia Savings and Loan Society. The clients were leaders of San Francisco's Irish community and they wanted an edifice that proclaimed the group's ascendance from scorned arriviste immigrants to established model citizenry. Or as city preservationist Chris VerPlanck observed in 2011: "After being poor and despised for a generation by many of San Francisco's Protestant ruling class, this bank was all about Irish pride."[6]

Pissis and Moore's majestic neoclassical design fired up the selection committee, easily outclassing rival entries. Completed in 1892, while Julia Morgan was studying engineering at the University of California, Berkeley, the building virtually "owned" the intersection of Market, McAllister, and Jones streets (FIG. 6). The bank is defined by a monumental semi-circular entrance and its four Corinthian columns. Crowned with a bronze dome, the element looks as if a temple were inserted to join its flanking angled facades. In fact, Pissis adapted Donato Bramante's (1444–1514) free-standing circular *tempietto* (a small temple) that the Italian designed as a martyrium for the convent of San Pietro in Montorio, Rome, 1502–1506. Pissis knew that in drawing his design from this source, he was linking the bank to a monument recognized for launching High Renaissance architecture. Extending ninety degrees from the bank's "temple" is a double facade Pissis created that employed an innovative Beaux-Arts re-combination of engaged columns, arches, mini-pediments, and roofline balustrades—a magisterial statement of the free classicism championed at the École.

If the members of the Irish community enthused over Pissis and Moore's exterior, they were surely ecstatic about the bank room that customers entered after passing through the *tempietto*. The two-story neoclassical interior with its encrusted gilt ceiling centered in a glass dome echoed the Palace of Versailles (FIG. 7). Gilded, corbeled beams rested on pilasters and fluted Tuscan columns. Cut and patterned marbles and granites in four colors paved the floor.

The bank's classic palatial beauty, however, proved less important than its structure when it went through the 1906 earthquake and fire. Thankfully, the architects had used steel-framed construction and the building survived to be renewed. In the 1908 reconstruction, Pissis designed an addition that incorporated a second and even larger patterned glass dome in an ovoid configuration, likely inspired by the expansive glass framework over the quad of the Cour Vitrée that the architect observed three decades earlier at the École des Beaux-Arts. In recent years the former bank has been restored, gaining new life as an event center.

BEAUX-ARTS ARCHITECTURE IN AMERICA
The 1893 Chicago World's Columbian Exposition and Its Influence on the Bay Area

The greatest boon to the Beaux-Arts academic movement in the United States was the design of the Chicago world's fair, or international exposition, of 1893. During the late nineteenth and early twentieth centuries, world's fairs came to be optimal venues for displaying the accomplishments of nations, states, and cities. Planned as ordered ensembles, they were departmentalized in displays of recent developments in horticulture, agriculture, industrial technology, the arts, and even the changing roles of women in society. New inventions were trumpeted. In their American settings, fairs were panoramas of progress and national pride. Philadelphia hosted the first official fair in the United States, the Centennial International Exhibition in 1876, attracting an astonishing ten million visitors. Civic organizers of subsequent fairs were keen to reap the benefits and hoped fairs would expand local industry, upgrade urban cores, attract outside investment, raise real estate values, and launch new cultural institutions. Ideologically, the fairs of the American Renaissance broadcast the nation's exceptionalism and its rising imperial ambitions.[7]

Previous and opposite
FIG. 6 AND FIG. 7 Albert Pissis and William P. Moore (Pissis & Moore), the Hibernia Bank Building, San Francisco, 1892 and 1908. The interior (opposite) shows the restorations completed in 1908, after the earthquake of 1906.

Fairs were also a godsend to American architects. Increasingly competitive, each exposition tried to outdo the previous one. As organizers were keen to attract visitors, this led to more magnificent layouts, bringing to life "dream cities" that quoted great architecture from the past. In what might be called a harmonic convergence, the only architects in the United States possessing the knowledge and experience for planning these idealized and temporary cities were those trained at the École des Beaux-Arts or apprenticed at American firms employing its methods. With their immersion in architectural history and training in functional planning, America's academic architects were highly qualified to conceive the order, grandeur, and beauty of fair sites with ever-more splendid ensembles of buildings.

The 1893 Chicago World's Columbian Exposition (CWCE) established Beaux-Arts as the dominant architectural style in the United States. Celebrating the 400th anniversary of Christopher Columbus's "discovery" of the New World, the fair also proclaimed America's future imperial destiny. Such a momentous aspirational undertaking called for an unprecedented level of artistic organization. Recruited to the task were none other than Frederick Law Olmsted (1822–1903, of New York's Central Park fame) as landscape architect for the 690-acre site and Chicago architect Daniel H. Burnham (1846–1912) as director of works. An advocate of the ascendant City Beautiful movement, Burnham oversaw an eclectic but tightly ordered array of some 150 buildings and sculptures that lined Olmsted's lagoon and canals. Upon its opening, the CWCE, defined by its avenues of monumental white neoclassical and Renaissance-derived structures, was dubbed "the Great White City" (FIG. 8). By the time the exposition closed, it had drawn more than 27 million visitors—nearly tripling the attendance of the Philadelphia fair seventeen years earlier.[8]

Standing out by sheer contrast to the dominant neoclassicist buildings coordinated by Burnham, the immense California Building designed by San Francisco's A. Page Brown (1859–1896) debuted the regional Mission Revival style to a curious nation (FIG. 9).[9] The combination of elements pulled from among the state's Franciscan missions—expanses of plain white-washed walls, massive arched corridors, sloping red-tile roofs, and, particularly, the Santa Barbara Mission's facade of terraced bell towers—could not conceal the Beaux-Arts principles of symmetry, integrated design, and spatial grandeur. Centering Brown's building, a very non-Mission Byzantine dome hovered over the reception area. Twenty years later, Brown's eclectic regional scheme influenced William Randolph Hearst's choice for his block-long Examiner building in Los Angeles, designed by Julia Morgan.

Among the throngs visiting the CWCE were three prominent Californians with visionary aspirations for the Bay Area and their state: Michael H. de Young, William Randolph Hearst, and Hearst's mother, Phoebe Apperson Hearst. De Young, the publisher of the tabloid-style San Francisco Chronicle, had long sought the social prestige he had been denied by the city's elites. Seeing an opportunity for the Chicago fair after it closed, he arranged for a portion of the CWCE's buildings and exhibits to be disassembled and transported to a 200-acre section of Golden Gate Park. The down-scaled version of the Chicago exposition (with a few local additions) opened in January 1894, promoted as the California Midwinter International Exposition. De Young's local gala made a modest profit, but more importantly prompted a "buzz" among San Francisco's leaders that the city just might be able to originate an exposition on its own.[10]

Hearst was even more prescient. In 1891, as the Chicago fair was in its design stage, the newspaperman commissioned local architect Willis Polk (1867–1924) to draw up a plan for San Francisco. The architect's drawings appeared in the Christmas issue of the San Francisco Examiner, portraying an immense, mile-long walled city with its interconnected pavilions forming—in effect—a single building. Polk's plan was revolutionary for California, demonstrating that expositions could function as laboratories for ordered urban design.[11]

Phoebe Apperson Hearst—the budding philanthropist and mother of William Randolph whose husband, the mining magnate George, died in 1891, as planning for the CWCE was underway—had developed an interest in education and women's rights and a belief in the capacity of grand architecture to ennoble human life and action. Now an extremely wealthy widow, she offered her patronage to the fledgling state university in Berkeley, which in the 1890s consisted of a smattering of Victorian buildings on a semi-rural sloping campus. With the canals, allées, and magnificent facades of the CWCE fresh in her

Opposite

FIG. 8
View of the World's Columbian Exposition, Chicago, 1893

Following spread

FIG. 9
A. Page Brown, the California State Building, World's Columbian Exposition, Chicago, 1893

A. PAGE·BROWN, Architect

COPYRIGHTED.

CALIFORNIA STATE
WORLDS COLUMBIAN
CHICAGO
18

H.S.CROCKER CO. S.F.

DIMENSIONS OF STATE BUILDING.
435 FT. LONG.
144 FT. WIDE.
113 FT. TO TOP OF DOME.
60,000 ☐ ON GROUND FLOOR. 40,000 ☐ ON SECOND FLOOR.

ATE BUILDING,
AN EXPOSITION,
O, ILL.
3.

mind, she chanced to meet Bernard Maybeck (1862–1957), possessed of a visionary outlook himself and recently hired to teach architecture at the university. Coincidentally, Maybeck was holding advanced architectural seminars in his home; among his students was Julia Morgan.[12]

Aroused by the City Beautiful movement, Phoebe Hearst was all ears when Maybeck, who trained at the École des Beaux-Arts from 1882 to 1886, lobbied her to sponsor an international competition for a master plan for the university. The philanthropist and her far-sighted architect overcame resistance from the provincially minded regents with energetic activism and eventually garnered their support. In 1897, the regents issued a competition, boldly calling for a "plan so perfect [that] there will be no more necessity of remodeling . . . a thousand years hence, than there would be of remodeling the Parthenon, had it come down to us complete and uninjured."[13] Two years later, the competition jury selected the winning entry: French architect Henri Jean Émile Bénard's comprehensive Beaux-Arts plan. The University of California would enter the twentieth century with the most ambitious construction campaign in its short history. Among the architects who would contribute to the design of the campus was Julia Morgan, who would return from Paris in 1902 as the first campus buildings were being realized.

SAN FRANCISCO AND THE CITY BEAUTIFUL MOVEMENT

Despite its spectacular natural setting and its growth as the West Coast's preeminent harbor, industrial region, and transit center (connecting with Oakland), San Francisco through the end of the nineteenth century remained a hodgepodge of cheek-by-jowl wooden buildings on a snug gridiron of narrow lots. Historian Kevin Starr described it as "a depressing lead-colored city."[14] Artistic buildings like Albert Pissis's Hibernia Savings and Loan Society stood out as exceptions to the tightly cluttered rule.

The model of the CWCE—the orderly classicist "White City"—persisted in the imagination of the Bay Area's elites as the twentieth century dawned. In January 1904, former mayor, civic leader, and banker James D. Phelan took action to transform San Francisco into a beautiful Beaux-Arts metropolis, forming the Association for the Improvement and Adornment of San Francisco (AIASF). (Two months

TELEGRAPH HILL, LO

NG EAST, SHOWING SUGGESTED ARCHITECTURAL TREATMENT

Previous

FIG. 10

Daniel Burnham and Edward H. Bennett, "Telegraph Hill. Looking East. Showing Architectural Treatment." Proposal prepared for the Association for the Improvement and Adornment of San Francisco, ca. 1905. These never-realized plans were submitted on April 17, 1906, the day before the San Francisco earthquake.

later, Julia Morgan would be certified to practice architecture in California.) Phelan gathered twenty wealthy grandees whom Kevin Starr described as "imperial, post-frontier in their style and culture, [but] frontier in their vigor and capacity for bold action, men of business, patrons of art and learning, cosmopolitan, determined to make San Francisco a world city."[15] By year's end, Phelan's association numbered nearly four hundred members, mostly from the city's merchant and banking class. Together they developed a "wish list" of civic improvements that included an opera house, an auditorium, a music conservatory, street and boulevard upgrades, and terraced parks to grace the hills of the municipality.[16] In the spirit of Chicago's "White City," they envisioned a classicized San Francisco; one contingent even clamored for the construction of a replica of the Athens Parthenon on Telegraph Hill.[17]

In the same year the AIASF was formed, Phelan invited Daniel Burnham, the CWCE's former director of works, to come west to devise a city plan "for all time," transforming the crude urban energy of the peninsula into a "fixed and splendid form."[18] With a 360-degree view from his studio in Twin Peaks—the geographical center of the city—Burnham (succeeded by his associate Edward H. Bennett) and his draftsmen sketched dramatic panoramas of Parisian boulevards slicing through existing grids; magnificent esplanades laid upon graded hilltops; steep, soaring stone stairs rivaling those of Aztec temples; and focal points of triumphal sculptures on towering rostral columns (FIG. 10). As a vision of classical imperial urban grandeur, his plan was unrivaled. The architect submitted his plans to City Hall on April 17, 1906. Early the next morning, a 7.8 magnitude earthquake shook San Francisco. Fire ravaged the peninsula for the next four days, destroying more than 80 percent of the city. Surveying the devastation, Phelan and the AIASF saw a ripe opportunity to implement Burnham's designs. But their hopes were dashed

when the city establishment ignored their bold and probably impractical proposal. Over the next five years San Francisco was largely rebuilt in wood along old lot-lines. The city would wait six more years before attempting another master plan, but with different means and ends: the 1915 Panama-Pacific International Exposition.

BEAUX-ARTS ARCHITECTS DESIGN HIGHER EDUCATION CAMPUSES IN THE BAY AREA

At the same time the AIASF was active, across the bay another major architectural plan was unfolding: Phoebe Apperson Hearst's international architectural competition to design the University of California, Berkeley. In 1899 the competition jury chose the plan submitted by the French architect and painter Henri Jean Émile Bénard (1844–1929), an alumnus of the École des Beaux-Arts who also received the coveted Prix de Rome in 1867. His ensemble design drew heavily on French neoclassical styles and city planning—a virtual translation of Paris onto the slopes of the Berkeley campus. This was the major factor in his selection, as Hearst's advocacy was informed by her conviction that a rational, noble, and beautiful design would infuse the campus community with moral and aesthetic uplift.

But the post-selection chemistry between Phoebe Hearst, the university regents, and Bénard grew vexed and discussions of his designs became contentious. This led to irritation with the Frenchman, while the fortunes of another competition entrant, the American John Galen Howard, rose.

In the competition for the campus design, the New York firm of Howard & Cauldwell placed fourth. The firm's plan bore both important similarities to and differences from Bénard's (FIG. 11). Moreover, Howard (1864–1931) had the imprimatur of having studied at the École des Beaux-Arts from 1890 to 1893.[19] Invited

Above

FIG. 11

John Galen Howard, *Campus Elevation*, University of California, Berkeley, pencil, ink, and watercolor on paper, early 1900s

Above

FIG. 12

John Galen
Howard, Greek
Theatre, University
of California,
Berkeley, 1902-03.
Julia Morgan was
the supervising
architect.

Opposite

FIG. 13

John Galen
Howard, Hearst
Memorial Mining
Building, University
of California,
Berkeley, 1902-07.

to the university in Berkeley in 1901 as frustrations with Bénard mounted, the affable and confident six-foot-tall New Yorker impressed the community and gained favor with the regents.

Also in Howard's favor were his shared interests with university president Benjamin Ide Wheeler, who was appointed in 1899. A classicist by training, Wheeler noted Howard's foundation in classical education at the Boston Latin School. Formerly a professor of classical Greek language and culture, Wheeler envisioned the campus as a Progressive Era Acropolis overlooking the Golden Gate, "the Athens of the West." With Bénard's viability in doubt, sympathy for Howard rose. Seeking affirmation of the American, Wheeler contacted John Merven Carrère, partner in the architectural firm Carrère and Hastings in New York. Successful at winning major Beaux-Arts commissions, including the block-long New York Public Library that was considered a masterpiece

of classicism, Carrère gave Howard high marks.[20] This satisfied Wheeler and he approved the regents drafting a resolution appointing Howard supervising architect of all campus construction.[21] Howard and his family relocated to Berkeley, arriving in the summer of 1902.[22]

A few months later, another architect arrived in the Bay Area. Julia Morgan, the first woman to ever receive the *certificat de capacité* from the École des Beaux-Arts, returned home to set up her first studio in her parents' Oakland carriage house and look for work. She was soon hired by Howard's office, which he kept staffed at around ten, including draftsmen and an engineer or two. Howard saw that Morgan, fresh from the École, was well-grounded in design, structural engineering, and the latest construction technologies.

Indeed, as Morgan biographer Sara Holmes Boutelle observed, after studying for five years in

Paris, she had "refined her talents and absorbed a classical idiom that would shape her architectural repertoire without constraining it. Barely breaking stride, she was ready to begin her life's work."[23] Morgan's first two design projects under Howard were ideally suited to her skills and knowledge: the Hearst Memorial Mining Building and the Hearst Greek Theatre.

The Greek Theatre (1903) was enthusiastically promoted by President Wheeler, the university's most ardent and influential Grecophile. It was funded by William Randolph Hearst at the urging of the university's principal patron, his mother, Phoebe. The semicircular structure is one of the most purely classical buildings Howard designed for the campus, owing to its imitation of the fourth century B.C.E. Greek theater at Epidaurus, recreated half-size at Berkeley (FIG. 12). With the vocabulary of classical forms fresh in her mind, Morgan was the obvious choice to

draft designs for the colonnade atop the scene building backing the stage.[24] In Howard's presentation drawing, twelve caryatids support the ornamented cornice, but budget shortfalls forced the university to eliminate this crowning feature.[25] Appreciating Morgan's engineering background and knowledge of ferroconcrete construction, Howard appointed her assistant supervising architect to bring the project to completion.[26]

Design for the Hearst Memorial Mining Building (1907) commenced the year Howard moved to Berkeley and Morgan returned to the United States (FIG. 13). It was commissioned by Phoebe Hearst in honor of her late husband, George, who made the family fortune in various mining operations in Nevada, Utah, Montana, New Mexico, and South Dakota. George Hearst also served as a U.S. senator for California. Unlike subsequent buildings Howard designed at Berkeley—Boalt Hall (renamed Durant

Above

FIG. 14

John Galen
Howard, vestibule,
Hearst Memorial
Mining Building,
University of
California,
Berkeley, 1902–07

Hall), Doe Library, and California Hall—that housed classrooms, offices, books, and documents, the mining building contained metallurgical laboratories. A deeper building than it appears from the facade, the mining college didn't just teach theory. It instructed students in the latest extraction methods, and housed smelters, rock crushers, drill rigs, and chemical fume hoods. Some twenty chimneys protruded from the roofs of its left and right wings. With its basement, the facility reached four stories, providing sufficient space for students to learn how to dig long, deep vertical airshafts and illuminate and ventilate them. The industrial hardware within was not evident from the building's facade.

An exercise in Beaux-Arts eclecticism, the outward face of the mining building combines classical,

Mediterranean, and California Mission elements in a restrained and balanced use of voids and solids. Howard's team designed the facade in a tripartite arrangement with the center section projecting from the main block. A flight of stairs precedes the arched openings, each of which frames a pair of Tuscan columns that support architraves. Understated classical motifs—laurel wreaths, figurative corbel sculptures, fillets, and dentils—announce the building's classical lineage.[27] Evoking California missions, prominent wooden brackets support the tile roof. Commenting on Howard's designs for the campus shortly after the dedication of the mining building, the architectural critic Herbert Croly noted that the California landscape from the Sierra Nevada mountains to the Pacific Ocean "is composed of extremely simple

Above

FIG. 15
John Galen Howard, Sather Tower, also known as the Campanile, University of California, Berkeley, 1903-16

elements . . . A landscape of this kind demands a type of building which has been simplified in the classic spirit. Their white walls and tiled roofs will look particularly well in the California sunshine and atmosphere."[28]

The familiar saying "and now for something completely different" aptly applies to the vestibule. Passing through the carved oak doors, the visitor is astonished to discover—instead of a classical interior—a novel industrial aesthetic (FIG. 14). The vestibule soars a full three stories to reveal a trio of translucent glass domes (skylights) framed in slender cast-iron pendentives—exhibiting a similarity to the engineering of Gothic churches. Rising from the floor, vertical iron beams support the pendentives, in which buff-colored tiles are set. The inspiration for Howard's design is credited to two sources. The first is Henri Labrouste's Bibliothèque Nationale and Bibliothèque Sainte-Geneviève in Paris. Trained at the École des Beaux-Arts and awarded the Prix de Rome, Labrouste (1801–1875) pioneered in combining cast-iron structures and cast-metal classical ornament in place of stone. Both Howard and Morgan visited these innovative masterworks while studying at the École. The second source is the patented iron vaulting and tile system developed by New York's Guastavino Fireproof Construction Company, whose widely renowned work Howard saw while practicing in the city. The Guastavinos were contracted to execute the structural work for the mining building vestibule, adapting from Howard's sketches.[29] The industrial classicist aesthetic of the vestibule was intentional, as the space served as museum to display the materials of modern mining technology. Howard considered the vestibule the most important design element of the building.[30]

Upon the building's completion, Howard summarized his achievement: "Within [the laboratories] everything is work-a-day. Yet the building is intended to take on a progressively more civilized aspect, and a more monumental beauty as one goes from the work shops of the rear toward the public portions of the front, and sounds the highest note of dignity and impressiveness in the great museum-vestibule. The [memorial] motive reaches on the exterior its first full development and orchestration . . . and [is]

Opposite
FIG. 16
Julia Morgan,
El Campanil,
Mills College,
Oakland,
California,
1903–04

Above
FIG. 17
Julia Morgan,
Carnegie
Library, Mills
College, Oakland,
California,
1905–06

further enriched by the recall of the classic type of architecture, which the . . . University as a whole will approximate. We have sought to secure beauty not by easy masquerade . . . , but by organic composition, working from within out, and letting the heart of the thing speak."[31] His closing sentence summarizes the core of Beaux-Arts theory: begin the design with a plan that serves the building's function. With that accomplished, the structure takes its shape—the ornamentation complementing its purpose.

Upon completing her work on the Hearst Memorial Mining Building, Morgan ended her relationship with Howard and formed a partnership with Ira Wilson Hoover in 1904 in San Francisco.[32] Their offices were in the new Merchants Exchange building, a Beaux-Arts skyscraper designed by Daniel Burnham and local architect Willis Polk.

Prior to Morgan's departure from Howard's office, plans got underway in 1903 for a prominent bell tower to honor the memory of Peder Sather, an early trustee of the university and prominent banker. Sather Tower, also known as the Campanile, is today the most recognizable of Howard's UC Berkeley projects (FIG. 15). Ever mindful of historical precedent, the architect looked to the sixteenth-century campanile of Saint Mark's Basilica in Venice for inspiration.[33] A decade's hiatus halted progress on the bell tower, during which Howard refined his designs. Construction began in 1913; the Campanile opened to the public in 1917. Sited at the end of a long esplanade bordered by balustrades, Sather Tower rises to more than three hundred feet, orienting the surrounding buildings that Howard designed.[34]

In a parallel to Howard's role as supervising architect at Berkeley, Julia Morgan was commissioned to design a number of buildings for Oakland's Mills College, then the only secular higher education institution for women on the West Coast. Concurrent with Howard's design of Sather Tower, Morgan's first Mills project was a freestanding 72-foot bell tower, El Campanil (FIG. 16). While Morgan designed it in the regional Mission Revival style, one cannot help but notice that, in its isolation, it is a severe abstraction of its Franciscan sources. On all four sides she made use of double-stepped buttresses, which she accented with red-tile mini-roofs. The most striking feature of the tower is her incorporation of ten pre-existing bells of different sizes into the design. Morgan's grasp of the Beaux-Arts principles of symmetry, proportionality, and rational order served her well in creating El Campanil.[35]

Her second Mills College commission was the Margaret Carnegie Library—designed in 1905 and completed the following year (FIG. 17). Its style appears similar to the Mediterranean classicism of Berkeley's Hearst Memorial Mining Building. Both El Campanil and the library were undamaged by the 1906 earthquake, thanks to Morgan's use of steel-reinforced concrete construction. She continued to work on other Mills College buildings up to 1925.

BEAUX-ARTS ALONG THE SHORE AND ON THE MESA
The 1915 Panama-Pacific International and Panama-California Expositions

SAN FRANCISCO

By the second decade of the twentieth century, the academic movement in America was reaching its zenith. National, state, and civic building commissions were routinely awarded to architects who had studied at the École des Beaux-Arts or graduated from American schools that adopted its pedagogy, such as the Massachusetts Institute of Technology, Columbia University, the University of Pennsylvania, and the University of California, Berkeley. (The latter's architectural program was founded by John Galen Howard in 1903.) In addition, the Beaux-Arts triumph at the 1893 Chicago fair influenced subsequent expositions in America's rising cities: Nashville (1897), Omaha (1898), Buffalo (1901), St. Louis (1904), and Seattle (1909). Further, more Americans were traveling abroad, and many planned their itineraries around major fairs like the Exposition Universelle in Paris presented in 1889 and 1900. The world's cultural capital and home of the École des Beaux-Arts, the City of Light set the highest bar for world's fairs, and many Americans took notice.[36]

If post-earthquake San Francisco—four square miles of shattered masonry and scorched wood—failed to rally around Daniel Burnham's 1905 Beaux-Arts plan to redesign the city, then another approach might rekindle grand scale urban renewal. With San Francisco's civic leaders keenly aware of the successes of American expositions since the Chicago

Opposite

FIG. 18

Burton Benedict, ground plan of the palaces and courts complex, published in *The Anthropology of World's Fairs: San Francisco's Panama-Pacific International Exposition of 1915* (Berkeley, California: Lowie Museum of Anthropology, 1983), p. 96. The ground plan is based on one featured in Juliet James, *Palaces and Courts of the Exposition: A Handbook of the Architecture, Sculpture and Mural Paintings with Special Reference to the Symbolism* (San Francisco: California Book Company, 1915).

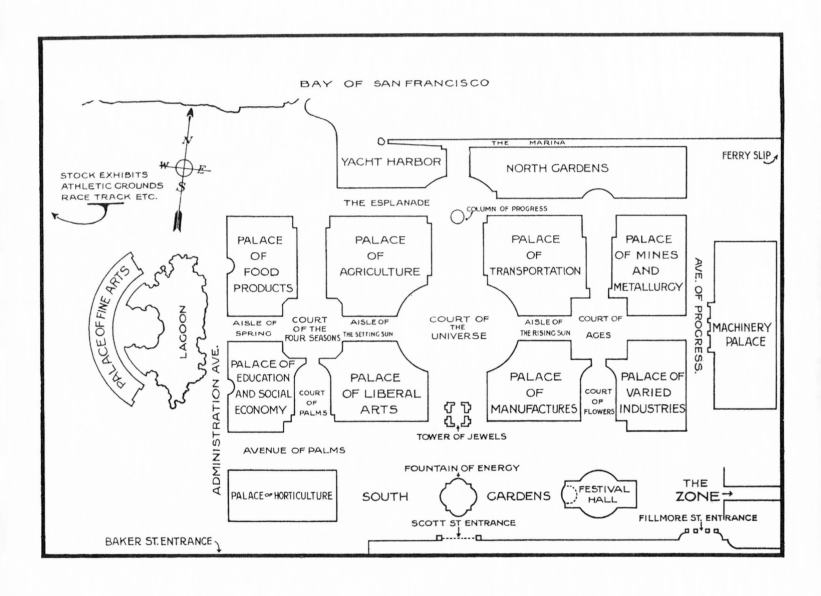

BAY OF SAN FRANCISCO

STOCK EXHIBITS
ATHLETIC GROUNDS
RACE TRACK ETC.

YACHT HARBOR

THE MARINA

NORTH GARDENS

FERRY SLIP

THE ESPLANADE

COLUMN OF PROGRESS

PALACE OF FINE ARTS

LAGOON

ADMINISTRATION AVE.

PALACE
OF
FOOD
PRODUCTS

PALACE
OF
AGRICULTURE

PALACE
OF
TRANSPORTATION

PALACE
OF MINES
AND
METALLURGY

AVE. OF PROGRESS.

MACHINERY
PALACE

AISLE OF
SPRING

COURT
OF THE
FOUR SEASONS

AISLE OF
THE SETTING SUN

COURT OF
THE
UNIVERSE

AISLE OF
THE RISING SUN

COURT OF
AGES

PALACE OF
EDUCATION
AND SOCIAL
ECONOMY

COURT
OF
PALMS

PALACE
OF LIBERAL
ARTS

PALACE
OF
MANUFACTURES

COURT
OF
FLOWERS

PALACE OF
VARIED
INDUSTRIES

TOWER OF JEWELS

AVENUE OF PALMS

FOUNTAIN OF ENERGY

PALACE OF HORTICULTURE

SOUTH   GARDENS

FESTIVAL
HALL

THE
ZONE

SCOTT ST ENTRANCE

FILLMORE ST. ENTRANCE

BAKER ST. ENTRANCE

fair, advocacy for the city as a host site began to coalesce in 1904. In a strategic stroke, the city's leadership decided to link their fair to the 1914 completion of the Panama Canal. A boom in shipping and trade would certainly follow—hence the oceanic designation Panama-Pacific International Exposition (PPIE). Prominent citizens joined forces and then redoubled their efforts after the catastrophic seismic upheaval. As 1906 ended, the city's business elites and leaders created the Panama-Pacific Exposition Company (PPEC) to make their dream a reality. An aggressive lobbying effort in Washington, D.C., secured San Francisco sole federal recognition in 1911, beating out the nation's capital and New Orleans. A year later, media mogul William Randolph Hearst hosted a sold-out black tie fundraiser in the ballroom of the Palace Hotel on Market Street, one of many events to finance the exposition.

In casting about for a site, the PPEC settled on the largely undeveloped Harbor View area on the north shore—today's Marina District. Its breathtaking vistas of the bay and proximity to many neighborhoods clinched the company's decision. Gazing down at the site from a nearby hilltop, Jules Guérin (1866–1946), the director of color for the PPIE, waxed poetic: Here was a "natural, even if not classical amphitheatre between the tawny Grecian hills and the blue Italian seas which are California's." Guérin envisioned a Latin-evocative design with orientalist undertones of the Islamic Near East.[37]

As expositions grew more ambitious, however, they required more rational and ordered layouts. The Harbor View site plan was developed by École alumnus Edward H. Bennett (1874–1954), who previously had worked with Daniel Burnham to produce the civic design for James D. Phelan's AIASF.[38] In what was officially known as the Block Plan, Bennett conceived a tight symmetrical arrangement of eight palaces, or exhibit halls, around a grand central court and four minor courts (FIG. 18). This arrangement was book-ended by a Machinery Palace on the eastern perimeter and a Palace of Fine Arts on the west. Landscaped gardens, oblong ponds, monumental fountains, and triumphal sculpture in the French mode defined the northern and southern boundaries of the block. The plan later was expanded along the southern perimeter to include the Palace of Horticulture, the Festival Hall, and the paired YWCA and Press Buildings.

West Coast architects with École des Beaux-Arts educations working on the palaces and courts of the PPIE included Bernard Maybeck, George Kelham, Robert Farquhar, Arthur Brown Jr., Édouard Frère Champney, and Julia Morgan.[39] In addition, the fair's architectural team included American-educated designers who had apprenticed with firms informed by academic theory (New York's McKim, Mead & White had employed Henry Bacon, Thomas Hastings, and William Baker Faville). Virtually all PPIE architects had made study tours in Europe.

Bennett's Block Plan concentrated the architecture, keeping its eclecticism within bounds. Guided by Beaux-Arts theory, the final result was a color-co-ordinated synthesis of historicist styles from Spain, Italy, and the Islamic Mediterranean. Louis Christian Mullgardt's Court of Ages incorporated elements from the forecourt of the Great Mosque of Córdoba and the Patio de los Naranjos of the Seville Cathedral (FIG. 19). Clarence R. Ward's Palace of Machinery echoed the Baths of Caracalla in Rome. Arthur Brown, Jr.'s Palace of Horticulture was an abundant exercise in free French baroque stylings with a great glass dome inspired by his visit to Istanbul, where he studied the seventeenth-century Blue Mosque of Sultan Ahmed I (FIG. 20).[40] East of the South Gardens, Robert Farquhar's Festival Hall may have been the most Francophile building in the fair, drawing on actual palaces, the Grand Trianon and Petit Trianon of Versailles.[41] Bernard Maybeck's misnamed Palace of Fine Arts—the one building to survive the fair—became the emblematic monument of the PPIE, a lyrical harmonization of dome, columns, temple, and colonnades hovering over a lagoon he had built to reflect his sublime classicist aggregation (FIG. 21 and FIG. 22).[42]

Édouard Frère Champney (1874—1929), a Seattle architect who studied at the École des Beaux-Arts from 1896 to 1900, was selected to design the YWCA (Young Women's Christian Association) building. Champney overlapped with Julia Morgan at the École, earning his diplôme two years before she earned her certification in 1902. As the PPIE came together, she joined him on the YWCA building. The pairing may have been due to pressure from Phoebe Hearst, a lifelong champion of Morgan, YWCA donor, and president of the PPIE's Woman's Board.[43]

To date, no detailed documentation of the building has been found. Champney is thought to have designed the building's exterior, but some scholars suggest he may at least have had assistance from Morgan in conceiving the series of paired caryatids

Opposite

FIG. 19

Louis Christian Mullgardt, Court of Ages, Panama-Pacific International Exposition, 1915

Right

FIG. 20
Arthur Brown
Jr. (Bakewell &
Brown), Palace
of Horticulture,
Panama-Pacific
International
Exposition, 1915

Following spread, left

FIG. 21
Bernard Maybeck,
Temple of the
Palace of Fine Arts,
Panama-Pacific
International
Exposition, 1915

Following spread, right

FIG. 22
Bernard Maybeck,
Colonnade of the
Palace of Fine Arts,
Panama-Pacific
International
Exposition, 1915.
The so-called
temple is just
visible through the
columns at left.

Y.W.C.A. BUILDING
PAN.-PAC. INT. EXPOSITION
SAN FRANCISCO, 1915

E99

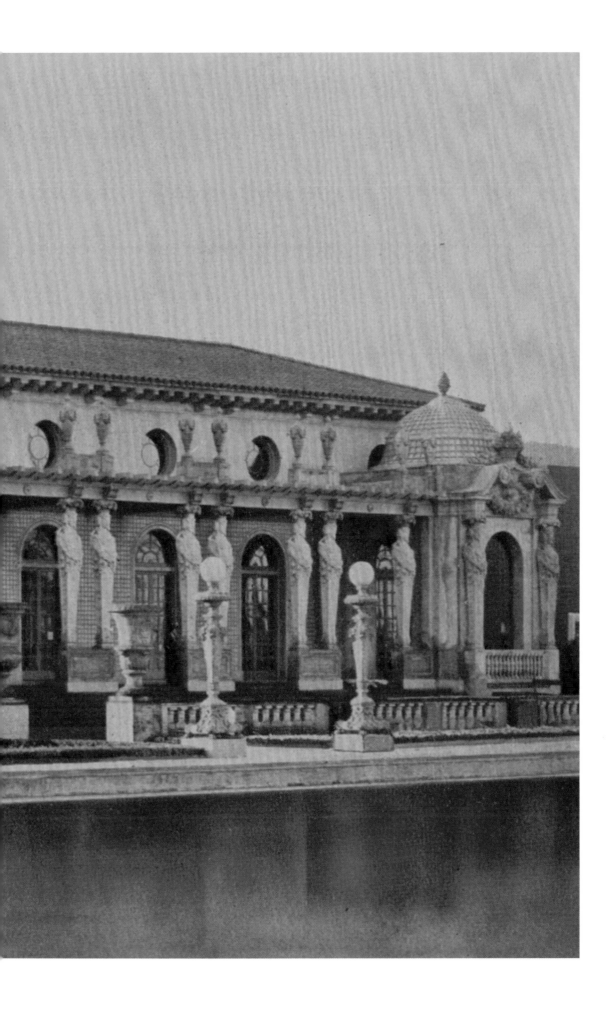

Left

FIG. 23
Édouard Frère
Champney and
Julia Morgan,
Young Women's
Christian
Association
(YWCA) Building,
Panama-Pacific
International
Exposition, 1915

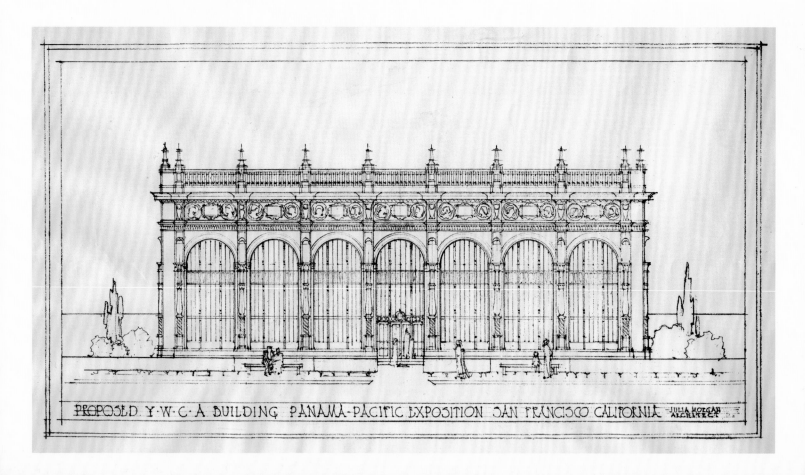

PROPOSED Y·W·C·A BUILDING PANAMA-PACIFIC EXPOSITION SAN FRANCISCO CALIFORNIA JULIA MORGAN ARCHITECT

that fronted the porch and sides of the structure (FIG. 23).[44] In classical sculpture and architecture, caryatids were maidens capped with baskets on their heads, functioning as columns supporting an architrave. Their position bearing the YWCA building porch roof, as well as presenting a phalanx of monumental women "greeting" visitors, may have been symbolic in this era of suffrage activism.[45] Curiously, the Department of Special Collections, Kennedy Library, Cal Poly San Luis Obispo, has a photostatic copy of Morgan's elevation sketch of the YWCA facade; her proposal lacks the final porch with its flanking domed pavilions (FIG. 24). Instead, her facade is composed of seven bays that each contain tall arched windows. Previous studies of Morgan's work on the PPIE YWCA building have isolated her participation to designing its interior, but given their time together in Paris, similar educations, and strong professional reputations, an overall collaboration between Morgan and Champney seems more likely.[46]

From 1893 to 1915, the interval since the Chicago fair, American inventions and technological breakthroughs had abounded. These were on display at the PPIE in the palace halls and also utilized to enhance the fair's presentation. Instead of the awkward electrical lighting via strings of bare bulbs of previous fairs, San Francisco's chief of illumination, Walter D'Arcy Ryan, conceived of a Total Illumination Plan for the fair. His team developed indirect wash and spot lighting with color filters to bathe and highlight the architecture. Color searchlights beamed into the night sky. Even the fair's pools and lagoons glowed with submerged colored lighting (FIG. 25). Centered in the courts, glass columns reaching 60 feet—topped by triumphant sculptures—were lit from within, glowing spectral white after dusk. The 435-foot-tall Tower of Jewels (designed by Thomas Hastings) was arrayed in 100,000 multi-colored cut-glass "jewels" (called Novagems, each 2 inches in diameter) that created shimmering sheets of color as they swayed in daytime breezes or glowed in the evening darkness when struck with spotlights. Nighttime visitors experienced the PPIE as a luminous nocturnal wonderland.[47]

Departing from the chalky classicism of "the Great White City" and succeeding fairs, the PPEC appointed muralist and illustrator Jules Guérin the PPIE's director of color. He created a tinted faux travertine "stucco" that gave the palaces an aged patina, and he also devised an integrated cluster of eight pigments to accent the buildings of the Block Plan.[48] Color decor was one of the most notable innovations distinguishing San Francisco from previous fairs.

Upon experiencing the PPIE's eclectic historicist Mediterranean architecture, halls of exhibits, extravagant effects, performances, and visual art displays, visiting art critic Christian Brinton concluded that "San Francisco boldly proclaims herself a world creation."[49] More than eighteen million visitors agreed.

SAN DIEGO

Alerted to San Francisco's efforts to host an exposition commemorating the opening of the Panama Canal, San Diego's business community roused itself to action. Though San Diego was a city of only 40,000 people, the chamber of commerce recognized that it was positioned to become the southernmost American port-of-call benefitting from the canal. Why should San Francisco get the jump on a town five hundred miles closer to the trans-oceans passage? Planning began in 1909 for what would become the Panama-California Exposition (PCE).

Unlike the imperial baroque Beaux-Arts "dream city" of the PPIE, a concept beyond San Diego's modest resources, the newly formed Panama-California Exposition Company (PCEC) early on stated a preference for Mission Revival architecture for the fair.[50] But after 1910, many architects found this style too limiting since its introduction at the 1893 Chicago fair. Impressed with John Galen Howard's design for the 1909 Seattle Exposition, the PCEC invited him to be the designer of the San Diego fair, but the UC Berkeley professor and Beaux-Arts proponent declined. With encouragement from colleagues to apply to the PCEC, New York architect Bertram Grosvenor Goodhue (1869–1924) lobbied hard for an audience with the company. A personal visit to San Diego and his visionary presentation won them over; Goodhue was appointed lead architect.

He proved to be the optimal choice. If the PPIE architects excelled in the "free classicism" of École des Beaux-Arts theory, Goodhue—temperamentally resistant to academicism—was a master of "free eclecticism." He was among the most gifted of American architectural draftsmen, and his dramatic pen-and-ink drawings revealed a love for a romanticized past informed by an historical consciousness. The styles in his previous commissions included elements from Gothic, Spanish, and classical traditions. A sojourn to study the architecture of viceregal Mexico in the early 1890s inspired Goodhue to develop the Spanish Colonial style, for which he is renowned. He applied it masterfully at the PCE.[51]

Goodhue sited the PCE on a mesa above a deep north-south arroyo known today as Balboa Park. Sightseers approached the exposition on El Prado, traversing the east-west 1,000-foot-long Cabrillo Bridge that spanned the arroyo. Arriving on the mesa, they passed through the Spanish West Gate arch to encounter what Goodhue described as "a city in miniature wherein everything that met the eye and ear of the visitor were meant to call to mind the glamour and mystery and poetry of the Spanish days."[52]

Standing in the Plaza de California, or California Quadrangle, one encountered the towering, densely ornamented facade of the California State Building and its tower, which Goodhue modeled after the Churrigueresque churches of colonial Mexico (FIG. 26). Attached to it was a large domed structure patterned with polychrome tiles, an element the architect borrowed from the Church of Santa Prisca y San Sebastían, Taxco. Proceeding eastward on El Prado, the PCE revealed itself as a tight arrangement of narrow alleys, esplanades, and plazas of varying proportions, as if one were strolling through pre-modern Rome, alternating from sunlit to shadowed environs.

The largest open space was the Plaza de Panama, Goodhue's equivalent of Mexico City's Zócalo. Turning south, the visitor walked the length of an esplanade and its pool, arriving at the outdoor semi-circular Spreckels Organ Pavilion, sponsored by sugar magnates John D. and Adolph B. Spreckels (FIG. 27). Designed by local architect Harrison Albright, the templelike structure with a Moorish sensibility served as the bandshell that housed an immense cluster of pipes within a deep and lacy arch. Wide, curving colonnades extend from both sides of the pavilion; their design is a novel mixture of classicist and Spanish baroque elements (FIG. 28). Glorified and sweeping walkways, they are similar in concept and function to Maybeck's Palace of Fine Arts.

After the PCE closed on January 1, 1917, the city fathers elected to retain permanently many of the buildings and grounds that Goodhue and his associate Carleton Winslow, Sr. (1876–1946) designed.[53] This was atypical, since most expositions were razed once they closed. Some of the PCE's other structures have been rebuilt in subsequent years, and this has left Balboa Park with a semblance of the original Spanish Colonial-themed exposition.

The 1915 California expositions were the high-water mark for Beaux-Arts architecture in the state. However, noteworthy structures in the style continued to be designed and built, such as the Carolands Chateau in Hillsborough (1916), Wheeler Hall, UC Berkeley (1917), Pasadena City Hall (1927), Los Angeles Board of Trade Building (1929), and the Los Angeles Theatre (1931). The San Francisco War Memorial Opera House (completed in 1932 and designed by Morgan's colleague Arthur Brown, Jr.) were among the last Beaux-Arts structures built in the United States. The Great Depression and the ascendancy of modernism sounded the death knell for the academic movement.

Even as the Beaux-Arts style declined, the architecture and art of the San Francisco and San Diego expositions made a lasting impression on certain men of power and wealth, especially those with a lifelong interest in history and culture. One such person was William Randolph Hearst. In his youth he took the first steps toward what would become the amassing of historical, architectural, and decorative objets d' art. With the death of his mother, Phoebe Apperson Hearst, in 1919, William inherited the family's mining fortune and sole control of its vast properties. Almost immediately he started planning to build a house on the heights overlooking the coastal hamlet of San Simeon. Hearst's early memories of his European travels, the impact of the historicist dream cities of California's expositions, and his self-regard as an inheritor of Renaissance ideals would become factors in the design of the Spanish Mediterranean complex he called La Cuesta Encantada (The Enchanted Ridge). All he needed was an architect with the skills and knowledge to realize his ambitious vision. Her name was Julia Morgan. ✿

Banc d'Œuvre.

John Howard
Élève de M. Laloux

1

THE ÉCOLE DES BEAUX-ARTS
AT THE FIN DE SIÈCLE

JEFFREY TILMAN

The École Nationale Supérieure des Beaux-Arts was the oldest and most significant and influential school of architecture in the Western world in the late nineteenth century. As the first American academic program was established at MIT only in 1869, just three years before Julia Morgan's birth, study at the French national school of architecture was a goal of many Americans of Morgan's generation who aspired to become leaders of the emerging profession of architecture. The decades that bookended the turn of the twentieth century saw a veritable flood of Americans traveling to Paris, with over three hundred Americans attending the school during these years.

The École des Beaux-Arts had its beginnings in the mid-seventeenth century in the royal academies instituted by First Minister Jean-Baptiste Colbert during the reign of Louis XIV. Shortly after the founding of the Academy of Architecture in 1671, François Blondel began to offer a series of public lectures on architectural history and theory, structures, perspective, mathematics, and construction. These lectures argued for an unchanging, universal standard of beauty. By 1717, a multi-year course of instruction under a single master was institutionalized, and this became referred to as the School of the Academy.[1] With the appointment in 1762 of Jacques-François Blondel, a distant relative of François Blondel's, as chair of the school, design instruction emphasized clarity of form, axiality, and monumentality—hallmarks of an architecture that in the United States would eventually be called the "Beaux-Arts" style.[2]

The academies were disbanded during the French Revolution, but the School of the Academy of Architecture was allowed to continue, largely because of the school's obvious usefulness. In 1795 the school was united with the schools of painting, sculpture and engraving to form what became known as the École des Beaux-Arts.[3] With the Bourbon Restoration, the École took on its stable nineteenth-century form. In 1816 the school moved to the Convent of the Petits Augustins, which was expanded with a set of new purpose-built buildings by Félix Duban in the 1830s (FIG. 1).[4]

The École des Beaux-Arts was an organ of the French state, and as such it was intended to educate promising young French citizens who would serve the state and the private sector after graduation. Thus, admission to the school was restrictive; students had to be between eighteen and thirty years old, and no more than one quarter of the student body could be foreign nationals. Until Julia Morgan's groundbreaking entrance in 1898, they were exclusively male. The structure of the curriculum, and thus of the student body, was divided into three parts and organized like a pyramid (FIG. 2). The largest group of students were those who aspired to be admitted to the school, but had not yet successfully passed the entrance examination—these were termed *aspirants*. Once formally registered as a student, one entered the second class (*deuxième classe* in French). Similar to what in the United States would be considered an undergraduate education in architecture, these students took coursework in architectural history, structures, and construction and participated in a number of design competitions specifically related to the second-class curriculum. After two or three years a student would move from the second class to the first class (*première classe*). First-class students took no coursework—they only competed among themselves in a set of monthly design competitions, hoping to gain enough credits

Previous spread
John Galen Howard student work, *Banc d'Oeuvre*, École des Beaux-Arts, March 3, 1893. This rendering depicts a so-called work bench, a type of bench reserved for special members of the church that was typically located in front of the pulpit.

Opposite
FIG. 1
Philippe Benoist, engraving of *École Impériale des Beaux-Arts*, ca. 1850

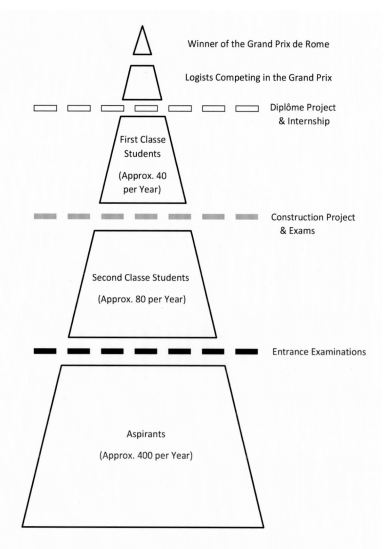

Winner of the Grand Prix de Rome

Logists Competing in the Grand Prix

Diplôme Project & Internship

First Classe Students

(Approx. 40 per Year)

Construction Project & Exams

Second Classe Students

(Approx. 80 per Year)

Entrance Examinations

Aspirants

(Approx. 400 per Year)

Graphical Description of Student Body at the Ecole des Beaux-Arts, c. 1900

Above

FIG. 2

Jeffrey Tilman, graphic showing the break-down of the student body at the École des Beaux-Arts around 1900.

(*valeurs*) to qualify for the *diplôme*, or to compete for and win the coveted Grand Prix de Rome and an all-expenses sojourn to Rome and other Mediterranean locations for four years' post-graduate study.[5]

Aspirants gained admittance to the École by passing a rigorous examination that lasted several weeks. In Morgan's time these exams were held twice a year, with about forty students being admitted each October/November and April/May. The examination was both artistic and academic. The artistic exams were exercises in the *trois arts*. *Aspirants* spent eight hours painting a still life, eight hours sculpting a small object in clay, and twelve hours designing an architectural element, usually a gatehouse or a portal. Each effort was juried anonymously, and received a score between 0 and 20. Any scores below 10 were disqualifying, and scores above 12 or 13 were usually required to gain admittance to the school. Those who had earned potentially qualifying scores in the *trois arts* were then allowed to take the academic exams, which focused on French literature and culture, French and world history, and mathematics and descriptive geometry, in that order. The examinations were given in French in the direct presence of a faculty member responsible for the area, and until the early twentieth century the faculty member was allowed to choose the questions, so that no two students received the same examination—this is why the professor of mathematics had the ability to bar Morgan from passing the entrance examinations in the face of her undoubted qualifications. In the end, the results of each exam were compiled using a complicated prorating formula and the would-be students were ranked—the top forty were admitted into the school, and the other several hundred aspirants were told retake the exam at the next opportunity.[6]

One could sit for the entrance exams as often as one wished, up until one turned thirty years old, even though admittance after age twenty-eight was unadvisable. *Aspirants* improved their chances of passing the entrance exams by joining one of the *ateliers préparatoires*; that of Jacques-Eugène Freynet (1862–1937) and Jules-Alexis Godefroy (1863–1928) was the most popular in the 1890s. There students practiced the artistic skills needed to pass the exams and, if foreign, spent time improving their French. By the late nineteenth century many French students came to the École by way of the network of regional Écoles des Beaux-Arts, which offered their own programs in art and design. Exceptional students won admission to the national school through regional competitions that guaranteed the winner admission and a stipend for attendance for up to four years. Others spent a few years at a regional school and then made their way to Paris to compete for admission with the rest of the *aspirants*; these students generally had an advantage, as their previous work was targeted to ensure success in Paris.

However one gained admission to the institution, it was equally important to gain entry to one of the *ateliers libres*, the affiliated studios, where most of the instruction in architecture was done. To the student, the atelier was the single most important organization at the École (FIG. 3). To join an atelier was to enter an exclusive club. The *patron*, or studio teacher, was the unquestioned authority of the atelier. He (and until the post-World War II period they were all men) came

to the studio twice or three times a week and might occasionally give a lecture, but generally spent his time reviewing and commenting on the design work of the senior students working in the first class. The actual management of the studio fell to the *massiers*, older students of extremely high standing, who rented the studio space, procured fuel and other supplies, collected dues from the other students, and enforced discipline among them. A code of behavior governed the students in each atelier, and a complex schedule of fines were in place that helped to support the enterprise, enforced by the *sous-massier*, the second in command. For the Americans, the most onerous fines were those for speaking a foreign language. In many of the ateliers one was fined ten centimes (about fifty cents) for each word of English spoken. It could be worse, though—the fine for a word of German was up to ten times higher! Upon entering the atelier and surviving the customary initiations, new students were inducted into the *nouveaux-de-service*, the corps of students in their first year who were charged with the maintenance of the atelier and providing assistance

to the older students, the *anciens*. This usually meant buying firewood or washing the floors, but during the final days of a project, it often meant mixing glues or inks, stretching paper over frames, and applying ink washes to a drawing, layer by layer, to achieve the depth of shadows that often won a student a competition. The work of *nouveaux-de-service* was directed by the third-in-command in the atelier, the *chef-couchon*, or "chief pig." Hardly a term of endearment, this name embodied the fear and disgust in which the *nouveaux* held their taskmaster; the *chef-couchon* could make one's first year in the atelier absolutely hellish if he chose.[7]

For most students the atelier became the center of their lives; ateliers were social as well as academic institutions. The *patron* set the character of the design work that was produced by the students, but the students created the atelier's distinct culture, much as in an American fraternity. There was an origin story and mythology for each atelier, and banners and songs that were distinctly each atelier's own. Entry into these societies was accompanied by an initiation

Above

FIG. 3

The patron Victor Laloux, studio teacher of a prominent atelier, is seated in the front row, to right of center, holding a top hat and umbrella. The *massiers* (older students who managed the studios), also with top hats, are to his left. A formal portrait like this was a yearly event for the larger ateliers, but Julia Morgan's solo work with Chaussemiche afforded no opportunity for such a portrait. Photo by Atelier Laloux, 1900.

ritual, often formalized into a pageant of sorts, and just as often involving nudity or fire, or sometimes both. Each studio's success in the design competitions that comprised the design education was carefully observed, and each victory was viewed as affirmation of an atelier's superiority over its rivals. A victory in one of the prestigious first-class *concours*—those that carried with them a monetary prize—was usually marked with a raucous celebration at a restaurant or other suitable night spot, much like a scene from *La Bohème*.

Each atelier had a distinctive character to its design work. Emile Paulin's studio, for example, was known for its conventional neoclassicism, and its commensurate success in the monthly *concours*. In contrast, the studio of Victor Laloux (1850–1937) embraced the free neo-baroque of the most forward-looking contemporary practitioners, as exemplified by Laloux's own Gare d'Orsay (now the Musée d'Orsay) or the Petit Palais, one of the signature buildings of the Exposition Universelle of 1900, designed by Charles Girault (1851–1932). A student chose an atelier based on sympathy for the design aesthetic espoused by the *patron*, but also considered other factors, such as the number of Grands Prix winners each studio could claim, or the lineage of the atelier. Many Americans chose Laloux's atelier because he took over the studio from Louis-Jules André (1819–1890), who had been Bernard Maybeck's patron in the 1880s, and André had been a student of Pierre-Jérôme-Honoré Daumet (1826–1911), who in turn was *patron* to Charles Follen McKim (1847–1909).[8]

Once students joined the *seconde classe* and an atelier, they began to take coursework at the École itself and to participate in the monthly *concours d'émulations*. These competitions formed the core of the design and skills instruction at the École. The format alternated every month between *esquisses-esquisses* and *projets rendus*. The *esquisse-esquisse*, or sketch-sketch, was an intense twelve- or twenty-four-hour design exercise. Students had to create and draw up floorplans, elevations, and sections of a building from a written program in one sitting. The *projets rendus*, or rendered projects, began the same way—students studied the program brief, found the inherent hierarchy within its text, and designed a corresponding set of plans, sections, and elevations within a twelve-hour time limit. But students were then asked to develop the designs further over the next two months. Each

element was to be reconsidered, from the relationships of the spaces to each other to the proportions of the classical orders on the elevations to the placement of the building on the site. The project was then formally presented in a fully rendered, water-colored composition that would usually take a week to produce. At the final jurying the submission was compared to the sketch produced two months earlier; if it varied too much from the initial ideas in the sketch, the project was considered *hors-de-concours* (out of the competition), and the student received no credit.

Although the sketch problems were generally executed in the same large drafting room used for the entrance exams, the *projets rendus* were developed and rendered in the ateliers. This permitted the more experienced first-class students to assist the second-class students, making suggestions and offering design alternatives that would improve their work.

Opposite
FIG. 4
Alexis Lemaistre, "Registering the Projects in the Salle Melpomène," published in *L'École des Beaux-Arts desinée et recontrée par un élève* (Paris: Firmin-Didot & Cie, 1989).

Above
FIG. 5
Alexis Lemaistre, "La Charrette," *L'École des Beaux-Arts desinée et recontrée par un élève* (Paris: Firmin-Didot & Cie, 1989).

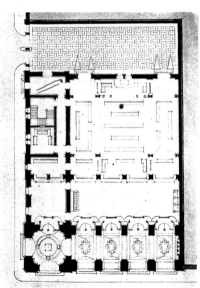

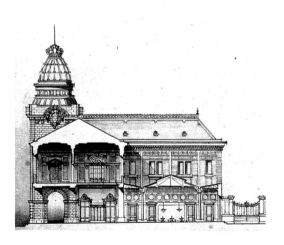

CONCOURS DE 2ᴹᴱ CLASSE

UN PETIT HOTEL DES POSTES ET TÉLÉGRAPHES

1ᴿᴱ MENTION : M. LESOUFACHÉ, ÉLÈVE DE M. LALOUX

Héliotypie FORTIER et MAROTTE, 35, rue de Jussieu, Paris

Librairies-Imprimeries Réunies, Éditeurs.

In return, the second-class students were expected to assist the first-class students with the menial rendering labor that was required for their much larger projects. This largely consisted of laying wash upon wash of watercolor onto sheets to build up the shadows and depth of the drawings. Once completed, projects were required to be presented to the registrar of the École on the day and hour they were due (FIG. 4). The *portier* closed the doors at the deadline, and if a student's drawing was not inside the room, it was considered *hors-de-concours* and eliminated from consideration. Since no one wanted to lose credit for two months' work, students would race through the streets of Paris, their drawings loaded on pushcarts, to make it through the gates in time. Were a student not quite finished, he might try to add some final details while running through the streets. It is from this mad dash to the École that we get the term working *en charrette*, or working on the cart; today architects often refer to the whole last-minute preparations of a set of drawings as a *charrette* (FIG. 5).

The curriculum at the École was concentrated in a few academic areas; students took courses in the history and theory of architectural design, in structures and building systems, and in construction. In fact, construction was the focus of the second class—students did exercises in wood, stone, masonry, and iron construction, and many of the studio projects required the use of new construction materials such as iron, steel, and, later, concrete (FIG. 6). Along with acceptable performance in artistic competitions in drawing, modelling, and ornamentation and a demonstration in architectural history, students were required to achieve competence in technical subjects, including mathematics, descriptive geometry (two- and three-dimensional constructions), perspective, and stereotomy (the cutting of stone for building vaults and the like). Typically a student earned half of the twenty *valeurs*, or competition points, required to move up to the first class in these artistic and technical competitions and the other half in the monthly competitions in architectural design. Successfully completing a project in the second class earned the student at least a *seconde mention* and one *valeur*. An exceptional performance might win one a first mention and two *valeurs*, and an award-winning entry earned the student a medal and three *valeurs*. Thus, one could move into the first class by earning the twenty *valeurs* and by completing the project for the construction course—a set of design development drawings detailing the construction of a building of the student's own design—in just over eighteen months. Very few students moved through the curriculum that quickly—accumulating the *valuers* usually took about two years, and most students spent four to six months completing the project and passing the final construction examination.

Work in the first class was focused on completing the requirements for the *diplôme* and on competing for the Grand Prix de Rome. The *diplôme* was a relatively recent creation at the École, as it was established in 1867, and most students did not pursue the degree until it was thrust into importance in 1887, when the École granted its *diplôme* to all living recipients of the Grand Prix. The degree required a thesis project and a year's full-time apprenticeship to a qualified architect. By the mid-1890s the degree was the goal of all who studied at the École and was the official endorsement of professional competency granted by the government.[9]

The primary vehicle for architectural instruction in the first class were the monthly design competitions, the *concours d'émulations*. The formats of these competitions were similar to those in the second year in that they alternated between *esquisses-esquisses*

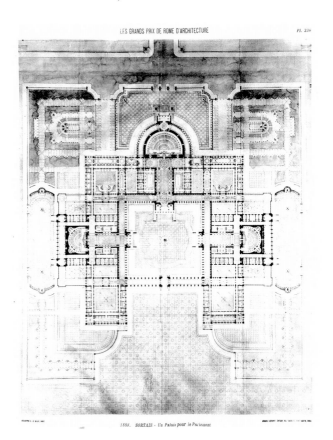

Opposite

FIG. 6
Charles-Louis-Marie Lesoufaché, "Un Petit Hotel des Postes et Télégraphes," 1901. Heliotype by Fortier et Marotte, published in *École Nationale Supérieure des Beaux-Arts: Les Concours d'École. Section d'Architecture, 1899–1902* (Paris: Libraries-Imprimeries Réunies, 1902), plate 123

Left

FIG. 7
Louis-Marie-Henri Sortais, "Un Palais pour le Parlement," Grand Prix entry, 1888. Sortais would win the Grand Prix in 1890. Heliotype by E. Deley, published in *Les Grands Prix de Rome d'Architecture, 1850–1900*, v. 4 (Paris: Armand Guérinet, 1904), plate 336

Above & opposite

FIG. 8

Paul Robine, "Une
Synagogue,"
medal-winning
Projet Rendu,
1900. Heliotype
by Fortier et
Marotte, published
in *École Nationale
Supérieure des
Beaux-Arts:
Les Concours
d'École. Section
d'Architecture,
1899-1902*, plates
60-61

and the *projets rendus*, but the projects were often more ambitious in scope. To succeed in these building design competitions, students had to employ the Beaux-Arts method, which demanded that they identify the implied hierarchy of the spaces described in the brief and find an efficient and pleasing circulation pattern that engaged the principal spaces—this circulation path was called the *marche*. It was axiomatic at the École that a graphically beautiful plan could be developed into a beautiful building in a number of historical styles, as long as the hierarchy of the program was respected within a geometrically pleasing figure (FIG. 7). The appropriate style for a project responded to the character of the building typology or the institution to be housed. So, most generally, the plan accommodated the programmatic functions of

the project and the elevations, or exterior appearance, satisfied its cultural and urbanistic requirements.

During Julia Morgan's studies in Paris, the professor of theory, the philosophical leader of the faculty, was Julien Guadet (1834–1908), who maintained the school's traditional stylistic orientation while introducing modern methods of construction and architectural practice. Guadet was a student at the École in the 1850s and early 1860s, having studied first in the atelier of Henri Labrouste (1801–1875), and then with his successor, Jules André. As an advanced student in the first class, Guadet worked for Charles Garnier (1825–1898), who was building the Paris Opéra from the early 1860s into the 1870s. The Opéra was one of the most technically advanced structures of the nineteenth century, utilizing the latest in theatrical equipment, lighting, and iron construction, yet it also embodied the social stratification of French society in its accommodation of rituals such as the *promenade*. Guadet's years with Garnier would have a lasting impact on him, as he would forever define architecture as the fusion of art and science demonstrated by the Opéra. In 1864, Guadet won the coveted Prix de Rome with a design for a "hospice in the Alps," ensuring his future within the architectural establishment. Guadet was installed as a *patron* of one of the *ateliers officiels* at the resumption of teaching following the Commune of 1871. He remained in this post until 1894, when he was appointed professor of theory.

Guadet attained this chair at a time when the ideological and stylistic struggles of past decades were largely settled. By the 1890s the battle between the Gothic and the classic seemed passé, and the technical curriculum of the École gave as full weight to iron as it did to wood and masonry; students were required to master iron detailing in the second class and to use this mastery in their designs in the first. Released from past agendas, Guadet was free to set his own. As professor of theory he further accentuated the professional orientation of the curriculum, an emphasis that had been a part of the École's teaching since the 1880s. Guadet shaped the pedagogy of the school and wrote the programs for the *concours d'émulations*; he used these programs to connect the École more strongly to the world outside its gates. Many of his programs directly confronted political or social events of the moment in which they were written, and others drew on social trends that had been apparent for decades.

Guadet's politics were staunchly Liberal-Republican, and he often used his architectural programs to communicate his party's social message to his students. For example, the programs for religious architecture highlight Guadet's intention to correlate work done at the École with political events. His proposal for a synagogue in October 1899 was issued just one month after army captain Alfred Dreyfus was convicted a second time for treason in a spectacular trial that confirmed for many a latent anti-Semitism within French society. The students' designs may or may not have shown a complete understanding of the liturgical requirements of a synagogue, but the exercise did require a sympathy with Jewish history and culture to produce a competent result (FIG. 8).

The judgement of the monthly *concours* was much harsher for the first-class projects than for the second. Fewer than half of the submitted designs might receive a *seconde mention*, worth half a *valeur*, or a *première mention*, worth a full *valeur*. Five percent of the submissions might receive a *première seconde médaille*, worth two valeurs, and usually only one or two entries would receive the *première médaille*, and the corresponding three points. The percentage of projects receiving recognition could vary considerably depending on the mood of the judges—in some *concours* less than a quarter of the submissions were awarded any kind of credit at all.

Along with the monthly *concours d'émulations*, first-class students competed in a series of extraordinary competitions for medals and cash awards.

Most of these special competitions focused on a specific design objective: the Prix Rougevin, for example, asked students to draw an ornamental object or a significant element of an interior, while the Prix Godeboeuf often focused on a building element. Julia Morgan achieved her greatest personal success with the Godeboeuf of 1901, when she won a *seconde médaille* for a "staircase for a palace."[10] The Prix Edmond Labarre was a one-day sketch problem that investigated progressive institutional types—there were no *valuers* awarded for the Labarre, just one cash prize (FIG. 9). The award for winning these competitions was substantial—as much as 750 francs (about 3,000 dollars in current U.S. dollars).[11] These short-term competitions, usually lasting no more than one week, were significant moments in the first-class student's year. The Godeboeuf was held in December, while the Rougevin was held in the second week of February; all of the work for the Rougevin was done *en loge*, that is, in small cubicles or rooms that could be secured, and no external assistance was allowed. Due to the timing of the Rougevin, usually right before Mardi Gras, the end of the *charrette* (at 5:00 P.M. sharp!) was celebrated with a massive procession from the Beaux-Arts buildings on the Rue Bonaparte up the hill past the Sorbonne to the Place du Panthéon, where the students lit an enormous bonfire of their sketches, stretchers, and anything else left over from the competition.[12]

The Grand Prix was the pinnacle of academic training in French architectural culture; only a select corps of students was allowed to compete for one of the loges used for the *projets rendus*. Unlike any other competition at the École, it required that the entrants be French citizens. It was typical for a student to compete for three to five years before winning the Grand Prix, and four entrants went through the grueling process at least seven times before winning! The reward was deemed worth the sacrifice. Winners were sent on a four-year residence in Rome (and later Greece) to study the greatest works of classical architecture; in return they were required to send a set of measured drawings of a building of their choice (called an *envoi*) back to Paris. Upon their return, winners were given important governmental commissions, which typically set them up to become *patrons* at the École and eventually members of the Royal Academy. Accordingly, *patrons* were as anxious to mentor their protégés to a Grand Prix as

their students were to be awarded it. A kind of esprit de corps would develop within a prizewinning studio that generated a momentum of its own; the successful students would teach their juniors the tricks of the trade, the atelier's reputation would attract more of the best students, and the *patron* would become more involved with the class. This could result in a studio becoming "hot" and producing several Grand Prix winners in succession.

The Grand Prix competition was conducted in two parts—a twelve-hour sketch problem, and a four-month rendering exercise. In the first part the student had to design a solution to the written program in one twelve-hour exercise. These sketches were then judged on their relative merits, and the contestants then ranked in order of probable finish. A few days later the top eight contestants (later ten) were identified and then each required over the next four months to render in large scale a plan, a section, and a principal elevation developed from their earlier designs. Upon completion, the rendered work was checked against the initial sketches; any projects that deviated too much from the initial *parti* were disqualified, although this rarely happened in the nineteenth century. Students were required to do their drawings *en loge*, so there was no possibility of a student claiming someone else's work as his own.[13]

The programs used in the Grand Prix were not formulated arbitrarily. The architect members of the Royal Academy or its equivalent selected three building types from a dozen or so that were proposed by the *patrons* and the professor of architectural theory. The final choice of building type from among the three was chosen by drawing lots. This would be done well in advance of the *esquisses*, as a formal program had to be prepared and published.

The Prix de Rome was the most prominent forum for the school's emerging professional orientation. Industrial building types accounted for one half of the Grand Prix programs during Guadet's term as professor of theory (1894 to 1908); factories, waterworks, and scientific stations were all deemed to be appropriate subjects for the Prix de Rome. Contestants faced with such programs often felt at liberty to employ more contemporary architectural forms and structural systems. Victor Laloux's 1902 program for a national printing house, for example, went further than most in confronting the competitors with an industrial type and encouraged the use of structural

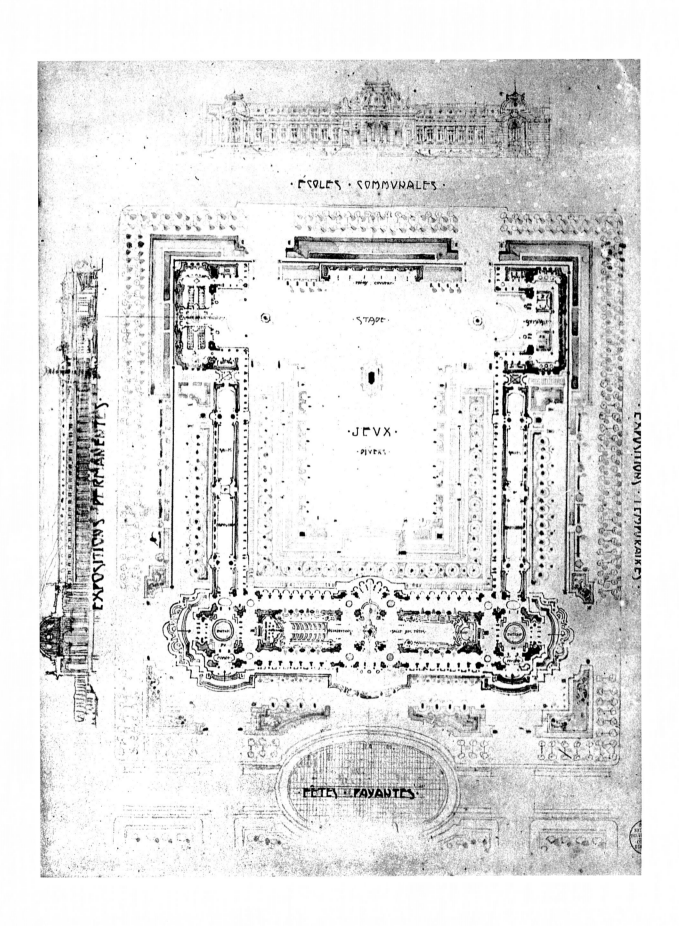

ÉCOLES · COMMUNALES ·

EXPOSITIONS · PERMANENTES ·

EXPOSITION · TEMPORAIRE ·

STADE

JEVX

DIVERS

FÊTES · PAYANTES ·

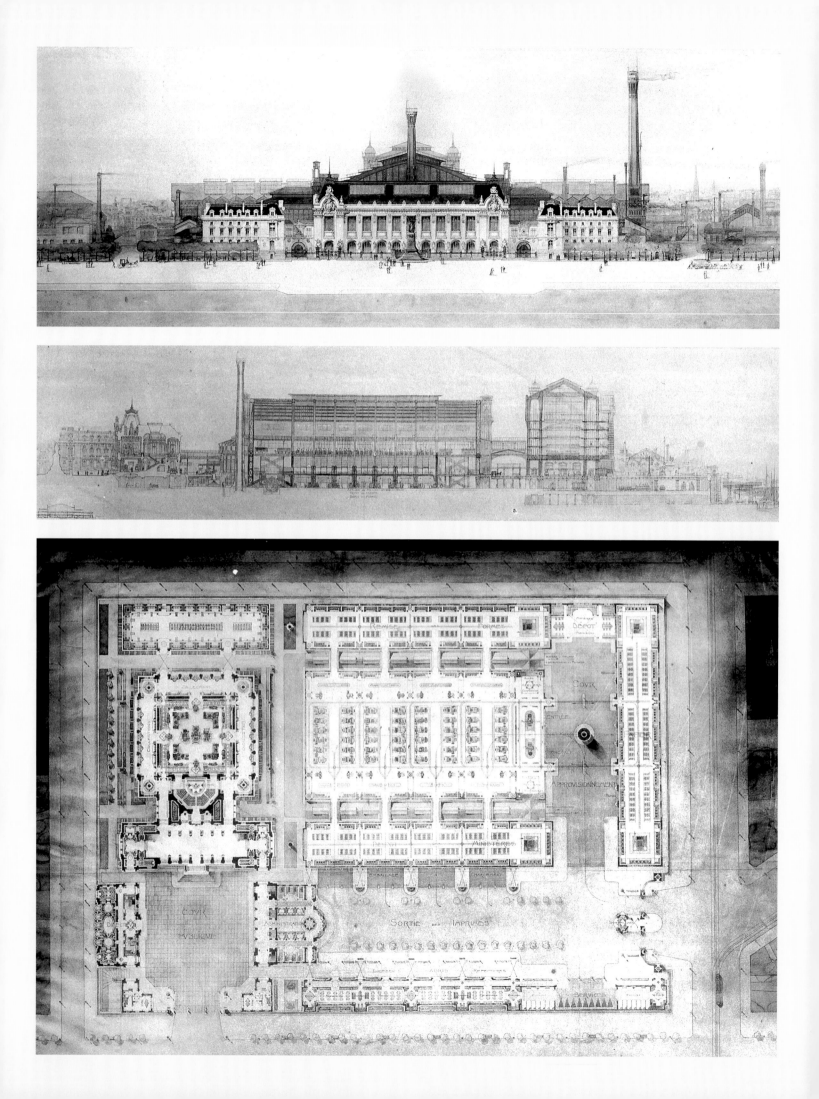

steel in an elegant and yet strictly functional manner that defied traditional stylistic categories (FIG. 10).

In the years of the French Third Republic (1871 to 1939) Americans made up the largest cohort of foreign students at the École des Beaux-Arts. Over three hundred fifty Americans studied at the École in those years, and there were usually at least twenty to thirty there at any one time. Julia Morgan came to Paris in the late 1890s, at the peak of the school's popularity with young American designers, and she was joined by nearly a dozen of her classmates from the University of California—all students, as she had been, of Bernard Maybeck, who had attended the school in the 1880s, studying under Jules André. Maybeck was not the first architect practicing in California to have attended the École; Albert Pissis studied there in the 1870s as a student of Julien Guadet and later established a practice in San Francisco.[14] Among Morgan's Berkeley confrères were Harvey Wiley Corbett, John Bakewell, Jr., Edward H. Bennett, Arthur Brown, Jr., Robert Farquhar, Édouard Frère Champney, and Loring Rixford. (See Gordon Fuglie's Introduction for a discussion of Pissis, Maybeck, and Brown.) Many of these classmates found success beyond the Bay Area upon their return from Paris. Corbett became very well known as a designer of skyscrapers in New York City, and Bennett became Daniel Burnham's chief assistant and one of the most prominent urban planners of the 1920s and 1930s. Morgan's childhood friend Arthur Brown, Jr. teamed up with his fraternity brother John Bakewell, Jr. to form the firm Bakewell & Brown, which designed dozens of Bay Area landmarks, including San Francisco City Hall, Temple Emanu-El, and many buildings on the Stanford campus. Brown later practiced alone and designed the San Francisco War Memorial Complex, Coit Tower, Pasadena City Hall, and the Labor-ICC complex at the Federal Triangle in Washington, D.C.

The Americans formed a distinct society within the École—they were typically older than the French students, and usually already had undergraduate degrees in civil engineering, or, later, in architecture itself. While the French students socialized nearly exclusively with those in the same atelier—to do otherwise was to risk being seen as disloyal to the *patron*—the Americans were less emotionally tied to their studios and had two sets of social identities, that as members of their ateliers and that as Americans. The Americans typically shared apartments, often located in the same buildings, and an elaborate system of subleases kept these lodgings in American hands for years.[15] The Americans made a point of celebrating holidays together, and the Fourth of July and Thanksgiving were particularly opportune moments for the students to proclaim their national identity. One well-known example of this sort of celebration was the football game played by the American students of the École on Thanksgiving Day 1897. The event was such a novelty that it was covered by the French press, who reported that the game was a seemingly incomprehensible brawl. The students arranged for a professional photographer to commemorate the event, and for many of the participants, this photo is one of the only pictorial records of their time in Paris (FIG. 11). (Incidentally, Yellow beat Red 6 to 0. Arthur Brown Jr. scored the only touchdown.) The Americans also participated in a yearly show with the larger expatriate community. Each December American students from several Parisian institutions staged a kind of vaudeville night, featuring stand-up routines, popular music, and short comedic sketches. Students would practice for weeks beforehand to perfect their routines, even though the timing of the event was such that it often conflicted with the most important exams, *rendus*, and competitions at the École.[16]

The highlight of the social calendar at the École des Beaux-Arts was the annual Bal des Quat'z'Arts (Four Arts Ball), more commonly referred to now as the Beaux-Arts Ball. Unlike many of its later imitators, the original Beaux-Arts Balls were themed costume parties. The first event was organized by Henri Guillaume, the chief *massier* of the atelier André, in 1892. He brought together the leadership of all the student bodies at the École: architects, engravers, painters, and sculptors. Together they planned a grand ball patterned in part after the official balls of the other *grandes écoles* in Paris. A hall and an orchestra were hired, and students spent weeks designing the decor and crafting costumes appropriate to the theme. It was a great success, and a second ball was held the following year at the Moulin Rouge. This event proved a scandal, as the famous artist's model known as Sarah Brown (actually Marie-Florentine Roger) arranged herself nearly nude atop one of the *tableaux vivants*, and was subsequently arrested for public indecency. The students of the Latin Quarter rioted in response, and in the end the government backed down.[17] The Beaux-Arts Ball was revived the

Opposite

FIG. 10

Léon Prost, "Une Imprimerie Nationale," Grand Prix winner 1902. Heliotype by E. Deley, published in *Les Grands Prix de Rome d'Architecture, 1850-1900*, v. 4, (Paris: Armand Guérinet, 1904), plates 190 and 191

following year, but subsequent balls were a bit more subdued and were held at more respectable locations (FIG. 12). By the end of the 1890s the most anxiety-inducing aspect of the event was often finding a date, and the ateliers were awarded prizes for persuading the greatest number of women to attend the event. It was into this highly charged gender-conscious atmosphere that Julia Morgan bid to enter the École des Beaux-Arts.

The story of Morgan's admission to the École has been told often. (But see Karen McNeill's "Parisian Foundations" in this volume for more on the gender dynamics of Morgan's time in Paris.) She was originally supposed to travel to Paris with Arthur Brown, Jr. and his mother, Victoria Runyon Brown, in 1894. Arthur was to spend a junior year abroad, and Morgan was to begin preparations for the entrance examinations. However, Victoria became ill, and the Browns cancelled their plans, forcing Morgan to delay her travel to Paris to the following year. Morgan took

the *examens d'admission* at least three times, performing well enough to earn admission if the faculty had been willing to admit her. However, the question of whether a woman could handle the rigors of the curriculum made her admission a political issue. Finally, with her excellent performance in the second exams of 1898, a change in the laws governing the *grandes écoles*, and the persistent lobbying of Bernard Maybeck, Julien Guadet and the rest of the faculty agreed to admit her. The official reaction of the architectural establishment was positive; *La Construction Moderne*, for example, wrote that "[F]or the first time since the vote on the law authorizing the admission of women to the École des Beaux-Arts, we learn of the admission of a woman to the section of architecture (2nd class): Ms. Morgan, nationality American, and, as one can see above, [she] has been admitted 13th of 40 successful aspirants. This is a great example for our refined young French women."[18]

Morgan's entry into the school did not go unnoticed. Many in the architectural community, fully aware of the spartan conditions of the school buildings themselves and the associated ateliers, used the occasion of Morgan's admittance to demand renovation of its facilities. Of chief concern were the toilets, which were primitive at best. A few weeks after the announcement of Morgan's achievement, an editorial in *La Construction Moderne* called for private dressing rooms for the female students near the school's drawing studios and women's restrooms, equipped with proper Western toilets, in contrast to the "Turkish" fixtures still present in the buildings. The article concluded, that "[W]e don't know if the *Egalité* that is inscribed between two other ideals on all our public buildings and on our money requires the admittance of women to the École des Beaux-Arts, but, we repeat, decency requires that women admitted to the École be treated there as women with the customs of the well-educated, and not that of cowgirls."[19] Whether the last term, *vachères,* was a direct reference to Julia Morgan, who, hailing from California, was thought by many in the French press to be a frontierswoman, akin to Annie Oakley, brandishing a T-square instead of a six-gun, one cannot tell.

Concern for Morgan's sanctity and safety greatly restricted her ability to shape her own education. She was barred, for example, from choosing an atelier. Instead, she was assigned to François-Benjamin Chaussemiche's *atelier officiel*, which had no separate studio space, no traditions, and no raucous esprit de corps. Morgan's initial assessment of Chaussemiche was not positive—he was very much the junior of the École's faculty, as he was only thirty-four years old when Morgan was assigned to him. While he had won a Grand Prix, he had only returned to Paris from his stay in Italy and Greece the year before and had not yet built anything. Morgan was almost certainly assigned to Chaussemiche because he had been taught by Jules André and mentored by Victor Laloux (like Chaussemiche, also from Tours). It was probably thought that if Morgan couldn't join Laloux's atelier, as some of her close male Berkeley classmates had done, she could at least be taught by one of his young acolytes. For his part, Chaussemiche may not have been thrilled with the assignment either, as he was faced with a difficult situation; whether he brought Morgan along into the profession as well as he could, or whether she wilted under the demands of

the curriculum and the inherent sexism of the institution, he was bound to make powerful enemies on both sides of the gender question. In the end, over the course of the nearly four years Morgan spent with Chaussemiche, they learned to work together despite the challenges that they had to overcome and despite Chaussemiche's long absences from Paris due to his historic conservation duties. When Morgan left Paris in 1902, Chaussemiche had become her champion and ally, and the two enjoyed a lifelong friendship.

Like many of the students at the École, Morgan struggled to maintain good health. She was very often sick, and minor colds and infections grew serious with the fatigue that set in with the long hours demanded by studio assignments. Victoria Runyon Brown often accompanied Morgan to the doctor, as young women were not to see a physician without a female companion. In a letter to her husband, Brown described one such bout of illness not long after Morgan's admission to the school, offering to take

Miss Morgan to the country. But she says she will not and she will do the Analytique which comes on right now. He told me that I must take care of her and not let her work so hard. But I can do nothing and [she] has an abscess in her ear. She was suffering very much. I went with her to see the doctor and she fainted in his office and I was frightened—she had a sort of spasm and was unconscious for some time. The doctor did not think the abscess very serious, but did think her general condition is, and told her positively she must rest and take care of herself and go away with her. She is very determined and she may go on all night.[20]

Morgan did recover from this abscess, of course, but her health was constantly under threat the entire time she studied in Paris.[21]

As Morgan advanced to the first class, she faced other challenges. For example, she had a great deal of difficulty finding second-class students to assist her with the rendering of her drawings. Typically the youngest students in an atelier assisted the first-class students with the menial work required to produce the large *projets rendus* that were the mainstay of the first-class work; this was the case even after one had completed a year as a *nouveau-de-service.* However, no Frenchman, *nouveau* or not, would work for Morgan, and while most of the Americans were willing, they often faced the same deadlines Morgan did, and were thus unavailable. Morgan found her assistants where she could; Mrs. Brown, in particular, took great pride

Opposite

FIG. 11
American students of the École, Thanksgiving Day, November 27, 1897. James Gamble Rogers, back row; Joseph Howland Hunt, back row, sixth from left; John Bakewell Jr., back row, third from right; Arthur Brown Jr., seated, fourth from left; Robert Farquhar, seated, fifth from left; Édouard Frère Champney, seated, second from right.

in assisting Morgan and in seeing her succeed at the École and later in practice in San Francisco.[22]

The influence of the École des Beaux-Arts on American architecture greatly diminished in the years after its closure for World War I. The proliferation of architecture programs in the United States between 1900 and 1930 meant that the Beaux-Arts method could be learned stateside (and in English) by professors who had been trained in Paris, alleviating the need to spend years overseas. By the 1930s the Beaux-Arts method and Classical Revival vocabulary became the bête noire of modern architectural theorists, and as modernism became mainstream, the École was slow to change its pedagogy. Rival institutions in Paris, such as the École Spéciale d'Architecture on the Boulevard Raspail, flourished as the Beaux-Arts struggled to find its identity in the post-World War II context. The end of a three-hundred-year history came in 1968, when French president Charles de Gaulle blamed the architecture students at the École for instigating the student riots of that year. The architecture program at the Beaux-Arts was relocated to several different suburban universities to ensure that the student body could never take over the streets of Paris again.

Interest in the École des Beaux-Arts was reignited in 1975 when Arthur Drexler, curator of architecture at the Museum of Modern Art in New York, launched an exhibition of Beaux-Arts drawings. Designers trained in the modernist pedagogy marveled at the fine detail and nuance of shade and shadow in the nineteenth-century drawings on exhibit, even though the historicism of the architecture left them nonplussed. The subsequent catalogue, published in 1977 as *The Architecture of the École des Beaux-Arts*, presented a serious appraisal of the Beaux-Arts by noted scholars such as Richard Chafee, Neil Levine, Robin Middleton, and David Van Zanten.[23] The book was fortuitously synchronous with the revival of interest in architectural history that accompanied the postmodern movement, and for a short time there was a reawakening of interest in the Beaux-Arts method, rooted as it was in the exploration of geometry and an analysis of program, i.e., the implied social and functional hierarchy of people and activities to be housed in a building. Although overt postmodern historicism quickly faded, attention has continued to be given to the American architects trained at the Beaux-Arts. Monographs on several of

Julia Morgan's compatriots have been published in the past twenty years, and organizations such as the Institute of Classical Architecture and Art sponsor research into traditional architecture in the United States and offer training in drawing the orders and in classical design methods.

Although the École des Beaux-Arts is no longer the center of architectural production it once was, its legacy of three centuries of traditional design instruction remains in the thousands of buildings designed using the Beaux-Arts method that grace France, the United States, and the Francophone world. The school's impact is particularly noticeable in California, where the work of Julia Morgan and her Berkeley classmates dominated the state's architectural profession between 1890 and 1930. Adapted to the state's unique context, the lessons Julia Morgan learned at the École were the foundation that supported her career as she became one of the state's most prolific and celebrated architects. ✥

Opposite

FIG. 12

Edward Cucuel, *The Grand Cavalcade*, illustration published in W. C. Morrow and Edward Cucuel, *Bohemian Paris of To-Day* (Philadelphia and London: J. P. Lippincott, 1900)

THE GRAND CAVALCADE

2

Signature de l'Élève

Julia Morgan.

CHAPTER 2

PARISIAN FOUNDATIONS

JULIA MORGAN AT THE ÉCOLE DES BEAUX-ARTS, 1896–1902

KAREN McNEILL

Julia Morgan boarded an eastbound train in California, at the western terminus of the transcontinental railroad, on March 25, 1896. She was on her way to Paris to study architecture at the École des Beaux-Arts, the most prestigious architectural program in the world. As the train pulled away from the station, one society columnist wrote, "Oakland will be very proud in the future of her woman architect."[1] With that, Morgan's role was cast: she bore the burden of blazing a career path that few women had tried to follow and still fewer had succeeded in navigating, and she did this under the scrutiny and admiration of a well-meaning but often ignorant public eye.

Morgan knew her heroic destiny was hardly certain. Gaining admission to the architecture program within the École des Beaux-Arts was daunting under the best of circumstances; the entrance examinations for architecture were notoriously difficult, and most applicants failed at least once.[2] Around the time Morgan was heading to Paris, the architectural faculty made admissions even more demanding: With the rise of modern construction technologies, like structural steel framing and reinforced concrete, the faculty elevated the mathematics requirements for all students. And in response to a dramatic influx of foreign students who crowded the ateliers and successfully competed against French citizens in the entrance examinations—effectively leading to a decline in the number of Frenchmen who could train at their country's most elite national institution—the École limited the number of foreigners admitted during any examination period to just ten. Beyond these challenges, Julia Morgan was a woman, and the École des Beaux-Arts did not admit women.

On November 14, 1898, however, Julia Morgan learned that she had passed the entrance examinations for the architecture program at the École des Beaux-Arts, making her the first woman to achieve that distinction (FIG. 1). Though she did not earn the highest degree for international students, the *diplôme,* she became the first woman to earn a *certificat d'études* from the École in February 1902. These are well-known and long-celebrated facts. Much less understood are the complexities of the gender dynamics that Morgan experienced throughout her six years in Paris. They fueled her ambitions with a purpose that transcended individual success and laid the foundations for her professional persona and approach to architectural design in the United States.

THE MORGAN ATELIER

All Beaux-Arts students studied with master architects in ateliers. For Julia Morgan, this proved to be an almost insurmountable obstacle. Just one woman threatened the fraternal culture of the ateliers that had developed over the centuries, and most of them refused to admit her. As a result, the ateliers that did open their doors to her came with significant compromises in the quality and nature of instruction—formal and informal.

Morgan arrived in Paris optimistic that her journey abroad would be more valuable than any training she might have undertaken in the United States, regardless of whether or not she would be able to study at the École. She immediately secured lodging at the American Girls' Club, an institution established to provide reasonably priced room and board for American women artists as well as an exhibition space for them (FIG. 2).[3] And within days, Morgan was invited to join the atelier of Marcel Pérouse de Monclos, a young architect who had earned his *diplôme* from the École in 1893.[4] "I'm glad I came," she wrote to Pierre LeBrun,

a family relation and second-generation member of a distinguished architecture family on the East Coast. "It wakes one up wonderfully more than Boston," where she presumably could have studied architecture at MIT.[5] Eight months later, alas, the atelier's work had fallen to virtually nothing, pupils were leaving, and Morgan was searching for a new mentor. As she had been advised early on, Monclos was adequate to begin her studies with, but had neither the prestige nor expertise to be her permanent mentor.

When Julia Morgan embarked on her search for a new atelier in the spring of 1897, however, she soon discovered just how unique the Monclos situation was. While most architecture students had little trouble securing places in one of the free ateliers at the École or, for a fee, any number of independent ateliers in the city, Morgan faced a daunting task. Initially, she

hoped to study under Jean-Louis Pascal (1837–1920). Unfortunately, Pascal had different ideas. When Morgan arrived at his door with Bernard Maybeck, her Bay Area architectural mentor and an École student in the 1880s, simply to seek Pascal's critique of her work, Pascal immediately assumed that she wished to join his atelier and promptly disabused her of any such notion. He did, however, like her work and thought she would perform well at the examinations. He suggested she try one of the official ateliers of the École, but those doors proved closed to Morgan as well.[6] Her search for a new atelier lasted nearly a year.

Morgan's ease at securing a space in the Monclos atelier can be attributed to a transatlantic network of American women who supported an increasingly broad range of educational and professional opportunities for women at home and abroad. Elisabeth

Opposite

FIG. 2

Garden of the Art Club published in Emily Meredyth Aylward, "The American Girls' Art Club in Paris," *Scribner's Magazine* 16, no. 5 (November 1894): 601. The club was located at No. 4 rue de Chevreuse.

Right

FIG. 3

Guy Rose, *An Architect at the Gates of the Beaux-Arts*, illustration published in John M. Howells, "An Architect at the Gates of the Beaux-Arts," *Harper's Weekly* (December 22, 1894): 1221. Rose's illustration depicts both the carnivalesque and studious life of architecture students at the École des Beaux-Arts.

Mills Reid, daughter of San Francisco banking tycoon Darius Ogden Mills and wife of newspaper magnate and American ambassador to France Whitelaw Reid, opened the American Girls' Club boardinghouse, where Morgan lived during her first year in Paris. Shortly after arriving at the club, Morgan met Katherine Budd, a fellow aspiring architect who studied with Monclos and introduced Morgan to him.[7] In turn, Monclos "had no doubts but [she] would come to him," making Julia Morgan the third American woman to join his atelier; the Pennsylvanian Fay Kellogg had been the first.[8] Importantly, Monclos was married to another Pennsylvanian, Katherine Cheyney Bartol. She was a contemporary of Morgan's, an American woman who came of age in the same post-Victorian culture that imagined young single women engaged in all sorts of pursuits outside of the home, and of the same class as Elisabeth Mills Reid, who adopted aspects of these modern ideas for her personal causes. As the Monclos atelier fell apart, Morgan commented to Pierre LeBrun, "I have not yet discovered how his [Monclos] having an American wife make[s] it any advantage to his students."[9] Perhaps Morgan had assumed Mrs. Monclos would be a factor in attracting American students to her husband's atelier, but that turned out not to be the case. Still, Katherine Monclos likely played an important role in acculturating her French husband to the notion that women could be architects and that his atelier could welcome female students. She also fostered a nurturing environment for women students; for example, after the exhausting experience of Morgan's first entrance examination in June 1897, Katherine Monclos was the person who encouraged the Californian to sojourn for a month in the country to recuperate. In short, she helped render the Monclos atelier a suitable place for women and the rare one to welcome them, if not, in the end, a great one in which to develop strong architectural training.

In contrast, without the safety net of the women's network, finding a new atelier was difficult precisely because Morgan presented a threat to the culture of masculinity and fraternity that had come to shape the architecture student's experience as powerfully as the curriculum of the École did. Every member of an atelier, for instance, endured an elaborate initiation ritual that involved deceit, humiliation, interrogation, and drunken revelry in the crammed quarters of the atelier or the smoke-filled rooms of a nearby café or boisterous bar.[10] In general, atelier life alternated between, or even

ACROPOLE D'ANXVR RES°

combined, hard work with smoking, drinking, group singing, and general fraternal revelry; it appealed only to a certain type of character, thereby creating an informal means of separating men who would likely succeed at the École from those who could not abide this culture and would abandon their formal studies (FIG. 3). Julia's brother Avery Morgan (who had no trouble finding a place in Victor Laloux's atelier when he arrived in the fall of 1898) enjoyed the actual work, for instance, but complained about atelier culture. If he invited one fellow atelier member to lunch at his apartment, at least five were sure to turn up. He sometimes came home wet from periodic dousing. Ironically, Avery noted, the greatest mischief makers produced the best work. This lifestyle did not suit Avery's nervous constitution; he returned to the United States after two years. While commercial images from fin-de-siècle Paris include women reveling in decadent pleasures in the bars and dance halls of Montmartre, no woman dared compromise her respectability or subject herself to the sophomoric male behavior by crossing the threshold of an architecture atelier. Similarly, no atelier would

Opposite
FIG. 4
François-Benjamin Chaussemiche, *Restoration of the Acropolis of Anxur*, watercolor, 1903, collection of Musée des Beaux-Arts, Tours

accept Morgan—whatever talents she could bring to it—as long as this spectacular culture of masculinity persisted. Or, as Morgan opined, "I don't think . . . that is a very possible arrangement."[11]

While a group of unionized women artists advocated for separate ateliers in all four disciplines at the École, hoping that the atelier situation would be worked out officially, Morgan turned for help to a familiar resource: her mentor Bernard Maybeck. During the spring of 1898, while Maybeck was in Paris to promote the international competition to design a new campus for the University of California, he learned that François-Benjamin Chaussemiche (1864–1945) had expressed interest in starting an atelier for women and introduced him to Morgan. Chaussemiche won the prestigious Grand Prix de Rome award in 1893. Noted for his superb draftsmanship, he was considered one of the most promising young architects in France (FIG. 4). The new mentor and student developed an affinity for one another, and their working relationship began in earnest in the fall of 1898.[12]

Although Julia Morgan found a mentor and ally in Chaussemiche, her atelier experience continued to differ significantly from that of her fellow élèves. While most students studied in large ateliers of thirty to eighty students, Morgan studied alone with Chaussemiche. This meant she was able to evade the notorious fraternal culture described earlier, but it also isolated her from the more beneficial aspects of atelier life. For example, she did not move through the atelier hierarchy from the novice, who had to tend to the most basic and tedious of tasks, to *massier*, a student veteran of the atelier who was elected to the position and made responsible for collecting dues and paying bills. And while a senior atelier member might delegate the inking of a competition drawing to a newer student and find colleagues to help frame his drawings and cart them to exhibitions, Morgan could not rely upon such assistance. Avery Morgan undoubtedly helped his sister while he lived in Paris, and Arthur Brown, Jr., a fellow student from the Bay Area, and his mother, Victoria Runyon Brown, helped from time to time as well. Victoria Brown left Paris around the same time as

Avery, however, and Arthur helped Morgan only if he had the time—no promises. It is, perhaps, no wonder that Morgan subsequently maintained close personal control over all aspects of her studio in San Francisco; that is effectively how she was trained.[13]

Julia Morgan's solitary study also denied her a space for intellectual exchange of architectural ideas. Normally, the atelier *patron* visited his studio a few times a week to critique the pupils' work. By contrast, a student who was the sole pupil of a *patron* usually worked as an apprentice in the business offices of his mentor. Like atelier members, this student benefited from interactions with colleagues and office critiques, progressing in a professional environment. He also gained insight into the practicalities of running an architectural firm, realizing the construction of actual buildings instead of École coursework, where one designed theoretical spaces. Morgan, in comparison, did not work in the business offices of Chaussemiche; her home doubled as her atelier. Consequently, Morgan did not enjoy regular discussions about architecture. Indeed, just weeks into her partnership with Chaussemiche, the French government sent him to Italy for two months to complete some restorations. Frequent absences were characteristic of Chaussemiche's mentorship of Morgan.[14]

In the absence of a regular atelier and patron, Morgan depended on the American expatriate community for intellectual engagement. Early on she met John Vredenburgh Van Pelt, a graduate of the École and the "laureate" of the French Société des Architectes des Beaux-Arts; he had earned more honors as a student than any other American to date. His mother ran an upscale pension in Paris, where she hosted social gatherings that included several architects. This provided an informal venue where Julia Morgan could discuss architectural matters with her peers. Similarly, Victoria Runyon Brown hosted teas and dinners for the American students in Paris, and whenever Bernard Maybeck was in town, he and his wife invited all the Californians for a repast and debriefing. Avery Morgan arrived in Paris in November 1898 and lived with his sister for two years. He was an eager student of architecture, but after securing a place in the atelier of Victor Laloux, he left his sister to work and think alone by day. The closest Morgan came to the constant exchange of ideas that men enjoyed in the ateliers was her ongoing correspondence with her cousin, Pierre LeBrun. In long

letters, she described in painstaking detail all of the sites she saw in the city—especially the buildings being constructed for the world's fair of 1900—and on her travels in Switzerland, Germany, Italy, and France. She sought his advice on everything from the best clothes to wear for drafting to the essential books to acquire for her professional library. LeBrun served as an outlet for Morgan to relate her observations. His letters to Morgan from these years have not yet come to light, but he did regularly send Morgan architectural magazines, including *Architect and Builder* and the British publication *Architecture* (her favorite), as well as newspaper clippings and articles of note. As important as Morgan's correspondence with LeBrun and interactions with the expatriate community were, neither could replace the atelier for the critical exchange of ideas. As Victoria Brown often lamented, Julia Morgan spent most of her time alone (FIG. 5).[15]

Like all serious students, Morgan took advantage of Paris and the easy access to Europe to study architecture, but in light of her restricted atelier circumstances, visits to actual historical buildings were even more essential to her education. She began as a tourist with her cousin Nina Thornton, college friend Jessica Peixotto, and a number of comrades visiting from California. From the outset, Morgan described Paris as a place that "wakes one up wonderfully" and "does not make you feel a stranger."[16] She spared no time in acquainting herself with the city and learned to navigate it with ease. Within the first three days of her arrival in Paris, Morgan toured the Luxembourg Gardens, the Church of the Holy Trinity, Notre-Dame Cathedral and the Île de la Cité, the Palais de Justice, the École des Beaux-Arts, and the famous Bon Marché—the grand retail complex and department store (where Morgan vowed she would never return) (FIG. 6 and FIG. 7). Less than a month later she had investigated nine churches, visited two salons, and took the omnibus to the Arc de Triomphe de l'Étoile, Père Lachaise Cemetery, and the Opéra Garnier.[17] Nearly four months to the day after her arrival in Paris, Morgan had thoroughly studied and explored the Left Bank from the Hôtel des Invalides to the Jardin des Plantes, as well as Ile de la Cité, Ile Saint Louis, and twenty-four churches.[18] Morgan's adventures took her beyond Paris as well. She traveled around Switzerland during the summer of 1896, and by the time she returned to California she had explored Germany, Italy, and much of France as well. Sometimes her journeys were well

Above

FIG. 6

Julia Morgan at
Notre-Dame de
Paris, 1901

Opposite

FIG. 7

Julia Morgan,
*Notre-Dame de
Paris, Triforium,
twelfth century,*
pen and ink sketch,
September, 1896

facade and immense glass and steel roof. And while Morgan deeply disliked the rococo decorations of the Pont Alexandre III, its steel-frame and reinforced concrete construction technologies fascinated her. She also witnessed and commented upon the excavations and installation of tunnels for the *métropolitain*, the Paris subway system.[20] As much as anything, Morgan found in Paris a laboratory for studying applied engineering and modern construction technology.

Julia Morgan's dependence on the city and travel to destinations outside Paris exposed her to a subject that the École ignored, but which profoundly shaped her career: the common person and everyday life. She tried to spend at least one hour every day to "see something new" or draw, but if she did not have a friend or chaperone to join her, Morgan restricted her movements in the city to traditionally feminine spaces. Thus, the Cluny Museum became a favorite spot (FIG. 10). The sprawling former medieval abbey and palace, constructed over partially exposed Roman baths, provided plenty of subject matter to draw, but Morgan liked the gardens, where children could always be found at play. "I have come to know twenty or more quite as good friends," she wrote to her cousin.[21] Unlike atelier students, who lunched and imbibed at nearby cafés or bars, Morgan regularly picnicked on a bench in the Luxembourg Gardens (FIG. 11), she said, "to watch the children with their nurses, the ducks in the little ponds, and all the fascinating daily panoramas of people and animal and vegetable life."[22] While Morgan's academic education taught her how to design complex buildings in a variety of historical styles, her informal education sensitized her to the beauties of everyday life and the insatiable capacity of children for fun and all things imaginary.

BREAKING DOWN BARRIERS
Women at the École des Beaux-Arts

In March 1896 Morgan boarded that eastbound train in Oakland with the understanding that the faculty of the École des Beaux-Arts was seriously considering opening all of its programs to women. It finally did so largely because of the organized efforts of women artists with whom Morgan interacted regularly during her first year in Paris. However, once the doors officially opened to women, gender discrimination did not end; indeed, the École tried to keep Morgan out. With Morgan's initial

planned, and other times they were not planned at all. When she and a San Francisco acquaintance decided to find a place outside of the city to sketch one day, they based their choice on the name of a place that struck their fancy and the cost of rail fare.[19]

Paris was undergoing a rapid and dramatic transformation as it prepared for the Exposition Universelle, or world's fair, of 1900. Its ornately decorated, mostly temporary buildings were constructed all along the Seine, from the Tuileries to the Trocadéro and Eiffel Tower. Few of them captured Morgan's fancy. She even had direct access to one of the most celebrated buildings of the exposition, Victor Laloux's Gare d'Orsay, because François-Benjamin Chaussemiche served as the supervisor for the construction of this grand railroad station. While Morgan may have learned something from the innovative design that allowed the waiting rooms and train tracks to occupy the same space, all she could say was that it looked "just like a Beaux Art Projet [*sic*]," perhaps suggesting, like contemporary critics, that the building looked more like an academic exercise than a creative and innovative work of art. Of far more interest to Morgan were the Grand Palais and Petit Palais and the Pont Alexandre III (FIG. 8 and FIG. 9). She particularly liked the use of mixed and contrasting materials of the Grand Palais, with its gleaming white

NOTRE-DAME DE PARIS.

TRIFORIUM - XII CENTURY - SEPT '96

Julia Morgan

successes at the École, the pressure grew to succeed still more. All the while, the international press chronicled Morgan's achievements—often inaccurately—and placed upon her the burden of becoming an icon of modern womanhood. Within this context, Morgan developed a gender consciousness that simultaneously fueled her will to achieve—not just for herself, but on behalf of her sex—and a need to manage unwanted public attention.

In all likelihood, Julia Morgan never would have crossed the threshold of the École des Beaux-Arts had it not been for the Union des Femmes Peintres et Sculpteurs (UFPS). Founded during the spring of 1881 by sculptor and teacher Léon Bertaux, this organization marked the first collective effort to fight the exclusion of women from the French art world. The UFPS employed several tactics to bring attention to itself and gain support for its goals, always embracing a brand of feminism that adroitly appealed to conservative and liberal—even radical—ends of the political spectrum. It published a magazine, *Journal des femmes artistes*, and the union's artists disseminated their work through popular media more generally. An annual banquet hosted by the UFPS also became a spectacular event that was well-publicized in the Parisian press. Starting in 1882, the union hosted its annual Salon des Femmes, the first, largest, and most well-known exhibition devoted exclusively to women artists. By 1896, the Salon des Femmes exhibited nearly one thousand works by 295 artists and served as a model for the potential achievements of women who were provided with adequate space to practice and display their work (FIG. 12). By the time Julia Morgan arrived in Paris, the UFPS was the most influential voice in the cause for women and the arts.[23]

In 1889, the UFPS decided to launch a campaign against the country's foremost symbol of masculine domination of the French art world: the École des Beaux-Arts, including all four of its divisions. This was not the first time women in the arts had raised this issue. Marie Bashkirtseff published an article in *La Citoyenne* railing against the practice of excluding women from the École. Arguing that each person should have the opportunity to pursue the career of his or her choice, she called for the École to open its doors to women in its four fine arts disciplines—painting, sculpture, engraving, and architecture. For the next several years, activists and artists debated the importance and wisdom of organizing around gaining access to the École. Eventually, the UFPS concluded that the battle had to be won as a matter of principle. Thus, in July 1889, during centennial celebrations of the French Revolution for freedom and equality, Bertaux stood before the Congrès International des Oeuvres et Institutions Féminines (International Congress of Women's Work and Institutions) and proposed the establishment of separate ateliers for the education of women in all four arts. Further, she stated, women should be able to compete for honors up to and including the Prix de Rome. Union members voted unanimously to support the cause.[24]

Despite this agitation, the faculty remained remarkably resistant to arguments for the entry of women to their institution, even as public opinion and the government increasingly favored such legislation. By the mid-1890s, the École faculty also found themselves under international pressure to admit women to its programs, including the architecture program. Fay Kellogg was the first woman to request to study architecture at the École. She wrote to the directors of the École des Beaux-Arts in 1895 requesting that she be able to work in the *loges*, small, semi-private studios where students sketched their initial responses to the school's competitions, or *concours*. These were problem-solving exercises that would be critiqued by École professors. Kellogg tried to assuage the directors' worries about the "impropriety" of a woman immersing herself in the masculine culture of the École by assuring them—in perfectly good French—that she did not speak much French; the male students' crude, rude, or otherwise inappropriate comments therefore would fall on deaf ears and leave the young woman uncorrupted and the masculine culture of the École intact. She also ingratiated the directors with compliments, but her parting words were "Universities everywhere are beginning to open their doors to women, and I don't think the École, the greatest school of fine arts in the world, will want to keep women from studying at the École forever."[25] The directors did not grant the twenty-four-year-old American woman's request, and Kellogg left Paris to embark on a successful architectural career in New York in 1896. Julia Morgan met "the famous Miss Kellogg" at the Monclos atelier, and while she "did not love her," she nevertheless was indebted to Kellogg for broaching the subject of women studying architecture at the École.[26]

Two years after Fay Kellogg's unsuccessful attempt to gain entrance to the École, Julia Morgan's supporters

again invoked the institution's international prestige to persuade the directors to admit a woman into the architecture program. Alumnus Bernard Maybeck, in particular, cast the École's decision to enroll women in degree programs in an international perspective. Julia Morgan had traveled all the way to Europe on reports that had long been circulating in the United States that the school would soon open its doors to women. "The École des Beaux-Arts has always shown so much good will towards foreigners," Maybeck continued, "that we have been encouraged to ask this new request of you and we sense the strong opinion that you will act in our favor. The decision now depends on you."[27] The United States, as represented by Julia Morgan, had long been waiting for the French school to modernize its admissions policies, much as American schools and institutions in other countries had already begun to do. To allow Julia Morgan to compete in entrance examinations would be an act of international good will and prove that the École des Beaux-Arts, as it had incorporated recent advances in science, math, and architecture, also could respond to social change, thereby maintaining its relevance in the modern world.

In 1896, after seven years of activism on the part of women and resistance on the part of the French government and École faculty, women gained limited access to the school. They were allowed to use its library and attend courses in perspective, anatomy, and the history of art with the promise that women would soon have complete access to the École. Thus, when Morgan arrived in Paris, she secured her paperwork to take advantage of the library and lecture courses currently available to women. Her participation in these courses placed Morgan in a stimulating environment of determined and diverse women. She studied with an international group students whom she described as "the first . . . I've seen of bohemianism." Morgan did not judge ill of the women, even if they smoked and drank tea, for she found them to be "fine strong workers, and very intelligent and good."[28] Activists of the UFPS were in these classes, too, and they were discontented with the modest concessions to women's access to the École. From the activists' perspective, neither the government nor the École moved quickly to secure the necessary funding for the instruction of women. Determined to see the government fulfill its promise, the UFPS thus continued to campaign vigorously for full rights to all courses, degree programs, ateliers, and competitions. Soon

enough, the activists emboldened the reserved young aspiring architect from California and worked with her on a plan to secure a place at the École.

In March 1897 the French Senate voted to fund the organization of complete instructional programs for women at the École des Beaux-Arts. According to Tamar Garb, the director of the École had outlined the conditions of women's entrance the previous year. They stipulated that "women students would take the same entry exams as prospective male students. On admission, they would be able to work in the drawing and sculpture studios between 8:00 and 10:00 a.m. every morning, where they would receive instruction that was separate from male students but identical to that received by them. In the afternoons, they would be able to attend the oral courses in perspective, literature, archeology, history of art, general history and anatomy." Other stipulations promised separate but equal instruction, along with the unequal distribution of awards. Separate ateliers and the Prix de Rome, however, remained off limits to women.[29] Nowhere in this list of stipulations did the director of the École specifically mention the architecture program, leaving Julia Morgan unsure about her prospects for taking the entrance exams. Working with members of the UFPS, she wrote a letter to the faculty requesting that they waive the entrance examinations for her and allow her to pursue a degree in architecture. Like Fay Kellogg before her, Morgan played into the notion that her presence would be an aberration, not a precedent, and as she would work in a private atelier outside of the École, she would pose no threat to the institution's masculine culture. Morgan's letter elicited a response that typified the faculty and administration's position on the subject of women and the school: "The decision of the Ministry that opened the École des Beaux-Arts to women created no special privileges for those in question. Mlle Morghan [sic], therefore, will have to go through the standard examinations if, as is her undeniable right, she wants to be admitted to the second class and take part in the concours."[30] Two things were clear: the rule protected a woman's right to enroll in any of the four divisions of the École des Beaux-Arts if she passed the appropriate examinations, and the faculty would do absolutely nothing more for women than honor the rules of the state.

Morgan finally learned about her status in mid-May, some five weeks before the next entrance examinations were scheduled. Having secured the proper documentation and letters of reference, she registered at the École des Beaux-Arts on May 28, 1897. Then, as Morgan wrote to her mother's cousins, Pierre and Lucy LeBrun, she had "a great deal" of preparation ahead of her—"Descriptive Geometry entirely, besides the *Esquisse* (sketch) work for the Architecture, modeling, cast drawing, Algebra, Geometry, one examination written, one oral, and the same in history from the Commandments [the biblical Exodus] to modern times."[31] Although she had been developing her architectural skills gradually over the previous year, Morgan now studied virtually non-stop for weeks on end.

On June 25, 1897, Julia Morgan commenced her first attempt to pass the qualifying examinations. In her account of the day to the LeBruns, she "did not go [to] it very fresh and vigorous," and things only got worse. Morgan's arrangements with the guards to see her into the examination rooms early fell through. She had hoped to shield herself from the gaze of her male competitors, not to mention the general chaos created by hundreds of *aspirants* who gathered in the courtyard of the École, waiting with their T-squares, triangles, drawing boards, paints, and brushes, and subject to taunts of other students already *en loge* (in studios working on their examination sketches) or paint-tainted water pouring onto them from the windows above. After a poor night's sleep in the sultry heat of the summer, Morgan arose at five o'clock to breakfast and dress, arrived at the École just before seven, and immediately learned that the guards "had made a mistake;" she would not be the first person to be let in, but the last. Morgan paced along the Quai Malaquais and watched the men against whom she was competing pass through the gates. At 8:30 a.m., half an hour after the exam officially started, the guards finally led Morgan through the smoke-filled corridors of the loge building to her 6- by 8-foot room, complete with a skylight for a ceiling and a window overlooking the courtyard. Almost eight hours later, her preliminary sketch nearly complete, Morgan realized that she had not yet mastered the metric system and had miscalculated the measurements for the entire project; she redid her work as best she could. Hot, tired, famished, and nerves shattered, Morgan returned home for dinner and a short rest. After a restless night, she awoke at three in the morning.[32]

Morgan completed the remaining four parts of the exam, which covered modeling, drawing from a cast, history, and mathematics. The mathematics portion,

as American student John M. Howells noted, was "the test which only the fittest (or the luckiest) survive." The students gathered in a gloomy auditorium, Howells recounted, where they sat until "it is all your lungs can do to suck in the hot garlic-tainted gas in which your head beats with semi-asphyxiation."[33] The examiner proceeded arbitrarily to call students one by one to stand on the stage in front of their peers, where they usually failed to answer correctly the mathematics questions posed. With three hundred applicants, this process could take days and, more often than not, was also a humiliating rite of passage. Morgan was the last of the *aspirants* to take this exam but had the "pleasure" of performing in front of a full house. Nobody wanted to miss the trial of the first female *aspirante*.[34] Morgan passed all the parts of this first examination, but her scores were not high enough to earn her a spot in the architecture program.[35] While gender issues surely shaped the course of her first examination attempt, Morgan understood the debacle as part of an initiation process that nearly all prospective architecture students endured—accepting their failure in stride. "As they say it is necessary to fail once, to know how to take the Examinations, perhaps it was best anyway," she wrote to her cousin, assuring herself. "Everyone takes their defeat in the most cheerful way, for you are always with the majority at least."[36]

Blatant gender discrimination elicited less equanimity. During the summer of 1897, while Morgan was, as suggested by Katherine de Monclos, taking a break from her studies in a quiet village outside of Paris, she told the LeBruns that she would probably leave Paris if she was not received into the school when she took the examinations again in October. She would be nearly twenty-six years old, and the unlikelihood of completing coursework to earn a *certificat d'études*, let alone complete the further requirements for the *diplôme*, made the idea of staying on in Paris seem like an expensive extravagance that offered little in the way of useful architectural training. Then, in October 1897, Morgan attempted the entrance examinations for a second time. Though she felt better prepared when she entered the exam and completed each part thinking she had performed better than before, she actually scored lower on every section and failed for a second time. "I felt very much ashamed and badly," she confessed to the LeBruns, "for I thought I'd made mistakes I did not recognize, carefully avoiding the Atelier and M de Monclos—he had been so ashamed

of me before." Morgan had understood where she went wrong in her first series of examinations; the idea that she could not understand where she had made mistakes in her second series of exams shattered her ego. Her comments also make clear that her quest to study architecture at the École carried more weight than mere personal ambition. She felt she owed her mentors—Monclos, Maybeck—and all those people who had supported her through the years a successful examination.[37] This second failure exacerbated her feelings of guilt.

Unable to avoid Monclos forever, Morgan finally ran into him one day on the street. Much to her surprise, he did not scold her or reprimand her in any way. She eventually learned that "the Jury had openly said they 'ne voudraient pas encouragé les jeunes filles' and that everyone said it would make no matter what I did." Morgan's only failure had been her failure to be a man. Others agreed that she had been judged unfairly simply because she was a woman. "It was such a relief I did not care much," she claimed, for at least such overt gender discrimination restored her confidence in her skills as an architect. But Julia Morgan was angry. She declared in her usual understated way, "I'll try again next time anyway even without any expectations, just to show 'les jeunes filles' are not discouraged."[38] Indeed, she told Victoria Brown that she would take the exams eleven times—every time the exams were open before her thirtieth birthday in 1902—or until she passed, whichever came first.[39] Prior to this incident, Julia Morgan had known it would be difficult to get into the École because she was a woman, but she accepted this more or less as the way things were and tried to work around obstacles as best she could. Now she personally understood the unfair consequences that gender discrimination produced, the very issues she heard the UFPS railing against since arriving in Paris. But the École faculty's plan to protect its institution and the field of architecture from the threat of a feminine invasion backfired. Instead, they lit a fire under "Mlle Morgan" to work harder than ever to pass the examinations.

In April 1898 Morgan tried and failed a third time to pass the entrance examinations, but as Victoria Brown observed, "She has grit enough to deserve to succeed."[40] So, in October 1898 Julia Morgan took the entrance examinations for the École des Beaux-Arts for a fourth time.[41] In a draft of his report to the director of the École on the status of women who participated

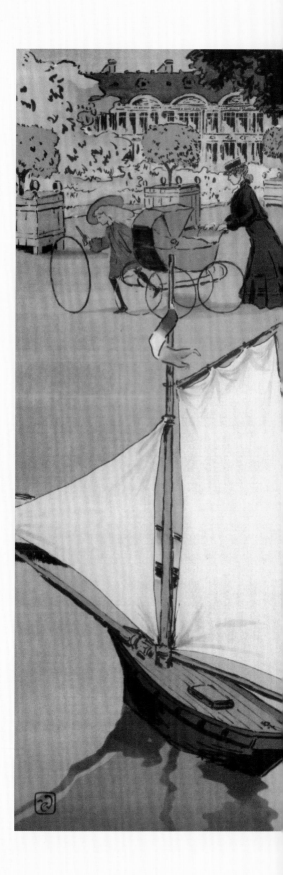

in that round of examinations, one juror characterized the work of the women artists as inferior and like that of commercial artists, "rather than those by students of our school." Of Morgan, however, the writer could only say, "Finally, a young American woman with satisfactory notes wants to be admitted in architecture."[42] This tepid approval may have indicated that he was not certain about Morgan's success. Nevertheless, with her fourth attempt, she passed the examinations with flying colors, ranking thirteenth out of 392 applicants. On November 14, 1898, Julia Morgan was now the first woman to be accepted to the architecture program at the École des Beaux-Arts. Once again, in her typically understated fashion, she wrote to Pierre LeBrun, "A mixture of dislike of giving up something attempted and the sense of its being a sort of test in [a] small way, of work itself overcoming its natural disadvantages made it seem a thing that really had to be won. Its [sic] not much but has taken quite a little effort."[43]

STUDYING ARCHITECTURE WHILE FEMALE

Once admitted to the École, Julia Morgan had just over three years before her thirtieth birthday to complete all the requirements to pursue the *diplôme* in architecture. To put this in perspective, the average École student took over six years to complete his studies from entrance examinations to the *diplôme*. Morgan worked at a relentless pace, ignoring illnesses as best she could—at times working without sleeping for days. No sooner did she complete a *projet rendu* than she went *en loge* to complete a new *esquisse* for her next *projet*. And it was not uncommon to go *en loge* in the middle of working on a *projet* either. Arthur Brown, Jr. and his mother often described Morgan as very *en charrette*—or quick tempered and stressed out from working up to the last minute—particularly when she was preparing her *rendus* for exhibition. Nervous, anxious, and taxed were also common adjectives Victoria Brown ascribed to Morgan. Morgan completed some of her work in the stifled air of the *loges* and all of it by dim candlelight. Perhaps not surprisingly, she suffered from headaches and severe eye strain. Soon, she required glasses. Frankly, none of this was unique to Julia Morgan; Arthur Brown's correspondence with his mother also details several American men studying in Paris who worked at a similar pace to Morgan's and suffered from the same bouts of stress-induced illness,

fatigue, and depression. Unlike them, however, Julia Morgan could never escape the additional burden of being the first and only female studying architecture at the École des Beaux-Arts.[44]

Sometimes the École exerted pressure on her that her male colleagues did not endure. "Everybody in Paris . . . knows Miss M," Jean-Louis Pascal said to Eliza Morgan, the architect's mother, upon being introduced to her by Bernard Maybeck in Berkeley. "[She will] get along nicely now." He meant his remarks as a compliment, but they underscore the pressure of the notoriety under which Morgan worked. It seemed everybody was monitoring her progress. She steadily earned *valeurs*, or points, toward promotion to the first class, earning a point every month or so for the first nine months—until she was ready to tackle the more challenging and time-consuming construction requirements. By November 1899, however, she was not sure if she would remain in Paris longer than another year. When Paul Dubois, director of the École, learned of this, he "asked as a favor to the board" that she try to reach the first class before she left. Implicit in his request was that he did not want the École to look foolish for having admitted a woman, only to have her fulfill sexist social expectations that a woman "naturally" was not fit to meet the rigorous demands of architecture. While her male counterparts could have left the school at any point, no questions asked, Morgan had to prove something. She succeeded and was admitted to the first class on August 6, 1900. Morgan decided to continue her studies toward the *diplôme*.[45]

As she worked her way through the first class, the pressure of the public gaze became a burden. She had been under special scrutiny since the announcement of her departure from Oakland to Paris in 1896. During the height of organized efforts to establish equal access to École programs and separate ateliers for women, the French media often singled out Morgan as the one woman, the American, who was defying history by pursuing architectural studies in France, "the first woman no doubt that ever won over this branch of art, indicating a new opening in feminists' advancements."[46] Back home, the Bay Area press was wildly enthusiastic about its native daughter's successful admission in 1898.[47] By and large, Morgan did not pay much attention to these notices. Media interest quieted until *American Architect and Architecture* published news of the *mention* Morgan earned for her historicist design (including a plan, section, and elevation, and

Opposite

FIG. 12

Marie Bashkirtseff, *In the Studio*, oil on canvas, 1881

Following spread

FIG. 13

Julia Morgan, *Concours Godeboeuf: Une Rampe au fer et bronze pour l'Escalier d'un Palais*, 1901, from Les Médailles des Concours d'Architecture à l'École des Beaux-Arts, 1901–1902

labeled with neo-medieval calligraphy and ornament) of a sculpted thirteenth-century church pulpit in May 1901. It noted that no riots ensued, as had happened when the École first opened its doors to women, and that Morgan's achievements were playing an important role in changing the sentiments of male students towards female architects. Then, in October of that year an article appeared in London's *Pall Mall Gazette* naming Morgan "The First Lady Architect." The *New York Times* reprinted the article and similar stories soon began to appear in several French papers. Across America, the "Julia Morgan story" was picked up by the *New York Sun*, *New York Herald*, *Brooklyn Eagle*, and, of course, the San Francisco and Oakland papers. Ultimately, at least twenty-five articles in thirteen states and three countries announced that Morgan was winning high honors at the École des Beaux-Arts,

and several of them falsely stated that she had already earned the *diplôme*. "Celebrity clippings" arrived daily at the Morgan home in Oakland.[48]

The flood of publicity was upsetting personally and professionally. Morgan's family grew increasingly impatient with frequent disruptions from nosy reporters knocking at the front door and did not hesitate to express their frustration in their letters to the family's "rising star."[49] Worse, the stories were not accurate. With just three months until her thirtieth birthday, the age when the École turned students away, Morgan had earned four and a half points, only three and a half of which were in architecture. She might be able to earn the one and a half points in architecture to secure a *certificat d'architecture*, but her pursuit of the *diplôme*, which required two points in drawing and modeling as well as six and a half more points in architecture,

Concours Godebœuf : Une Rampe en fer et bronze pour l'Esc

ARMAND GUÉRINET, ÉDITEUR, 140, FAUBOURG SAINT-MARTIN, PARIS

d'un Palais - Mlle MORGAN, Elève de M. CHAUSSEMICHE

Left
FIG. 14
Julia Morgan
student work,
sketch in portfolio,
pencil, ca. 1900

Following spread
FIG. 15
Julia Morgan
student work,
sketch in portfolio,
pencil and
watercolor, ca.
1900

seemed all but lost. "I am very, very sorry indeed," wrote Eliza Morgan to her daughter just days before the *Pall Mall* story began to circulate, "after all your work and hopes that you lost. It was too sad. I hoped so much you could 'make your Diplome.'"[50] The gulf between the idealized Julia Morgan who was written about in the papers and the lived experience of the real Julia Morgan simply added to the pressure and frustration the aspiring architect felt as she struggled to earn the points. Would years of hard work and personal battles come to naught? How would Morgan live down the crushed expectations of so many people? How could she make up for the invasions of privacy and daily disruptions her family experienced for attention that, in the end, she felt she did not quite deserve?

But then success began to come Morgan's way. During the nine-week period between November 26, 1901 and February 2, 1902, Morgan earned *mentions* in drawing and modeling, a medal for her design of a vestibule, a medal in the prestigious Prix Godeboeuf (FIG. 13), and a *mention* for her design of a grand ballroom in a palace. The *certificat d'architecture* was now secure, and only two points in architecture separated her from embarking on a thesis for the *diplôme*. As her points added up, Morgan knew that Victor Laloux, one of the most prominent French architects, and several other men were trying to persuade École director Paul Dubois to grant the now thirty-year-old Morgan an extension so she could earn her last two values and pursue the *diplôme*. But Dubois would not relent. Julia Morgan's career at the École des Beaux-Arts was over.[51]

PARISIAN FOUNDATIONS

As Julia Morgan prepared to leave Paris, a new article about her began to circulate in the international press. In it, the journalist scoffed at French newspapers' idealized feminist vision of Morgan "running up ladders and scampering over scaffolding, no doubt in a costume suited to the requirements of the profession." Further, the reporter stated, the practical Morgan assumed that her career, "like that of other women architects in America, would consist largely of office work and plan preparation."[52] In fact, Morgan knew that eager clients were already waiting for her in California to design their homes. Within weeks of her arrival in Oakland, she was in contact with John Galen Howard, another École alumnus, about working for him on the design of new University of California Beaux-Arts style buildings.

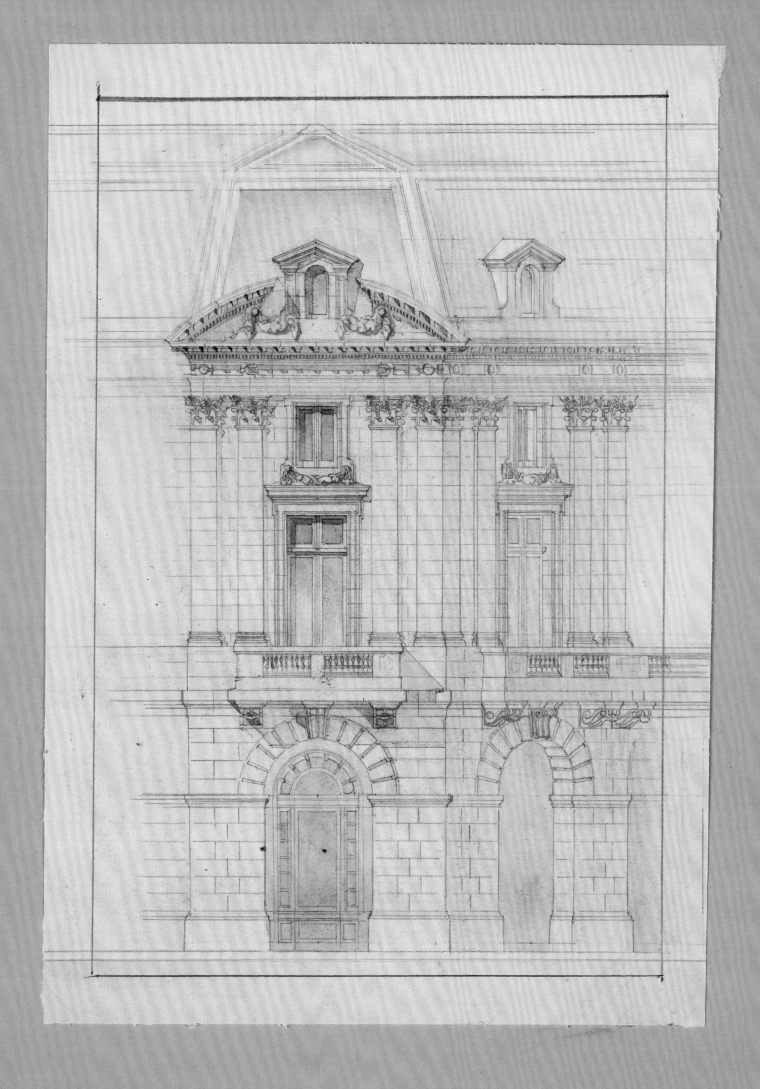

If the journalist's account of Morgan's words are accurate, Morgan was likely managing public expectations of her future career and trying to turn the disruptive spotlight away from her Paris achievements. Tellingly, though, it was easier for the journalist to accept her self-deprecating assessment than the French feminist vision of the future. The article captures perfectly the mixed legacy of Morgan and the École des Beaux-Arts, the still challenging path that awaited Morgan as she pursued a career in architecture, and the tactics she would deploy as she charted that new territory.

The gender dynamics at the École des Beaux-Arts proved resistant to significant change. Despite Julia Morgan's accomplishments in the architecture program, she long remained an anomaly. Meredith Clausen has summarized the post-Morgan era for women at the institution: a second woman, also an American, Mary Rockwell Hook, took the entrance examinations in 1906; male students supposedly doused her with buckets of water as she fled the school grounds. A third woman took the examinations and failed in 1913; only three women took the exams between 1914 and 1920. Jeanne Surugue, a French woman, became the second woman to pass the examinations in 1918, and in 1923 she became the first woman to earn a *diplôme d'architecte*. In June 1920 four of six women who took the entrance exams for architecture passed and were admitted to the École, and over the next decade about fifty women took the examinations and nineteen succeeded. The numbers were rising, but to put this in perspective, the percentage of admitted women students, *élèves*, in architecture rose from .014 percent in 1920 to 2 percent in 1925 and 1930, then "skyrocketed" to 6 percent in 1931 before dropping to 1 percent in 1932. In sheer numbers, change was indeed slow to come, and of the experience of these women who followed Morgan at the École we know very little.[53]

If Julia Morgan did little to change the gender dynamics of the École des Beaux-Arts, her time in Paris changed her life significantly. She achieved her primary goal, to gain a formal education at the most prestigious architectural institution in the world, and she developed an architectural philosophy in the process. She appears never to have subscribed completely to the Beaux-Arts way of design, once commenting to Pierre LeBrun in reference to an assignment, "It's on the principle, 'in the Beaux Arts region, do as the Beaux Arts do,' only I'd promise that, given one to build, it would not be like this one."[54] She made similar comments about other assignments. Not surprisingly, then, François-Benjamin Chaussemiche noted that his young pupil liked to mix styles a little bit too much, rather than adhere to historical purism. Morgan did, however, adhere closely to the École's methods of composition. Working from the inside out, the architect first created a plan that took the function of the site into consideration. The elevations followed the plan, and any number of styles could adorn the building's facades or interiors. Modern technology fascinated her as well, and the use of it became a hallmark of her architecture, from the daring reinforced concrete technology and exposed aggregate of the *campanile* at Mills College in 1904 to the Gothic Moorish 1929 Berkeley Women's City Club building, which both showcased the infinite plasticity of the material and, according to long-time structural engineer Walter Steilberg, was one of the most complex reinforced concrete buildings in the state of California when it was built.[55] Most importantly and unusually—if not uniquely—for an École graduate, Morgan found inspiration in everyday life—for example, creating secret spaces for children in houses she designed, and providing kitchenettes for women who lived in YWCA residences so they could entertain friends.

Paris also engendered in Morgan a complex worldview and sense of purpose. As mentioned earlier, she was struck by the diversity of her female classmates in the other divisions of the École. Nearly twenty years later, when Morgan recounted her Paris years to Aurelia Reinhardt, president of the Mills College, a women's college in Oakland, these women still stood out in her memory.[56] She valued them for their work ethic, their minds, and their treatment of others. These cosmopolitan women intrigued her and made her more accepting of cultural differences. Ultimately, Morgan also adopted some of their feminist politics. She had left Oakland on a personal and uncertain journey to get an education that no school in the United States could provide. The sense of injustice she felt when the École jury purposefully failed her entrance examinations made her understand that her battles were part of a larger story about gender inequality; the personal had become political. From this point forward, Morgan devoted much of her life and career to creating greater opportunities for women in work, education, politics, social reform, urban development, and more. Reserved in nature, averse to the press and public attention, her actions, as is often said of her buildings, speak for themselves. ✿

YOUNG WOMENS

MARBLE

DETAILS OF TERRA-COTTA WORK ON FRONT OF THE

3

CHRIS

MARBLE

SCALE 3/4"=1'-0"

Y.W.C.A. BUILDING OF OAKLAND, CAL. ❈ JULIA MORGAN ARCHT. ❈

CHAPTER 3

A TWENTIETH-CENTURY REVIVAL
JULIA MORGAN'S RENAISSANCE PALAZZO IN OAKLAND

JOHANNA KAHN

Julia Morgan's 1913 design for the Young Women's Christian Association (YWCA) building in Oakland, California, involved a complex historicist architectural program that projected a distinguished urban presence while conveying the civic and spiritual mission of its patron. With the national consolidation of the YWCA in 1871, the association grew, founding new chapters and commissioning new buildings into the twentieth century—concurrent with the growth of American cities. Morgan's Oakland design from this era demonstrated propriety and sophistication by means of her thorough understanding of architectural precedent, specifically the Italian Renaissance palazzo, or palace. Although she had studied recent designs for other YWCA chapters and sought to conform to the emergent national standards of the organization, she adopted a distinctly historical style and plan that complemented other new and historicist buildings in Oakland's developing city center. Her ability to accommodate clients' wants, understand users' needs, and employ architecture as a medium that represented the identity of the institution in its urban setting led to a positive reception for her design in the East Bay city, as well as subsequent commissions for the YWCA nationally.

THE ORIGINS OF THE AMERICAN RENAISSANCE
Classicism Translated Through the École des Beaux-Arts

As is well known, the Italian Renaissance was a flowering of the humanities, sciences, and fine arts during the late fourteenth century through the sixteenth century. This rebirth was largely inspired by a renewed interest in *all'antica* ("after the antique," or "in the ancient manner" of the Romans) sources. In addition to the profusion of technological, scientific, literary, philosophical, and artistic advancements in this era, remarkable innovations in architecture also define this period. This was grounded in a new appreciation of Italy's classical heritage and led to experimentation with dimension, proportion, volume, pattern, detail, and form—drawing upon ancient Roman models while devising new building technologies and design solutions. As this new body of knowledge accumulated, it was aided by the invention in 1450 of the printing press, allowing for the widespread circulation of architectural treatises that were illustrated with drawings of ancient and modern buildings. These ranged from works by the Roman architect Vitruvius (first century B.C.E.) to the seminal sixteenth-century treatise by Andrea Palladio (1508–1580).[1] Some of the best known Renaissance architects and designers were influential theoreticians and also *ingegneri* (those known for their *ingegno*, or "talent" and "genius"), that is inventors, problem solvers, and devisers of innovative building solutions.[2]

The nineteenth-century rediscovery of Italian Renaissance humanism and its architects, such as Palladio, Michelozzo di Bartolomeo Michelozzi, Leon Battista Alberti, Michelangelo Buonarroti, Raffaello Sanzio, and other *ingegni*, had a major impact on American architecture and extended into the twentieth century. As a result, many examples of Italian Renaissance architecture, predominantly *palazzi* (plural of palazzo), came to represent the civic aspirations of this era. Renaissance-style works first appeared in the first half of the nineteenth century, a phenomenon known as Neo-Renaissance or Renaissance Revival.

Previous spread
Julia Morgan, *Details of Terra-Cotta Work on Front of the Y.W.C.A. Building of Oakland, Cal.*, pencil and colored pencil, ca. 1913

Opposite
FIG. 1
John Notman, the Athenæum of Philadelphia, 1845-47

Following spread
FIG. 2
Edward Clarke Cabot, Boston Athenæum of Philadelphia, 1847-49

The palazzo became a model for social clubs (such as Charles Barry's 1832 Travellers Club in London) and places of learning in Europe. The first palazzo-inspired architectural designs in America were for athenaeums (learned libraries) in Philadelphia (FIG. 1, constructed from 1845 to 1847) and Boston (FIG. 2, constructed from 1847 to 1849), designed by John Notman and Edward Clarke Cabot, respectively.[3]

It was during the 1840s that the word "Renaissance"—in the sense of the influence of classical architecture in early modern Europe—became known and used by educated Europeans and Americans. In the following decades, American fascination with the Italian Renaissance and its various European derivations escalated, and scholarship of that period resulted in an artistic invigoration that significantly influenced the built environment. This first Renaissance Revival lasted from the mid-1840s into the post-Civil War era in the United States and was accompanied by an array of other "revivals," including Greek, Gothic, and even Egyptian, and was evident in cities undergoing rapid development.[4] The architectural revivals of this era coincided with momentous events, such as the Civil War, Manifest Destiny expansionism, Transcendentalism, and developments in American arts and letters.

Toward the end of the nineteenth century, designers of institutional and residential architecture in the eastern United States embraced a more sophisticated and ambitious Renaissance classicism that was distinct from the earlier movement. This approach is epitomized in the works of the New York firm of McKim, Mead & White, whose 1884 Villard Houses (FIG. 3), as described by contemporary English architect Charles Reilly, resembled "a group of magnificent seventeenth-century Italian palaces, fine and strong as the [Palazzo] Farnese itself, and crowned with a very similar cornice," and whose University Club (1899) was considered "a palace worthy to rank with the Farnese, the Massimi [Palazzo Massimo alle Colonne, Rome], or any of the great Italian palazzi."[5] In this era, urban-scale adaptations of classically inspired architecture—including historicist variations of Greek, Roman, and Italian Renaissance styles—were built, most notably at the 1893 World's Columbian Exposition in Chicago. The massive scale and complexity of this landmark event and other subsequent projects are what distinguish the second, or late, Renaissance

Revival in the United States, spanning from the mid-1880s through the 1920s.

This second manifestation coincides with the era known as the "American Renaissance" (1876 to 1919), during which time the grand traditions of history (especially those of Renaissance Italy) came to embody the national identity of the United States and its post-centennial aspirations.[6] The prospect of civic and federal architecture in America during the American Renaissance was announced by Senator James McMillan, chairman of the Senate Park Commission of the District of Columbia, when he wrote in 1902, "It is the general opinion that for monumental work, Greece and Rome furnish the styles of architecture best adapted to serve the manifold wants of today, not only as to beauty and dignity, but as to utility."[7] A broad-based classicism had indeed been embraced as an expression of American national identity and cosmopolitan ideals; it eventually would spread across the United States. But one must carefully distinguish between classical (i.e., that of the ancient Greeks and Romans) and Renaissance Revival styles of architecture. Whereas the aesthetic principles of classical architecture (and especially that of the Romans) informed the designs of artists and builders during the Italian Renaissance, the period of the Italian Renaissance came to embody cultural and stylistic associations of its own. It is the sophistication, multivalence, and inventiveness of Renaissance architecture that differentiates it from its ancient sources and that made it such a fertile field of study and inspiration for architects during the American Renaissance. (For an additional treatment of the American Renaissance in architecture, especially in California, see Gordon Fuglie's Introduction to this volume.)

Architectural expressions of Renaissance historicism during the nineteenth century were guided more by a building's function and its architectural details than by the principles put forth in theoretical treatises from the fifteenth and sixteenth centuries that prescribed suitable architectural applications for their time.[8] Because the architects of ancient Rome were viewed as masters of structure, orders, and ornament, and since a revival of Roman traditions engendered the Italian Renaissance, Italian architecture therefore represented a paragon for architects in late nineteenth- and early twentieth-century America.[9] Further, the survival and availability of ancient Roman and Renaissance buildings and structures provided examples of inestimable worth to architects during the American Renaissance. Of great significance was the incorporation and study of Italian Renaissance architecture through the curriculum at the École des Beaux-Arts in Paris, the most prestigious architecture school in the world in the late nineteenth century.[10] In addition to fostering the study of design principles, the École also held a trove of models, decorative architectural elements, sculpture, and an unparalleled reference library—a veritable academic museum of art and architecture.[11] Moreover, its central building, the Palais des Études, was conceived in the form of and ornamented as a Florentine palazzo, with its facade inscribed with the names of the most influential artists of the Italian Renaissance (FIG. 4). It is not difficult to imagine the impression this grand building made on students during their time at the École, especially young Americans keen to learn the history and artistry of architecture (FIG. 5).

Despite the absorption of Beaux-Arts theory and practice at a number of academic institutions in the United States, many American students desired first-hand experience at the Parisian academy. Americans were admitted to the École's architecture program beginning in 1846, and the first woman to be accepted was Julia Morgan in 1898.[12] (See two other essays in this volume: Karen McNeill addresses the challenges Morgan faced while at the École; Jeffrey Tilman discusses the coursework, atelier life, and competition sequences American students underwent at the École.) In addition to her formal instruction and use of the collections at the Palais des Études, Morgan studied her Parisian surroundings. During her six-year residence, she observed the urban transformation resulting from the extensive building programs for the 1900 Exposition Universelle, many of which were designed by École professors or distinguished graduates.[13]

When Morgan returned to her native Oakland in 1902, she was a sophisticated lady with a certificate from the world's premier architecture school. Her first professional position was as a draftsperson for John Galen Howard, "a devoted Beaux-Arts man" and the supervising campus architect of Morgan's other alma mater, the University of California, Berkeley.[14] After becoming certified as a California architect in 1904, Morgan practiced in San Francisco until the devastating earthquake and subsequent fires on April 18, 1906, caused extensive destruction throughout

Opposite
FIG. 3
McKim, Mead, & White, Villard Houses, west facade, 1882–85, at 451–457 Madison Avenue and 24 East Fifty-first Street, New York, NY, 1890.

Following spreads
FIG. 4
Palais des Études, École des Beaux-Arts, Paris

Pages 116–17
FIG. 5
Julia Morgan, *Building for the Young Women's Christian Association of Oakland, California*, pencil, colored pencil, and ink wash, ca. 1913

BUILDING FOR THE YOUNG WOMEN'S CHRIST

STIAN ASSOCIATION

JULIA MORGAN ARCHITECT

AN ASSOCIATION OF OAKLAND CALFORNIA

the city and across the region. This led to the urgent need for architects to rebuild the city, proving advantageous to Morgan's nascent career.

Considering the theoretical rigor and problem-solving approach that informed a Beaux-Arts education, as well as its favor in the United States, it is understandable that Morgan relied on its principles and methods throughout her career. Years after Morgan's death, Dorothy Wormser Coblentz, a former associate in Morgan's office, recalled that her design philosophy was essentially Beaux-Arts in approach, observing: "[Morgan] didn't build in a style. [Rather,] she built functionally; the plan came first. Nothing was built from the outside in; everything was from the inside out."[15] True to Beaux-Arts principles, once the utility and efficiency of the architectural program was determined, it could be complemented by aesthetic treatments.[16]

A PALAZZO FOR OAKLAND'S YWCA

Throughout the later nineteenth century, Oakland developed in the shadow of its increasingly fashionable and sophisticated neighbor across the bay, San Francisco. But the seeds for growth were planted early. In the 1850s, one of the first commercial ports on the Pacific Coast was built along Oakland's waterfront. In the next decade, the city became the western terminus of the transcontinental railroad when the line was completed in 1869.[17] The port and rail line made Oakland a principal gateway to the San Francisco Bay Area, as well as the link to inland western and midwestern cities via rail.

The destruction caused by the 1906 San Francisco earthquake and fires led to an influx of evacuees from across the bay, and during the early decades of the twentieth century Oakland quickly grew from an industrial freight and commuter hub to a populous and prosperous city. Largely responsible for the creation of Oakland's civic growth and cultural sites was Mayor Frank Mott, who served from 1905 to 1915. He envisioned and accomplished a reformed urban plan influenced by the City Beautiful movement, bringing wide boulevards, monumental civic and institutional buildings, and landscaped parks to the city.[18] By 1914, Oakland boasted a Beaux-Arts-style city hall and civic auditorium, a lakefront boulevard with recreational space around Lake Merritt, and high-rise buildings designed in a variety of revivalist styles that lined the new downtown corridor along Broadway.[19] It was in this part of Oakland that the new YWCA was sited and built.

As a charitable organization, the YWCA focused its efforts on providing accommodations, education, and community to younger women in need of assistance or transitioning to city life. One of the organization's maxims stated that "the Association is not the building, but the membership."[20] Suitable buildings, however, were essential for accommodating the lodgings, classrooms, cafeterias, offices, and recreation spaces required to provide these services for its female members.

In the early decades of the twentieth century, the YWCA experienced a considerable increase in membership, and many urban chapters, including Oakland, outgrew their facilities, prompting building campaigns across the United States. In 1916, Elizabeth Wilson, the executive secretary of the national board, described some considerations and virtues of a thoughtful design for a modern multipurpose association building:

When a building or the building is the embodiment of the loyalty and enthusiasm of the members, that glorifies it as nothing else can adorn it, from the swimming pool in the basement to the moving picture installation and soda fountain on the roof. It is also praiseworthy according to its figurative windows and doors. From how many windows do the workers look out upon the community and see all the girls as they move about in all directions? Are there plenty of doors on the four sides for girls to come in—large doors for great assemblies, and little doors for everyday wants?[21]

Although the circumstances of Morgan's selection as architect for the Oakland YWCA remain unclear, she likely was given the job through one of her many professional or social connections.[22] It is probable that Grace Fisher, president of the Oakland YWCA since 1908 and a sorority sister of Morgan's at UC Berkeley, was instrumental in the appointment of her old friend as the designer. Further, Morgan's association with Phoebe Apperson Hearst, a patron of the arts and UC Berkeley and a prominent YWCA benefactor for whom she had worked for nearly a decade on other projects, also may have played a role. In 1912, the year before Morgan designed the Oakland YWCA, Hearst recommended to the national board that Morgan be hired to design the beachfront YWCA conference center in Pacific Grove, California, which

Y. W. C. A., St. Louis, Mo.

P-25083

was later named Asilomar (derived from Spanish and meaning "refuge by the sea").[23]

To acquaint herself with the requirements of a modern association building, Morgan toured recently constructed YWCA clubhouses in the Midwest and the eastern United States. Her goal was to assess which amenities were sufficient and the features that were most valued by young female occupants, as well as becoming familiar with the specifications and aesthetic standards promoted by the national board.[24] Among the YWCA buildings Morgan visited in 1912 were those in Brooklyn, St. Louis, Pittsburgh, Cleveland, Philadelphia, and the new national headquarters in New York City, built in 1911. Her list of concerns included swimming pools, gymnasia, cafeterias, employment offices, classrooms, and facilities for vocational training.[25] In April 1913, upon reviewing Morgan's design, *The Architect and Engineer of California* announced that the architect of the Oakland YWCA incorporated "all the newest features to be found in the finest buildings of this type in the East."[26]

Another article reported that Morgan "was much impressed with the [YWCA] building at St. Louis, which is six months old. The lighting and general cheerfulness of this structure appealed very much to Miss Morgan, and they will be incorporated in the local building [in Oakland]."[27] The St. Louis YWCA included a swimming pool in the raised basement; two gymnasia on the first floor; a mezzanine level with administration offices; classrooms; an auditorium; a chapel on the third floor; twenty-one bedrooms on the fourth floor; and a cafeteria and roof garden on the uppermost floor.[28] If Morgan appreciated the building's interior qualities, it is clear from a cursory comparison of the two buildings that the facade of the St. Louis YWCA must also have given her inspiration for the Oakland building (FIG. 6 and FIG. 7).[29] The imposing edifice was conceived in the style of an Italian Renaissance palazzo, the symmetrical brick facade with a double staircase and a pronounced cornice creating an impressive presence on Locust Street.[30] Other decorative elements included terracotta door and window surrounds and lion heads on the primary facade. Morgan's interest in the St. Louis YWCA aligned with the attributes of the second Italian Renaissance Revival discussed previously and is evident in her design for the Oakland building.

Morgan's Oakland YWCA draws heavily upon the

Above

FIG. 6
St. Louis YWCA, ca. 1912

Above

FIG. 7
Julia Morgan, Oakland YWCA, 1913–1915

Opposite

FIG. 8
Michelozzo de Bartolomeo, Palazzo Medici, 1445–1455

palazzo in both plan and elevation. Historically, the palazzo could function as the residence of a noble or wealthy family, as well as housing the family's business enterprises. Large palaces had been built throughout Europe since the time of the Roman emperors, but the palazzo—urban, block-like, fortified, and compact, as opposed to a sprawling compound—developed during the later Middle Ages and reached new levels of refinement by the mid-sixteenth century. Centuries later, the historical, civic, and social associations of the palazzo, along with its commodious proportions, made it an ideal model for new YWCA branches that were known for providing urban places of domestic refuge, community, and educational opportunities for

young women. This likely led the association's governing boards to conclude that their mission was best served by a palazzo-like building that also symbolized the notion of renewal of the American Renaissance.

In a Renaissance city, the palazzo was among the foremost expressions of stateliness and magnificence in addition to the cathedral and district, monastic, and convent churches. It was intended to beautify the neighborhood as well as enhance the reputation of the patron. The building type was revolutionized by the design Michelozzo di Bartolomeo Michelozzi (1396–1472) created for the Palazzo Medici (renamed Palazzo Medici Riccardi in 1659) in Florence (FIG. 8). Begun around 1445 and completed

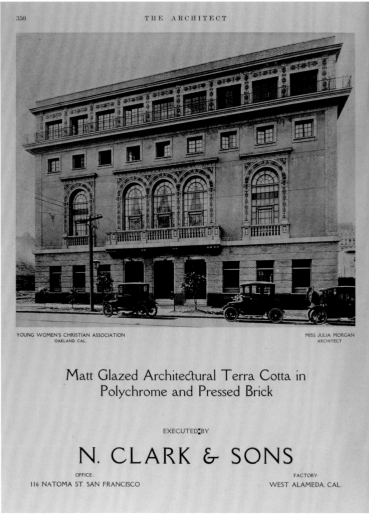

YOUNG WOMEN'S CHRISTIAN ASSOCIATION
OAKLAND. CAL.

MISS JULIA MORGAN
ARCHITECT

Matt Glazed Architectural Terra Cotta in
Polychrome and Pressed Brick

EXECUTED BY

N. CLARK & SONS

OFFICE:
116 NATOMA ST. SAN FRANCISCO

FACTORY:
WEST ALAMEDA, CAL.

Above

FIG. 9

Advertisement for
N. Clark & Sons,
1916

Opposite

FIG. 10

Julia Morgan,
matte-glazed
polychrome terra
cotta tiles used as
window surrounds,
Oakland YWCA

a decade later, it became the prototype for subsequent Florentine and Tuscan palazzi.[31]

In fifteenth-century Florence, the Palazzo Medici represented a revolutionary and harmonious combination of local materials and building traditions while incorporating the *all'antica* traditions of Rome into its design. One can identify in the palace facade such traditional Florentine elements as *bifore* (pairs of lancet or round arched windows) and the rusticated and rough-hewn stone cladding of *pietraforte* (a common building material of locally quarried sandstone). The view from street level gives the appearance of a massive, fortified foundation. Additionally, a variety of *all'antica* elements can be found on the interior and exterior. These include a tripartite stone facade divided by stringcourses modeled after the enclosing wall of the Forum of Augustus in Rome and a central courtyard based on Vitruvius's description of domestic Roman architecture. This courtyard is bordered by an arcade inspired by the monastic cloister.[32] The combining of architectural elements from different periods of

Italy's architectural history was recurrently applied in Florence. Approximately thirty palazzi were erected in the city between 1450 and 1475, and this model continued to influence local and regional architecture for centuries.[33]

With varying degrees of subtlety, Renaissance architects made sophisticated references to historic buildings and structures while they incorporated local materials and traditions. A building's significance, therefore, lay in its historical associations rather than displays of costly materials. In fact, the facades of many of the grandest palazzi are composed primarily of modest components. Various methods were used to simulate costly techniques, such as using stucco to simulate stone, or stone veneer instead of solid stone construction.[34]

Morgan took a comparable approach in her design for the Oakland YWCA. As her colleague Walter Steilberg noted, "Since the object of the [YWCA] is service it is necessary to constantly exercise a strict sense of economy in design and detail in order that the building may serve as many [women] as possible."[35] Morgan's steel-reinforced structure was made primarily of common brick.[36] Other modest materials such as plaster and cast iron appear throughout the building. More sumptuous details were conservatively applied to best advantage. For example, the lintels and lateral faces of the recessed entrance on Webster Street are clad with marble veneer, and the entrance doorframes are of carved oak. Steilberg's reference to economy also pertains to Morgan's usage of locally sourced materials. The ornamental polychrome terracotta tiles that surround the windows above the entrance were manufactured in nearby Alameda by N. Clark & Sons (FIG. 9), a maker of bricks, terracotta tiles, and "kindred clay products." The manufacturer obtained clay from deposits in northern California and supplied products to various architectural jobs throughout the West.[37] Morgan also specified matte-glazed tiles in five hues in her design of the decorative window frames on the second and top floors. These feature dolphins and California flowers and fruits (FIG. 10).

Several exterior elements illustrate the Oakland YWCA's close resemblance to the Palazzo Medici Riccardi. The facades of both buildings include three distinct horizontal registers, each exhibiting a unique surface treatment. In the Florentine model, these divisions are representative of the spatial and social hierarchies within the palace, with the *piano nobile* (the

Above

FIG. 11

Julia Morgan,
Oakland YWCA
with original side
garden, ca. 1918

Opposite

FIG. 12

Michelozzo de
Bartolomeo,
bottom illustration
showing ground
floor plan of
Palazzo Medici

main floor of the house, above the ground floor) being the most exclusive.

By contrast, the YWCA's facade attempts to visually disguise its five floors within the three horizontal registers while still conveying the importance of the *piano nobile*, which contains one of the building's most important social spaces, the assembly room. With their repeating window patterns, the facades of the Florentine and Oakland buildings are intended to impart order, solidity, and domestic security. Both buildings are capped with cornices, or cornice-like elements, resolving the uppermost zones of their facades.

Another important similarity between the Palazzo Medici Riccardi and the Oakland YWCA is that both are prominently sited in their urban settings. By amassing a number of adjacent properties, the Medici acquired a conspicuous location to build their palace along a processional route near the Cathedral of Santa Maria del Fiore. In Oakland, the YWCA originally included a garden running the length of its south elevation (through

which 15th Street was later extended), effectively buffering the building from adjacent edifices and giving the impression of a spacious corner lot (FIG. 11).[38] In addition, since the Palazzo Medici Riccardi and the YWCA are located at intersections, both simultaneously display two elevations.

In conceiving the Oakland building, Morgan drafted a plan that echoes that of the Palazzo Medici Riccardi. For comparison, the ground floor plans have been color-coded to indicate spaces of comparable form and placement (FIG. 12 and FIG. 13). The axial vestibul in each building guides the visitor directly to a central light-filled courtyard. The location of the main staircase is nearly identical in both plans. Another shared feature is the large space beyond the courtyard. In the Palazzo Medici Riccardi this contained a walled garden, but in the Oakland building it was occupied by a cafeteria. As mentioned above, the second floor of the YWCA includes a large, high-ceilinged assembly room that occupies more than half the

Das Lebensprincip der toscanischen Fassade ist die völlig gleich-
mässige Behandlung, das Verschmähen jeder besondern Characteristik
der Mittelpartie oder der Ecken, des sog. Gruppirens.

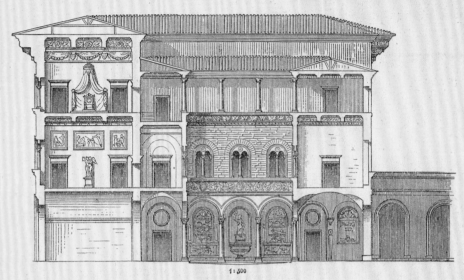

1:500
Fig. 105. Pal. Riccardi zu Florenz.

Beweis einer hohen Anlage der florentinischen Kunst, die in einem
schmuckliebenden Zeitalter auf Alles, was irgend die Aufmerksamkeit

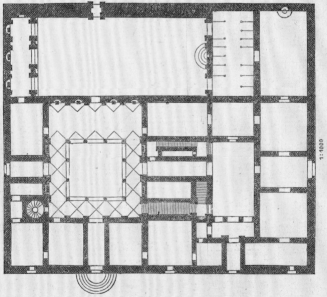

Fig. 106. Pal. Riccardi zu Florenz.

theilen konnte, auch auf Prachtpforten verzichtete, und die Mittel gleich-
mässig auf das Eine Ganze verwandte.

length of the Webster Street facade. This corresponds to the grand gallery in the Palazzo Medici Riccardi.

In addition to these and other similarities of the YWCA to the Florentine palazzo, there is also a faithful reworking of a well-known Italian Renaissance architectural space. This is the cloister adjoining the church of Santa Maria della Pace in Rome, created by Donato Bramante (1444–1514) around 1500. Morgan adapted Bramante's open-air cloistered courtyard for the interior enclosure of the YWCA (FIG. 14 and FIG. 15).[39] Considering the alterations that Morgan made to Bramante's design, it seems likely that she was interested in the cloister primarily for its organization of an interior gathering space. Bramante's cloister provided a means for nuns to pass between the church and the monastery complex. In comparison, the YWCA's courtyard is the heart of the interior, providing easy circulation across the first floor, enabling communication between the first and second floors, and encouraging socialization among the building's occupants. Additionally, the courtyard originally featured a Morgan-designed fountain with polychrome ceramic details that matched the color scheme of the building's exterior. Centrally placed, it featured sculpted Greco-Roman mythological figures and had a distinctly Mediterranean aspect that Morgan would further develop in her landscape design at Hearst Castle (FIG. 16 and FIG. 17). A further adaptation from Bramante's cloister is the use of an inscription as a proclamation. The Roman cloister frieze commemorated its patron, Oliviero Carafa, Cardinal of Naples, and dedicated the structure to the Virgin Mary, the spiritual patroness of the church.[40] In the Oakland YWCA, all four of the friezes overlooking the interior courtyard are inscribed with Psalm 19:1–2, proclaiming its identity as a Protestant Christian institution:

THE HEAVENS DECLARE THE GLORY
OF GOD
THE FIRMAMENT SHOWETH HIS HANDIWORK
DAY UNTO DAY UTTERETH SPEECH
AND NIGHT
UNTO NIGHT SHOWETH KNOWLEDGE[41]

In adapting the palazzo model to serve the needs of the YWCA, Morgan modified Bramante's cloister design in order to unify the courtyard visually and increase its utility. Most apparent is the addition of the timbered skylight that covers the YWCA's courtyard above the second floor. Traditionally, a

Right
FIG. 13
Julia Morgan, original blueprint of the ground floor plan of Oakland YWCA, ca. 1913

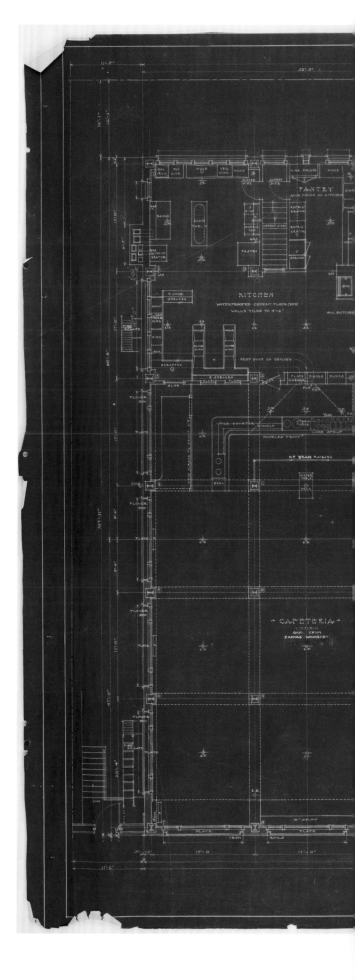

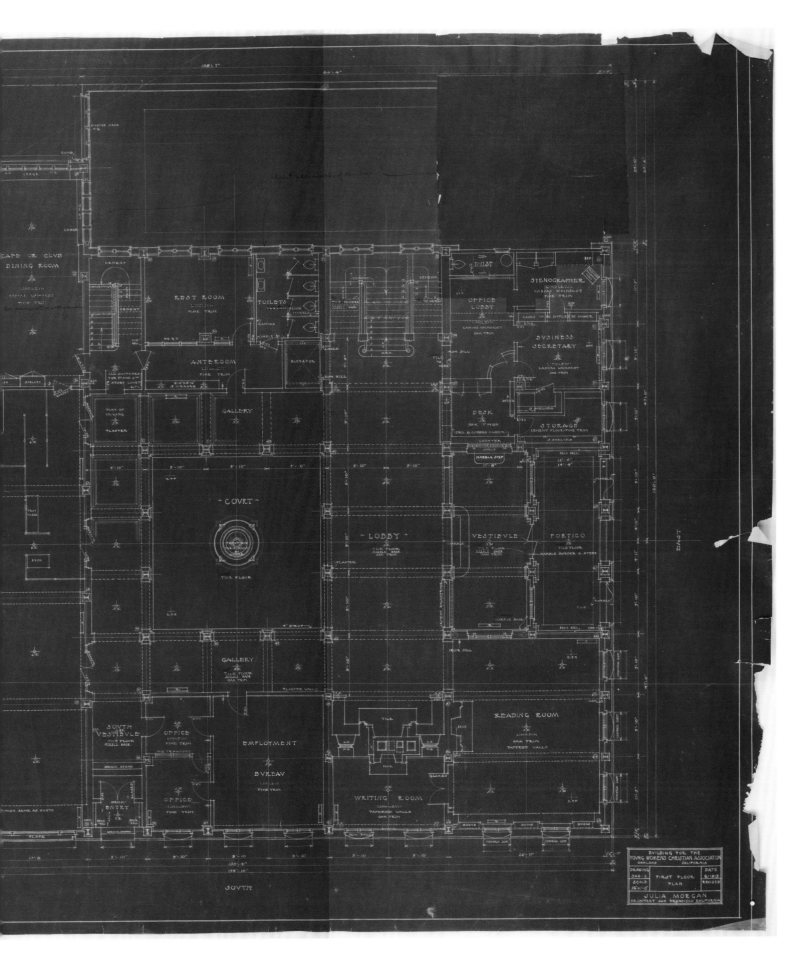

Below
FIG. 14
Donato Bramante,
cloistered
courtyard of Santa
Maria della Pace,
1500–1504

Opposite
FIG. 15
Julia Morgan,
courtyard in the
Oakland YWCA

cloistered courtyard is open to the sky, but by covering the space Morgan maximized its utility, allowing it to be used regardless of the weather. The inspiration for the glass-paned ceiling may have come from the Cour d'Honneur in the Palais des Études at the École des Beaux-Arts, which Morgan visited frequently during her student years (FIG. 18). Beneath the skylight, she extended the consoles above the second-story colonnade by designing a trellis that projects horizontally over the courtyard. This feature, typically found in an outdoor garden, contributes an Arts and Crafts aspect to the otherwise classicized interior. The galleries on both levels of the YWCA courtyard feature flat coffered ceilings, and the smaller square pattern of the upper gallery corresponds to the grid of the skylight above. Moreover, it is worth noting that the scale of the YWCA court is two thirds the size of Bramante's open-air cloistered courtyard, and a more intimate

interior space was achieved by this reduction.[42]

Morgan's partnership with the YWCA was one of her longest and steadiest professional affiliations, and over the course of her career she designed more than thirty buildings for the institution.[43] Reflecting on this relationship to her associate Walter Steilberg, she offered this advice:

Don't turn down a job because you think it's beneath you, because you think you want to do something larger . . . One of the smallest jobs I ever had was a little two-room residence in Monterey [California] . . . when I first started in practice for myself. The lady for whom I did it was most pleased with the job, and now the lady is the chairman of the board of the YWCA. And from that has come all these fine big jobs we have.[44]

In appreciation of her designs for new YWCA buildings, the national board in New York invited Morgan to officiate as the association's supervising

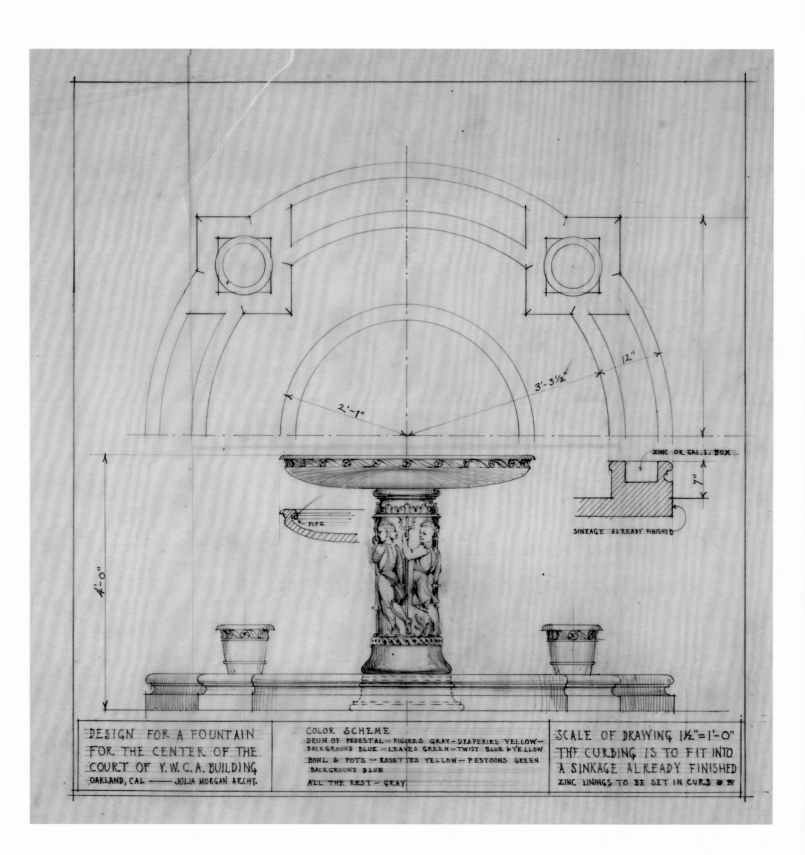

DESIGN FOR A FOUNTAIN
FOR THE CENTER OF THE
COURT OF Y.W.C.A. BUILDING
OAKLAND, CAL — JULIA MORGAN ARCHT.

COLOR SCHEME
DRUM OF PEDESTAL - FIGURES GRAY - DRAPERIES YELLOW -
BACKGROUND BLUE - LEAVES GREEN - TWIST BLUE & YELLOW
BOWL & POTS - ROSETTES YELLOW - FESTOONS GREEN
BACKGROUND BLUE
ALL THE REST - GRAY

SCALE OF DRAWING 1½"=1'-0"
THE CURBING IS TO FIT INTO
A SINKAGE ALREADY FINISHED
ZINC LININGS TO BE SET IN CURB

ZINC OR GAL. I. BOX

SINKAGE ALREADY FINISHED

PIPE

architect in 1919.[45] Although she declined the offer in order to remain near her family, she received many more commissions from the grateful institution. Morgan's historicist design for the Oakland YWCA played an integral role in her development as an architect, and several of her later designs for the organization similarly reflect Italian and Mediterranean stylistic influences, including those for facilities in San Francisco, Los Angeles, Fresno, and Honolulu. She adopted modified palazzo schemas for other projects, such as the concurrently designed San Jose YWCA (completed in 1915, demolished in the 1960s) and the extant Emanu-El Sisterhood Residence in San Francisco. (It was completed in 1923 and was the Jewish counterpart to the YWCA. The building now houses the San Francisco Zen Center.)

Morgan's understanding of historic styles and precedents continued to inform her design method and vision.[46] Her study of historical precedent at the École des Beaux-Arts would serve her career for another thirty-five years, during which time she received commissions for numerous educational, social, healthcare, and religious organizations. Bolstered by her training in Beaux-Arts architectural principles, which profoundly influenced the American Renaissance, Morgan repeatedly looked to the Italian Renaissance as a source of inspiration, not only as a model for institutional buildings and a hilltop mansion in San Simeon, but also for the spaces that served hardworking people, like the low-wage young women who flocked to the new jobs created in the growing cities of early twentieth-century America. ✿

Opposite
FIG. 16
Julia Morgan, *Design for a Fountain for the Center of the Court of Y.W.C.A. Building,* pencil and ink, 1912

Above
FIG. 17
Julia Morgan, courtyard in the Oakland YWCA, 1918

Following spread
FIG. 18
Courtyard of the Palais des Études, École des Beaux-Arts, Paris

4

JULIA MORGAN'S LOS ANGELES EXAMINER BUILDING
A BEAUX-ARTS VISION OF SPANISH COLONIAL ARCHITECTURE

ELIZABETH McMILLIAN

During the California Spanish architectural revivals—first in the Mission phase (1885–1915) and thereafter in the Spanish Colonial phase (1915–1940)—Julia Morgan played a major role in applying Beaux-Arts methods and practices in her major commissions.[1] Her design of the Los Angeles Examiner Building is a standout example of the emerging Spanish Colonial style (FIG. 1). In *California Colonial*, I wrote that "[t]he first notable Spanish Colonial Revival building in Southern California was the Los Angeles Examiner Building, 1914, by San Francisco architect Julia Morgan with J. Martyn Haenke of Haenke and Dodd as the local architect. Morgan, who studied at the École des Beaux-Arts, Paris, designed the block-long newspaper plant for her chief client, William Randolph Hearst. True to the historical eclecticism of the revival, she incorporated a Mission Order gable and Moorish domes, as well as Italianate and other Western European elements in the overall design."[2]

The Los Angeles Examiner Building is an example of the development from the preceding Mission Revival that became widely known with the California State Building at the 1893 World's Columbian Exposition in Chicago (FIG. 2). Subsequently, American architects developed an increasingly complex variant known as Spanish Colonial architecture that was most strongly expressed in the Spanish Colonial style of the buildings at the 1915 Panama-California Exposition in San Diego. The earlier fair saw the Beaux-Arts method and style become the leading architectural trend in America. Twenty-two years later in San Diego, Beaux-Arts continued as the foundation for the emerging Spanish Colonial Revival, a prominent style for California, as well as for Florida, Texas, and New Mexico—states with a Spanish-Mexican heritage.

After 1915, architects influenced by the Beaux-Arts tradition extended the California Spanish Revival into the 1920s and 1930s in a variety of commissions. Julia Morgan continued this style in a "Mediterranean" vein for William Randolph Hearst in La Cuesta Encantada, the hilltop complex that was his home in San Simeon, California—an amalgam of Spanish-Moorish, Italian Renaissance, and Greco-Roman sources. Morgan's California roots, her Berkeley and Paris educations, and the West Coast cultural environment in which she practiced favorably disposed her to realizing and integrating various Spanish and Southern European styles at Hearst Castle. The result is a composite and a pronounced example of the architectural eclecticism of the late phase of the American Renaissance.[3]

1902-1914
Early Hearst Patronage

After returning to California in 1902 upon earning certification at the École des Beaux-Arts, Morgan began her own practice. At the same time, Phoebe Apperson Hearst encouraged Morgan to join the architectural team implementing the Hearst masterplan for the University of California, Berkeley that she had sponsored. Morgan worked on two projects under the campus architect John Galen Howard (1864–1931), also an École alumnus, who had been appointed to found the university's architectural program.

Previous spread
Julia Morgan student work, sketch in portfolio, pencil, ink, and watercolor, ca. 1900

Opposite and following spread
FIG. 1
Julia Morgan, Los Angeles Examiner Building, 1914-15

Above

FIG. 2

A. Page Brown,
California State
Building, World's
Columbian
Exposition,
Chicago, 1893

Phoebe Hearst was among Morgan's first and most supportive patrons, and soon she hired Morgan to renovate her unfinished Spanish-Mexican rancho compound, Hacienda del Pozo de Verona, near Pleasanton. From 1903 to 1910, Morgan designed additions to the site in a fusion of Mission and Pueblo styles, substantially remodeling the original A. C. Schweinfurth (1863–1900) design.[4] When the hacienda was completed, it was a sprawling horizontal and towered ninety-two-room compound that prompted comparisons to a Spanish colonial presidio (FIG. 3 and FIG. 4). It included a banquet hall, music room, ballroom, bowling alley, and tennis courts. Morgan added multiple garages to accommodate automobiles that had not been envisioned

in the 1890s, when the first phase of the hacienda's design took place.

Morgan's work on the hacienda was accompanied by another Spanish-themed commission: El Campanil (INTRODUCTION, FIG. 16) at Mills College in Oakland, a tower accommodating ten bells with red-tile roofing and numerous open arches and buttresses.

Throughout her practice, Morgan stayed current with newly published works illustrating historical architecture and art. Her library included many studies by Arthur Byne (1883–1935) and Mildred Stapley Byne (1875–1941), renowned curators, collectors, and, eventually, dealers of historical Spanish artifacts and architectural elements. Morgan had known both since her student days in Paris. During construction of La

Cuesta Encantada, the Spain-based couple became agents for William Randolph Hearst in building his collection, procuring antique furniture, ornamental wooden ceilings, various architectural fragments, and Spanish-Moorish tiles.[5]

After the 1906 earthquake hit San Francisco, Morgan's speedy renovation of the Fairmont Hotel earned her particular notice, especially for her use of reinforced concrete structuring that would withstand future tremors. This and her growing reputation brought her numerous commissions for residences, schools, and churches. Sometime in early 1913, she began her first large commission from Phoebe Hearst's son, William Randolph Hearst. He wanted to construct a Spanish-style newspaper building in Los Angeles.

LOS ANGELES EXAMINER BUILDING, 1913-1914
The Commission and Design for William Randolph Hearst

In 1887, William, the young Hearst scion—an only child who would become a businessman, politician, and newspaper and media mogul—was given control of the *San Francisco Examiner* by his father, George Hearst. The senior Hearst turned over the newspaper to his son after he was elected to the U.S. Senate. Seven years later, William bought the *New York Journal*, and over time he acquired a chain of nearly thirty newspapers in major American cities. Hearst subsequently expanded to magazines, creating the nation's largest newspaper and media company, Hearst Communications. He was twice elected to the U.S. House of Representatives and then ran unsuccessfully for president in 1904; he founded the *Los Angeles Examiner* in 1903 to boost his political popularity during that campaign.[6]

By the mid-1910s, Hearst decided to increase his media presence in the Southern California market, and he commissioned his mother's favorite architect, Julia Morgan, to design the new headquarters and press building for the *Los Angeles Examiner*. It occupied an entire block south of the city center, facing Broadway between 11th and 12th Streets. In 1913 Hearst had paid one million dollars for the land, acquired from railroad magnate and fellow art patron Henry E. Huntington.

The original drawings and documents for the Examiner Building remain to be found, but it is generally assumed that the structure was completed by the end of 1914. A November 1918 article written by Morgan's structural engineer, Walter Steilberg, in *Architect and Engineer* dates the structure to April 1915, while showcasing renowned local metal artisan Edward Trinkkeller's iron grille in the lobby (FIG. 5).[7] In the same article, Hearst expressed his satisfaction with the finished project:

> *What do I think of it? Why, it is well within the bounds of a conservative judgment to say that it is creditable to the city and to the newspaper which it houses.*
>
> *Miss Morgan, the architect, commendably accomplished the task of constructing a building that is thoroughly practicable, for all newspaper demands and which, I am glad to note, combines with its efficient qualities those pleasing traits reminiscent of an architecture with the beautiful and romantic history of Los Angeles and of California. I think she has accomplished the result happily and effectively from all points of view.*[8]

With its rich historicist design, including six polychrome tile domes, a massive central tower, and a luxuriant baroque foyer, the Los Angeles Examiner Building seems more like a palace than a newspaper plant. Further, except for its Mission Order gable entrance with bell towers, it has very little in common with any of California's Spanish missions. The lobby interior, with its elaborate split staircase, gives an impression of real grandeur, largely due to the gilding of its arches and the plateresco wall reliefs that recall fifteenth- and sixteenth-century Spanish Renaissance styles (FIG. 6).

On the main-entrance facade, the central bay is distinguished by an arched entry pierced with a Moorish pointed star window (FIG. 7). Adding to this, the entrance is framed by a scalloped gable flanked by a pair of two-story bell towers, called *espadañas*, giving it the appearance of a church. These form the Mission Order gable typical of the California missions and seen in the Mission Revival style popular from 1890 through 1915. (And, in our time, handily adopted for its commercial appeal by the fast food chain Taco Bell.) Rising above and behind the central bay and bell towers is a double-story structure crowned by a drum tower with a cupola. Defined by open loggias along the front and sides, the thick tower calls to mind the Summer Palace (Palacio de Generalife) on the heights above Granada, Spain.

The corners of the long entrance block are capped with colorful geometric-patterned blue- and yellow-tiled domes (FIG. 8). The entire building is roofed in red clay tiles; its walls are finished in beige stucco. Across the facade is a ground-level arcade, typical of a Spanish mission compound. Now infilled, the arcades were originally glazed to allow sidewalk viewing of the *Examiner*'s massive printing machinery.

On entering the lobby, the impression is secular, neither high ecclesiastical nor provincially decorated like the Franciscan missions. Instead, it is structured and decorated like the great hall of a Spanish Baroque palace (FIG. 9). The double-story space is crowned by massive wooden ceiling beams. Ornate chandeliers provide dramatic lighting. The floors are paved in decorative patterned tiles and the walls and columns are detailed with plateresco-style bas-relief panels in terra cotta (FIG. 6). The highlights of the lobby are two series of polychrome arches that span the center section, and, as in a palace, two richly decorated staircases ascend to the second floor, one from each side of the spacious room.

Once the building was completed, it is not hard to imagine the overpowering impression of grandeur conveyed to visitors upon entering the *Examiner*'s lobby. Perhaps Hearst wanted to set the stage for those venturing into the vast interior expanse that housed enormous whirring presses and clattering typesetting machinery. Appropriate for a structure housing a modern newspaper, Morgan engineered the block-long industrial building using the latest construction technologies: reinforced concrete deployed a proprietary type of structural support for the load-bearing floors, known as Kahn Bar—an early twentieth century innovation. A key component of that system includes corrugated metal-formed joists that are still visible throughout the interior of the building.[9]

In 1921 and 1930 Morgan was called back to the *Examiner* to remodel some of the upstairs interiors. In 1976, the building—then housing a successor paper, the *Herald Examiner*—was further refurbished, though without any major alterations.

A DESIGN SOURCE FROM THE 1893 CHICAGO WORLD'S COLUMBIAN EXPOSITION

In its overall massing and symmetry, Morgan's Los Angeles Examiner Building design is notably similar to the California State Building, or pavilion, at the 1893 Columbian Exposition in Chicago (FIG. 2). The emphatically horizontal and multi-towered structure

Opposite

FIG. 4

A. C. Schweinfurth and Julia Morgan, Hacienda del Pozo de Verona, entry gate with main block directly beyond, 1894–1898 and 1903–1910

Below

FIG. 5

Edwin Trinkkeller, ornamental metal grille, ca. 1914. One of a number of grilles installed in the lobby, Los Angeles Examiner Building

Following

FIG. 6

Julia Morgan, lobby, Los Angeles Examiner Building, 1914-15

was designed by A. Page Brown (1859—1896). It marked the first instance in which the stylistic elements of California's more ornate Spanish missions were worked up into monumental forms. Its symmetrical plan, however, reveals its Beaux-Arts origins. Brown absorbed the academic approach in the early 1880s while drafting designs for the firm McKim, Mead & White—then America's foremost proponent of French classicism. In 1889, Brown came west and established a practice in San Francisco.

A popular attraction for fairgoers, the California State Building exemplified how a Spanish interpretation could derive from Beaux-Arts practice. Both the Los Angeles Examiner Building and the California State Building are aggrandized Spanish Mission–like blocks with arcades and bell towers punctuating each corner, elements that Hearst would later identify as "reminiscent of an architecture with the beautiful and romantic history … of California."[10] No records have yet been found to link Morgan's design to the iconic work by Brown. But there is no doubt that Morgan—as well as her client—knew Brown's design could be adapted for the newspaper printing plant in Los Angeles. The Chicago pavilion's interior was a vast open exhibition hall and it is easy to imagine it accommodating a newspaper plant.

Brown, himself a recent arrival in California, was intrigued by the development of a "Spanish" style and responded to the social, historical, and geographical environment of the forty-two-year-old state and the issue of its identity. The state commission overseeing the competition liked his proposal, and his office became the commission's choice to design the pavilion for the Chicago fair.[11] The popularity of the California State Building boosted the Mission Revival style, which lasted into the second decade of the twentieth century, impacting its successor, the Spanish Colonial Revival.

The Columbian Exposition was a national sensation, as well as announcing the arrival of the Beaux-Arts movement in the United States and forecasting its dominance into the twentieth century. That it occurred while Morgan was studying at UC Berkeley and considering applying to the very school that designed the Chicago fair means that it must have been a factor in her decision to study in Paris.

DESIGN INSPIRATION FROM THE 1915 SAN DIEGO PANAMA-CALIFORNIA EXPOSITION

It is also likely that Morgan and Hearst found more recent inspiration for the Los Angeles Examiner Building, in addition to the famed 1893 California State Building. As they were contemplating designs, planning for the 1915 Panama-California Exposition in San Diego was getting underway. Given the ongoing publicity for the fair to the south, Morgan and Hearst surely became aware of the exposition designs through the competitions and discussions appearing in newspapers and magazines. Located in Balboa Park, the San Diego fair was held between January 1, 1915 and January 1, 1917. By contrast, San Francisco's Panama-Pacific International Exposition ran from February 20, 1915 to December 4, 1915. It largely continued the classicist Beaux-Arts style of Chicago's "White City," but differed from it in its conception of a walled "Orientalized city" and use of a coordinated color scheme on the facades of its buildings.

Planning for the San Diego fair began in 1911.[12] Officials originally favored Beaux-Arts academician John Galen Howard to oversee the design, perhaps due to his recent role in Seattle's Alaska-Yukon-Pacific Exposition in 1909. Howard was uninterested, however, so they chose Bertram Grosvenor Goodhue (1869–1924), a brilliant historicist architect known for his skillful synthesis of styles and virtuoso draftsmanship. He was assisted by Carleton Winslow, Sr. (1876–1946), an alumnus of the École des Beaux-Arts who would later become a leading advocate for the Spanish Colonial Revival.

Goodhue's familiarity with and preference for Spanish Colonial baroque architecture in Mexico won over the fair commission, and the Spanish Colonial Baroque was chosen as the dominant style, reversing an earlier inclination toward a combination of the Pueblo and Mission Revivals. This contrasted the San Diego design with the previous American and European expositions and their neoclassical Beaux-Arts plans that placed grand formal structures around symmetrical expanses, deployed extravagant water features, and punctuated the grounds with towering sculpture ensembles.

Opposite
FIG. 10
Bertram Grosvenor Goodhue, California Building, Panama-California Exposition, San Diego, 1915

For his inspiration, Goodhue used drawings and photographs from his travels in Mexico, as well as illustrations from recent publications on historical Spanish and Mexican art and architecture. His core buildings in the Plaza de California (also known as the Quadrangle) are noted for contrasting expanses of bare walls with rich Mexican and Spanish Churrigueresco embellishment and additions of Persian and Islamic elements from the Moorish Revival then in vogue. Goodhue's strongest design was the California Building, the largest and most ornate structure on the site (FIG. 10 and FIG. 11). According to architectural historian Carolyn Pitts, he drew inspiration from the Spanish Colonial church of San Diego in Guanajuato, Mexico.[13] This repeats the precedent of using a religious architectural form for a secular building, as Brown and his design team did for the Chicago fair with their aggrandized composite of California's Franciscan missions. These and other contemporary examples—secular bell towers at American universities inspired by Spanish *campanarios*—may later have encouraged Morgan and Hearst to adapt the Renaissance Church of Santa María la Mayor in Ronda, Spain, as the inspiration for the facade of Casa Grande, the main building of Hearst Castle.

Arrayed along and extending from El Prado, the axis of the exposition, Goodhue and company's buildings presented a virtual history of Spanish Colonial styles in North America, from Renaissance European sources to Spanish Colonial to Mexican Baroque to the vernacular styles of California's Franciscan missions. Nearly fifty years after the San Diego Exposition, California Historian Kevin Starr insightfully described this amalgam of influences in the first volume of his multi-volume history of the Golden State, *Americans and the California Dream, 1850–1915*:[14]

To Goodhue Spanish Colonial stood for a revisionist, anti-industrial aesthetic. As a Mexican tradition, it had emerged from a society which was organized around religion and a peasantry, both of which Goodhue saw as essential to a thriving art-sense and which he found lacking in the civilization north of the Rio Grande. He became a leading exponent of Spanish Colonial in the United States, a revival especially appropriate, he thought, in the American Southwest, where Mexican civilization had once held sway.

In that journey [to the twentieth century] Spanish Colonial proved an important stage. It satisfied two needs in Goodhue: a need for history and a need for suggestions on how to handle form, mass, texture, and color in that way of the future haunting his imagination. . . .

Like Maybeck's Palace of Fine Arts [for San Francisco's Panama-Pacific International Exposition], Goodhue's California Quadrangle, especially the cathedral-like California State Building, conferred romantic historicity upon a rather raw American city. It was variously compared to the Giralda Tower of Seville, the cathedral of Cordova, the Balvanera Chapel of the Church of San Francisco in Mexico City, the cathedral at Oaxaca, Mexico, or the church of Montepulciano in Italy. The very roll call of these names gave satisfaction. Such were the associations San Diegans had to evoke.[15]

The 1915 Panama-California Exposition led to California's assimilation of Spanish Colonial Revival architecture as its dominant historical regional style through 1940. It also became the mode for the rebuilding of Santa Barbara after the 1925 earthquake, in no small part due to Winslow's efforts in persuading the city to adopt it as the official civic style in 1929. Consequently, the coastal city's characteristic Spanish nature was drawn from local Mission Revival precedents, as well as Goodhue and company's San Diego designs.

CONCLUSIONS

By 1915, Morgan and Hearst's Los Angeles Examiner Building was completed, establishing a paradigm for commercial use of the Spanish Colonial style. Contemporaneously, a historicist phase of period styles was spreading across the country and was supported by America's ascendant architecture schools and the American Institute of Architects. In addition, there was a growing appreciation among the general populace for buildings that had sophistication, historical associations, and European ornamental detailing. Alongside Tudor, Italianate, and French Normandy designs, Spanish-style works arose in abundance in the Southwest, particularly in California, where the style's advocates used it to claim the region's lineage as a colony of Spain and the inheritors of Spain's civilization.

Following the San Diego fair, city halls, churches, commercial districts, office buildings, mansions, bungalows, country clubs, dance halls, and even gas stations were designed in variations of the Spanish Colonial Revival style. These could be formal,

Casa del Prado
1650 El Prado

SAINT VINCENT'S CATHEDRAL. LOS ANGELES, CAL.

T 269

60142

symmetrical Beaux Arts–inspired projects, such as the commercial Los Angeles Examiner Building, or might draw upon an ecclesiastical plan—as in the 1925 Saint Vincent de Paul Church, also in Los Angeles by A. C. Martin (FIG. 12), or the 1918 Rew-Sharp House in Coronado with its intimate plaza and fountain by Elmer Grey,[16] or one of the many homes or "haciendas" of Santa Barbara designed by George Washington Smith in the 1920s. California, with its Mediterranean climate and landscape, took the lead in Spanish-themed architecture, largely due to its architects, designers, and city leaders becoming the principal proponents of the style.

During the Spanish Colonial Revival (1915 to 1940, paralleling Morgan and Hearst's work on La Cuesta Encantada), these proponents and their patrons increasingly looked overseas to Spain to borrow forms and elements from its rich wealth of centuries of styles. (See Victoria Kastner's chapter in this volume.) There was particular interest in southern Spain, where the Moorish impact infused the region with rich, complex crafts in tilework, metalwork, and wood and stucco carving. The historicist precedents established during the American Renaissance and rise of the Beaux-Arts movement laid the groundwork for the emergence of the Spanish Colonial Revival.

David Gebhard, an architectural historian and a force behind the preservation of Santa Barbara's Spanish-style architecture, noted the impact of the Beaux-Arts movement on the California Spanish Revival in his foreword to *Casa California*:

> *The way in which Spanish architecture and decorative arts entered the twentieth-century American consciousness is itself a fascinating and complex tale, an outcome of several centuries of European enchantment with Islamic architecture and decorative Arts . . . Spain and Spanish imagery, then, played an intriguing role in American architecture of the late nineteenth and early twentieth centuries. From the 1850s on, Spain entered the American consciousness through the idea of the romance of the Moors. Just before and after the turn of the century, exponents of the Beaux Arts enriched this fascination with Islamic Spain by expanding their palette to include Spanish and Italian Renaissance sources. This 'respectable' use of Spanish prototypes joined the remarkably popular, nationwide fascination with California's 'native' mission revival style, with its stucco walls and tile roofs.[17]*

Four years after the Los Angeles Examiner Building was completed, in a letter to Morgan on December 31, 1919, William Randolph Hearst affirmed that "[t]he San Diego Exposition is the best source for Spanish in California. We picked out the towers of the Church at Ronda [Spain]. I suppose they are Renaissance or else transitional, and they have some Gothic feelings, but a Renaissance decoration, particularly that of the very southern part of Spain." He expanded on the subject, writing that his preference was for the Spanish Renaissance style for San Simeon, then entering its first stages of design.[18]

In August 1977, the Los Angeles Herald Examiner Building—"Herald" had been added to its name in 1962—was designated a Los Angeles Historic-Cultural Monument. In 1989, the newspaper ceased operations. Since 2015, Georgetown Company, a New York real estate developer, has been making restoration and renovation plans for the building with the global design firm Gensler. Detail research is being done by Historic Resources Group, a Pasadena-based historic preservation consulting firm. The redesign includes restaurants and shops on the ground floor facing the street, while the upper offices and central printing plant spaces will be occupied by Arizona State University's Walter Cronkite School of Journalism and Mass Communication. This brings an interesting return to the media legacy of William Randolph Hearst and sparks interest in Julia Morgan and her historicist forms for a new generation in a vibrant Southern California city. ✿

Opposite
FIG. 12
Albert C. Martin Sr., St. Vincent de Paul Catholic Church, Los Angeles, 1925

5

HEARST CASTLE
A BEAUX-ARTS SPANISH VILLAGE OF THE AMERICAN RENAISSANCE

GORDON L. FUGLIE

The quasi-peaceable gentleman of leisure . . . not only consumes . . . beyond the minimum required for subsistence and physical efficiency, but his consumption also undergoes a specialization as regards the quality of the goods consumed. He consumes freely and of the best . . . Since the consumption of these more excellent goods is an evidence of wealth, it becomes honorific; and conversely, the failure to consume in due quantity and quality becomes a mark of inferiority and demerit.[1]

—THORSTEIN VEBLEN,
The Theory of the Leisure Class, 1899

Winding its way up the serpentine road that crests at the hilltop of the California State Parks historic residence known and trademarked as Hearst Castle, our tour bus halts at the North Terrace. Above us looms the grand ensemble of buildings and grounds designed and built between 1919 and 1947 by architect Julia Morgan (1872–1957) and her indefatigable and changeable patron William Randolph Hearst (1863–1951). We disembark to be greeted by a guide who directs us up to another terrace—named the "Earring" for its circular plan—from which we can stroll the circuitous esplanade to view the site or join a tour of specific structures of Hearst San Simeon State Historical Monument, one of five trademarked names for the state park.

Year round, from morning until late afternoon, platoons of curious visitors arrive to gawk at the indoor and outdoor pools, gardens, and guest houses, and the towering cathedral-esque abode of its former media mogul occupant (FIG. 1). Should the visitor purchase the Grand Rooms Tour, he will be steered through the high-ceilinged and art-filled rooms of Casa Grande, the main building. And if one arrives on a clear day, she will enjoy a vantagepoint 1,600 feet above the Pacific Ocean from which to marvel at breathtaking panoramas of mountains, sky, and sea.

While visitors can spend up to four hours at Hearst Castle, most are done in less time, often departing to other area tourist sites—the Central Coast package.[2] At day's end, how will they recall their time at Hearst Castle beyond the usual clichés (awesome, amazing, wonderful, spectacular)? But who can blame them for resorting to cliché? More than likely, their all too brief experience on the hill felt like an avalanche of culture and nature.

To absorb the rich array of architecture, art, and landscape design of the hilltop complex takes an effort only the most dedicated visitors are willing to make. Moreover, teasing out the fuller meaning of Hearst Castle means overcoming a residual prejudice against the site because of its association with Hearst himself—his yellow journalism, the stain of the fictional film *Citizen Kane*, and, of course, his flamboyant lifestyle. Then there is the reputation of San Simeon in the architectural community. It has long served as a whipping boy for modernist architects in their rejection of historical continuity, classicism, ornament, and Beaux-Arts theory—key elements in the design of the complex. In the name of "formal purity" modernists style-shamed and mocked the buildings of their predecessors schooled in the academic movement. Finally, there is the sexism that has tracked the profession since the nineteenth century, its idolizing of heroic *masculine* creativity, exemplified by the fictional architect Howard Roark in Ayn Rand's 1943 novel *The Fountainhead*. (For the sexism encountered by Julia Morgan at the École des Beaux-Arts, see Karen McNeill's essay in this volume.)

Previous spread
Julia Morgan, *Casa Grande Exterior Front Facade*, pencil and colored pencil on paper, ca. 1919-20

Opposite
FIG. 1
Aerial photograph of Hearst Castle with hand coloring by David F. Stevens, 1948

Above

FIG. 2

Hornblower and
Marshall, *Maryland
Ranch Building,*
watercolor on
paper, 1914. The
mansion was later
named Maryhill by
its founder Sam Hill.

It wasn't until the 1980s that San Simeon began to be reckoned with more seriously, some forty years after construction came to a halt. Architectural historian Sara Holmes Boutelle made a skeptic's visit to the hilltop complex and found herself charmed by its diverse architecture. But she was dismayed to learn that its architect was poorly credited. Boutelle subsequently spent more than a decade researching Julia Morgan's career, especially her Hearst commissions, resulting in the first serious biographical study, *Julia Morgan: Architect.*[3] This sparked further scholarly efforts; two professional studies devoted to San Simeon appeared in the next decade.[4] And as recognition of women's contributions to the arts began to blossom in the twenty-first century, the *New York*

Times redressed a sixty-two-year oversight, publishing a lengthy obituary for Morgan in 2019.[5]

To make sense of the phenomenon now known as Hearst Castle, we need to locate the complex within its era, in addition to probing the motivations of its patron, William Randolph Hearst. (Other chapters in this volume touch on the life and work of its architect, Julia Morgan.[6]) First of all, he was both shaped by and a shaper of an art and architectural movement known as the American Renaissance.[7] This cultural trend originated in 1876 with nationwide celebrations of America's one hundredth anniversary—particularly the Philadelphia Centennial International Exhibition—and extended into the next century until losing momentum in the 1920s. Hearst

was an impressionable and affluent teenager when the American Renaissance became America's cultural ideal. The ambitions that eventually shaped San Simeon had been coursing through his imagination for decades. Further, he and his imperious mother already had been planning and constructing baronial estate homes in California, such as her sprawling hacienda near Pleasanton in 1895 and a medievalist castle in 1902 on the banks of the forested McCloud River in Siskiyou County. In New York City, William had been remodeling his apartment home for many years before he hired Julia Morgan in 1919 as his designer and builder at San Simeon.[8]

The renaissance that was embraced by America's ruling, educational, and cultural elites in the late nineteenth century was Italian, French, and imperial. They saw inspiring precedents in the dukes of Florence whose patronage transformed their medieval town into a humanist city; the Bourbon kings who built the palaces and gardens of Versailles; and the emperors of Rome who renovated the Republican city into an imperial power center with forums, stadiums, theaters, basilicas, temples, public baths, and triumphal columns and arches. The leaders of an industrial and expansionist America could do no less. Out in booming California, Beaux-Arts architects worked in eclectic regional styles in addition to classicist, French, and Italian Renaissance modes.

One of these regional styles was a blend of Spanish Colonial—think of viceregal Latin America—and the

Above

FIG. 3
Bertram Grosvenor
Goodhue, proposal
for the Dr. Frederick
Peterson House,
near Brewster, New
York, mixed media
on paper, 1915

Spanish Renaissance of the sixteenth century. This look premiered at the Panama-California Exposition in San Diego (from 1915 through the end of 1916). Morgan and Hearst created a variant of this style for his Los Angeles Examiner Building. (See my Introduction and Elizabeth McMillian's essay.) In the former Spanish and Mexican territories of California and the Southwest, culturally attuned white arrivistes felt the region's distinct history and landscape called for an architecture that responded to its Latin legacy and Mediterranean environment; trends in the East or upper Midwest would be out of place. At the turn of the century, many of California's political, business and cultural leaders believed that the state's distinct origins and Western circumstances made it an exception, arguing that the state should go its own way in pursuing development.[9]

It is in this sense that what we call Hearst Castle is exceptional, and the term certainly applies to its builder's aspirations. However, he never referred to his Central Coast estate as his patronymic "castle." Speaking casually, Hearst and his family called

it "the ranch"; when more specificity was called for, San Simeon was the designator. And when he desired a more vivid and formal appellation for his Spanish-Mediterranean *latifundium*, it was La Cuesta Encantada (The Enchanted Ridge). Henceforth, I will employ the names that Hearst himself used.

But if the site's architecture and Hearst's approach to art collecting were peculiar to a California identity, the building of sumptuous villas and mansions has a long history, dating to the Roman Empire. Like San Simeon, these villas and mansions incorporated works of art, murals, mosaics, colonnades, bathing complexes, fountains, and libraries. Most were owned by members of the senatorial class, who bought or "appropriated" Greek vases and statuary to adorn their estates in Italy, Sicily, and Gaul, similar to Hearst's purchases of art and antiquities in Europe after World War I.[10] During the American Renaissance, Hearst was among a number of very wealthy and culturally aspirational Americans who collected European art, antiques and architecture, housing them in historicist mansions designed by

Beaux-Arts trained architects.[11] Among the better known of these Gilded Age estate holders are J. P. Morgan (1837–1913), Cornelius Vanderbilt II (1843–1899), George Washington Vanderbilt II (1862–1914), and Henry E. Huntington (1850–1927).

Moreover, while La Cuesta Encantada is renowned for its siting, it was not atypical for great houses of this era to be envisioned or erected on lordly heights. Railroad executive Sam Hill (1857–1931) purchased 5,300 acres along the rim of the Columbia River Gorge, engaging Hornblower & Marshall to design his mansion—originally called Maryhill in 1917—a crisp Beaux-Arts block with a pair of rotundas incorporated into ramped terraces extending from its eastern and western facades (FIG. 2).[12] Like San Simeon, it was intended to house the owner's art collection. At the opposite end of the continent, the pioneering psycho-analyst Frederick Peterson (1859–1938) entertained building a medieval aerie on the crags near Brewster, New York.[13] Bertram Grosvenor Goodhue (1869–1924) was commissioned by Peterson to do a series of drawings in 1915. The romantic studies were more evocative of Wuthering Heights than Westchester County (FIG. 3). Alas, Peterson's aspirational com-plex was never built.

What also sets San Simeon apart from other American Renaissance mansions is the influence on William Randolph Hearst of the architecture of the American world's fairs between 1893 and 1915.[14] The Beaux-Arts designs for the expositions were con-ceived as settings for "showcase architecture," and this appealed to the media mogul's sense of dramatic flair. I contend that it is this Hearst-ian sensibility that sets apart San Simeon from the classicist Beaux-Arts mansions like The Breakers in Newport, Rhode Island, and the Biltmore Estate near Asheville, North Carolina, both from 1895. The former, erected by male scions of the Vanderbilt family, is closely modeled on Italian Renaissance palaces in Genoa and Turin; the latter is a stylization of a French Renaissance château. In addition, both are unitary axially ordered blocks. The two estates are sited on flat and open expanses of turf; the main buildings alone define their sites.

By contrast, San Simeon is a work of composite architecture. The complex also presents varying site levels and styles: upper, middle, and lower terraces connect via networks of stairs; an autonomous Greco-Roman fantasy pool extends over a drop; a main building that stretches in five directions (its ground plan resembles a Lego-block exercise); a remote enclosed pool is roofed by a tennis court; and tow-ering monumental fountains are topped by gilt and bronze sculpture. Further, mix-and-match assem-blages of historical and contemporary figurative sculpture are generously placed around the encircling esplanade and throughout the grounds, similar to the varied sculptures that were located around the Palace of Fine Arts, Bernard Maybeck's (1862–1957) popular classicist caprice at the Panama-Pacific International Exposition of 1915 (Introduction, fig. 22). Moreover, one wonders if the bold but impractical Beaux-Arts plan architect Daniel Burnham (1846–1912) created for hilly San Francisco in 1906 was in some way inspi-rational to Hearst and Morgan as they created their Spanish Mediterranean village on the heights above the sea (Introduction, fig. 10).[15] Hearst had a lifelong fascination with large-scale visionary projects.

LA HOSPITALIDAD DEL GRAN SEÑOR DE LA CUESTA ENCANTADA

Previous studies have documented Hearst's mercu-rial approach to the planning and construction of La Cuesta Encantada. His frequent changes of mind on designs, numerous alterations, and requests for redos would have exasperated any architect. In her long labors on San Simeon, Morgan found ways to manage her inconstant client, anticipating his changeability as just one part of the design and building process. But even as Hearst was prone to revisions, he remained a knowledgeable patron. He had years of European travel under his belt, and years before he hired Morgan was personally involved with the redesign of his New York homes. In addition, his acquisition and intense study of the oversize photo-illustrated volumes of histori-cal architecture that began appearing in the 1890s and during the construction of San Simeon primed his active mind with ideas. (See Victoria Kastner's essay on the libraries that Morgan and Hearst con-sulted.) Finally, throughout the years of designing and building "the enchanted ridge," the client and his architect maintained a mutually cooper-ative relationship, and the results bear that out. Even though the rear of Casa Grande—a stillborn Venetian daydream—was unfinished and Hearst and Morgan's plans for a great hall—an art gallery and

Following spread

FIG. 4

Julia Morgan, early elevation sketch, pencil and ink, ca. 1919-20. The rendering looks east, with guest houses A, B, and C in the foreground. Casa Grande with two towers is at the center. Morgan and Hearst wrote the notes in the margins.

ballroom—on the eastern side of the complex were never realized, the existing ensemble is remarkable for combining diversity and coherence.

When Hearst began to envision a larger plan for his property in 1919, he and Morgan worked up sketches that led to the residential complex that came into being in the 1920s: in the foreground, three guesthouses placed in a semi-circle; further back on the hill, the main building, Casa Grande (FIG. 4). The only major change was to move the guest houses westward, producing a stepped cascade down the slope, and to pull Casa Grande further east. The former permitted the building of extensions from the rear of their higher up blocks, including belvederes, loggias, split staircases, patios with towering sculptural fountains, and wide terraces overlooking the coast. It also ensured unobstructed views from the upper floors of Casa Grande. The house farthest north Hearst named Casa del Monte (House of the Mountain, also known as house B); the middle house was called Casa del Sol (House of the Sun, house C); and for the southernmost residence he chose Casa del Mar (House of the Sea, house A). These names corresponded to the views offered from the rear of each building.

Despite the seeming resemblance of the *casas* as they are encountered along the esplanade, there is variation between the plans and capacities of each. Houses A and C are each three stories. The former measures 5,350 square feet and has twenty rooms; the latter is 3,620 square feet and has twenty-one rooms. House B is two stories at 2,550 square feet and twelve rooms.[16] The esplanade rings the complex, encircling Casa Grande, flanking the central plaza, and connects by stairs to terraces—the Earring on the north, a barbell-shaped space on the south—and cambers along gardens, sculpture appointments, and the entry courts of the guesthouses. Viewed on the site plan (FIG. 5), the esplanade (marked in green) is shaped like a pair of pincers, encompassing the four buildings and the central plaza.

Per Beaux-Arts theory, the plans for the guesthouses are symmetrical. Each is longitudinal with a red-tiled entry court bordered by protruding wings. Curved Spanish tiles roof the buildings, lending a Mediterranean look. All three have extensions from the rear of their central blocks with doorways onto split staircases allowing occupants access to walkways on the level below.

This idea of loggias
and stairs of house
put on house it makes
it much I think of
a good many for
the middle [illegible]

Rough isometric sketch
    of house location.
as per last telegram —
                    JR —
Some liberties taken with exteriors.
How do you like the idea? With
the long towers it might be very effective.

Morgan's coursework at the École des Beaux-Arts and the sketches she made from its collection of classicist architectural casts provided an excellent grounding for designing Hearst's Spanish Renaissance recreation. Further, one cannot say enough about influential publications like *Renaissance Architecture and Ornament in Spain* by British designer Andrew Noble Prentice (1866—1941). Prentice's illustrations of elevations, sections, and architectural details of the Spanish monuments he studied in his travels were a valuable source for Morgan and Hearst as they designed the eaves, windows, and doorframes of the guesthouses.[17]

House B, Casa del Monte, was the first of the three guesthouses to be completed (1922) and housed Hearst and his family during their visits. Subsequent

guests must have appreciated the intimacy and elegant design of its entry court and facade as they relaxed on the marble benches, greeting strollers on the esplanade (FIG. 6). The greenery in full bloom added to the enchantment of the enclosure. The eaves of Casa del Monte are made up of cast stone corbels of winged putti between which are a band of multicolor tile panels designed by Morgan and produced by The Tile Shop, later California Faience, Berkeley. (See Kirby Brown's essay in this volume.) The central window in the court is enveloped by a tile surround extending from the ground to the eaves. Over the two entries, cast stone roundels are bordered by cupids carrying garlands. The entry from the esplanade is defined by two marble statue groups after classical models—a pair of wrestlers and a seated athlete.

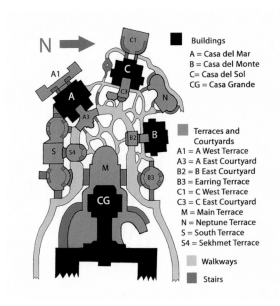

Opposite

William Randolph
Hearst and Julia
Morgan, ca. 1920s.

Above

FIG. 5

Site plan of the
Hearst Castle
complex by Kirby
S. Brown

Following spread

FIG. 6

Entry court, Casa
del Monte, house B

Page 172–173

FIG. 7

Rear facade, Casa
del Monte, house B

Page 174–175

FIG. 8

Entry court, house
C, Casa del Sol

The two-story rear facade of house B presents an aspect both crisp and lordly (FIG. 7). One enters the ground floor by ascending a wide stair defined by a pair of large consoles and lampstands created by the Morgan studio. A single door with a grid of gold knobs is at the top of the stairs; it is crowned by a scroll-work shield and enclosed by a tabernacle frame. The split staircase leads to the upper floor and a roofless gallery with a protruding balcony of the type from which nobles and clerics addressed their subjects. High upon the wall behind the balcony, Hearst placed a shield with his initials, WRH, supported by cherubs bearing garlands of the fruits of the earth, an image signifying the abundance of the lord's estate.

Proceeding south on the esplanade, house C, Casa del Sol, is the next residence (FIG. 8). While the layout of its entry court is similar to that of house B, its decor draws upon the southern Spanish Renaissance, the style from that part of the Iberian Peninsula once ruled by the Almohad Empire (Moors). But this is no simple recreation of sites in Seville or Córdoba; rather, the Spanish-Moorish style of the court was determined by Hearst's catholic collecting tastes and Morgan's Beaux-Arts training, which encouraged eclecticism in design over aping historical masterworks. For house C, Hearst wanted the main feature of the eaves to be purple and turquoise tiles rather than the cupid-head corbels of Casa del Monte. The tiles were installed in alternating bands of three, using a turbaned Moor's head motif—a motif that appeared in Spanish coats of arms during the Reconquista. The two main entries are framed in identical tile surrounds

with gilt borders. Above the doors are gilded tympani with relief sculptures of basins from which craftsmen emerge holding their tools. This area is overlaid with an angular arabesque pattern. The doors below are screened with intricate gilt wrought ironwork of curlicues into which human heads and mythical beings are incorporated. Between the doors is one of the many mix-and-match assemblages placed about the grounds. The centerpiece is a multi-tile mural produced during Iran's Qajar Dynasty. Dated to the early nineteenth century, the scene depicts three lavishly attired nobles—two women and a sultan—gathering in a garden as a servant brings beverage vases. Similar to pleasure imagery in Roman art, it displays the deluxe leisure of ruling elites, a suitable subject for the master of La Cuesta Encantada. The Persian mural is framed by a pair of twist-fluted *salomónica* columns. These became popular in Spain in the seventeenth century and were also used in the churches of its Latin American colonies.

Imagine yourself as a first-time guest at San Simeon assigned to Casa del Sol, or house C. Delighted by the exotic beauty of the entry court, and passing through the house and onto the three-arched loggia, you are stopped in your tracks by the spectacular 180-degree view. Your gaze then returns to your immediate surroundings. The loggia is part of a gallery that runs the length of the rear facade. Below is a sunny patio from which curved sweeping staircases extend and spill onto a court and a small circular plaza with a fountain. Wide stairs open the court onto a grand plaza. It took a considerable feat of engineering to make it level against the sloped terrain. With your arms resting on the plaza's balustrade, gazing onto the oak-studded hillsides below, you are treated to a magnificent view. Then, as you turn around to take in Casa del Sol from the plaza up to its red-tiled roofline, the word that comes to mind is "palatial" (FIG. 9).

To bring order to precipitously sited house C, Morgan relied on Beaux-Arts principles: begin with a sound plan, use rational symmetry in defining space, hold the structure's elements in balance, and integrate the ornamentation into the design. Thus prepared, she and Hearst thumbed the pages of their architectural books for ideas. As Victoria Kastner has noted, part of the western exposure of house C is derived from Austin Whittlesey's photograph of a building in Cordóba.[18] (See Victoria Kastner's chapter in this volume.) On the upper story, the rectilinearity

Left
FIG. 9
Rear facade, house
C, Casa del Sol

Following spread
FIG. 10
Lower patio, rear
entry, house C,
Casa del Sol

of the walls, windows, and single door is enlivened by bands of relief sculpture of swirling plant tendrils. Balcony facings were defined by pairs of circular stone medallions. Directly below the loggia is a patio for the lower floor of the guesthouse, featuring a door with a window on each side (FIG. 10). The door is enclosed by a tabernacle frame rimmed with polychrome tiles. Like the doors of the entry court off the esplanade, the patio door and windows are screened with intricately patterned gold metalwork, and each is topped by heraldic birds flanking a shield.

To reach the circular fountain plaza below the patio, guests descended one or the other of the curved-run stairs. The centerpiece of this space is a soaring triple-basin marble fountain in five sections—a conglomeration of Beaux-Arts components (FIG. 11). Crowning the monumental fountain is a bronze figure of the youthful biblical hero David, a reproduction of the original by the Italian Renaissance sculptor Donatello (1386–1466). It depicts David nude, standing casually over the severed head of Goliath, whom he has just slain (I Samuel 17:51). Monumental fountains of Hearst's time, such as the Fontaine du Palmier in Paris constructed in the early nineteenth century, were typically found in cities and had a public presence. (Morgan surely saw the Fontaine du Palmier while at the École.) Sculptural fountains of this height, however, were rare in private residences. Coincidentally, the original *David* was commissioned by the Florentine art patron and banker Cosimo de' Medici for the family's Palazzo Medici. Foreshadowing the placement of the San Simeon *David*, Cosimo had his sculpture mounted on top of a high pedestal in the center of his palace courtyard, so viewers would have to look up at the young conqueror from below. Was Hearst emulating Cosimo?

The high walls of the fountain plaza are softened by shrubs shaped on espaliers. Against the greenery and behind the *David* fountain is an unusual sculptural arrangement: two female nudes in white marble and an *Adam and Eve* in dark bronze (FIG. 12). According to Nancy Loe, *Adam and Eve* was acquired in 1930 directly from its sculptor, Arthur George Walker (1861–1939), a British academician.[19] Framed by a bower, the work depicts the first parents with their faces registering guilt and fear, just after they have eaten the fruit of the forbidden tree and realized their transgression. At the left and right of the bower are two nymphs who clutch long strands of flowers to

their chests. The figure on the right does so chastely, but the one on the left arches her voluptuous body, embracing the bouquet as she would a lover. The nymphs may be companions to Flora, the Roman goddess of flowers and spring. Just what sort of meaning this combination of pagan and Judeo-Christian imagery intends to convey invites speculation.

The southernmost guesthouse is Casa del Mar, house A. Its facade and entry court vary from those of B and C in that its ornamentation is more Italian Renaissance than Spanish, classicizing in effect (FIG. 12). On either side of the single doorway the entrant is greeted by identical Greek herms, freestanding square pillars surmounted with sculpted heads. In ancient Greece these served as boundary markers. The tightly curled hair, long sidelocks, and beards correspond to representations of Hermes, the god known for crossing over the lines demarcating the human and divine realms. The facade itself is plain except for the relief framing of the door with a pair of slender columns with floriated capitals supporting an architrave. Cherubs stand at the base of the columns. Above the architrave and at either end, kneeling cherubs shoulder a garland that stretches between them, draping over a medallion with a male portrait head. The gilt wrought-iron window and door screens are less intricate than those in guesthouses B and C. The ornamentation of the eaves, however, is nearly identical to that of Casa del Monte (house B).

The southwestern or rear-facing facade of house A sits on a very steep slope, limiting the usable space beyond the main block (FIG. 13). Morgan and Hearst decided to extend the structure by attaching upper and lower transverse sections parallel to and wider than the house itself. At either end of the lower section—in actuality a wide patio—Morgan appended quads to accommodate a pair of monumental marble fountains similar in scale to the *David* fountain outside house C. Ascending from octagonal bases, the fountains have two smaller basins between their decorative columnar components and their top-mounted sculptures. These are gilt bronzes of two lithe nude nymphs by the German sculptor Gustav Adolf Daumiller (1876–1962), who trained in the sculpture program at the École des Beaux-Arts. The figure on the fountain closest to Casa del Sol is *The First Rose* (FIG. 14). The nymph is shown inhaling the fragrance of a rose, symbolizing the coming of spring. Topping the fountain at the opposite end of the patio, another

nymph gazes on a frog she holds in the palm of her hand (FIG. 15). Titled *The Frog Prince*, the work illustrates the German fairy tale in which a princess aids a frog who is actually a prince prior to being cursed by a witch. Her kindness to the frog restores the prince to his humanity. Guests staying in Casa del Mar could appreciate the towering fountains from top to bottom by descending from the first floor to the half-turn stairs to a lower patio, then taking the split staircase to the transverse section below, encountering the fountains at their basin level.

Proceeding southeast from house A, strollers would enter the South Terrace, a barbell-shaped expanse bracketing a rectangular extension built over the slope, presenting a vista for contemplating the hills and sea below (FIG. 5). At either end of the circular bells on the barbell are marble Renaissance wellheads Hearst acquired in Italy.

CASA GRANDE
A Cathedral Residence
for a Media Magnate

In designing the hilltop complex, Morgan laid out seven access points along the esplanade where one could approach Casa Grande, the principal structure of the ensemble. All of these entries delivered guests into the central plaza, a large half-oval fronting the four-story, twin-towered structure (FIG. 16). Centering the plaza is a lily pond in the shape of a quatrefoil, a medieval motif. In its western lobe Morgan placed a marble sculpture of the sea nymph Galatea languorously entwined with a dolphin. Its creator, Leopoldo Ansiglioni (1832–1894), a favorite of Phoebe Hearst and her son, William, was known for incorporating sensuality in his classical subjects (FIG. 17). Ringing the curvature of the plaza are four marble benches bracketed with marble-columned electric lamps. This welcoming space encouraged guests and residents to gather and imagine themselves in the leisure of Roman elites, similar to the lounging ladies above the Mediterranean Sea in Sir Lawrence Alama-Tadema's (1836–1912) painting *Silver Favourites* from 1903 (FIG. 18).[20]

Phoebe Hearst was raised in a Presbyterian home that emphasized duty and discipline, if not Christian formation.[21] As an adult she was an infrequent churchgoer; nor did she see to her son's religious education. Not one of Phoebe's architectural commissions was

Opposite
FIG. 11
David Fountain, house C, Casa del Sol

Following spread
FIG. 12
Entry court, house A, Casa del Mar

Right

FIG. 13

Rear facade, house A, Casa del Mar

Following spread, *left*

FIG. 14

Gustav Adolf Daumiller, *The First Rose*, 1911; Julia Morgan, fountain design, Casa del Mar, house A

Following spread, *right*

FIG. 15

Gustav Adolf Daumiller, *The Frog Prince*; Julia Morgan, fountain design, Casa del Mar, house A

religious. Neither were any of her son's. With this in mind, contemporary visitors to San Simeon often wonder why William wanted the main building, his personal residence (which also hosted VIP guests), to resemble a cathedral from Catholic Spain. I suspect that during the secularizing American Renaissance and the birth of scientific art history, Catholic art and architecture from the medieval and Renaissance eras were appreciated by WASP elites for their formal beauty and not their spiritual rationale. This was little different than admiring Greek and Roman art while denying any call to pagan devotion. Further, during the American Renaissance the new wealthy class of collectors acquired religious art from Catholic Europe as part of their cultural stewardship, regarding themselves as the rightful inheritors of an idealized past and forebears of a new golden age.

Morgan was not religious either. But her studies at the École des Beaux-Arts exposed her to the numerous churches in Paris and many of her later design assignments were for ecclesiastical foundations or components. Shortly after her return to California, Morgan began receiving commissions for church buildings, mainly Protestant.[22] Her Oakland Chapel of the Chimes, a columbarium with oratories for religious services, was designed at the same time she was working on the Casa Grande. A blend of Italian Romanesque and Gothic elements, the chapel has many parallels to the main building at San Simeon.[23]

Casa Grande was under construction in two stages: 1922 to 1937 and 1945 to 1947. A four-story structure, its twin towers—topped by open metalwork Christian crosses—reach 137 feet. It contains some 60,000 square feet and 115 rooms of various usage. Prior to communal meals, visitors typically gathered in the assembly room, which was entered from the plaza through a sixteenth-century Spanish wrought iron doorway (FIG. 19). On their way to the assembly room they may have stolen a guilty glance at the titillating neoclassical sculptures in the vestibule.[24] Inside they were greeted by Hearst and his waitstaff serving cocktails. Here, beneath mural-size tapestries crowded with dramatis personae enacting episodes of mythological and ancient history, Hearst would hold court as the quintessential grandee. When meals were ready to serve, the company would be summoned into the adjacent medievalesque refectory, a richly ornamented version of a monastic dining hall. Exuding cheerful informality as he surveyed the

Left
FIG. 16
Central plaza and facade of Casa Grande

Following spread, *left*
FIG. 17
Leopoldo Ansiglioni, *Galatea on a Dolphin*, 1882, and marble bench in background, central plaza

Following spread, *right*
FIG. 18
Sir Laurence Alma-Tadema, *Silver Favourites*, oil on panel, 1903, collection of Manchester Art Gallery, Manchester, England

Pages 192–193
FIG. 19
Sixteenth-century Spanish metalwork door screen and ornamental stone door frame, facade of Casa Grande

long table, Hearst presided over the gathering as a kind of secular abbot hosting pilgrims from near and far.

The facade of Casa Grande is a cut-and-paste composition deriving from a number of sources and incorporating various artworks acquired via Hearst's ceaseless buying sprees. It is a tribute to Morgan's design acumen and her patron's focus on details—seeing in the parts the outcome of the whole—that the western part of Casa Grande coalesce. One example of the "methodology" informing San Simeon is Hearst and Morgan's consulting Austin Whittlesey's illustrated survey of the architecture of southern Spain for inspiration.[25] In viewing the photograph of the architecturally jumbled Santa María la Mayor in Ronda, Hearst saw in its single tower the basis for his twin-towered Casa Grande.[26] Further scanning Whittlesey, his eye fixed on the ornamental framework of a porte-cochere block in Seville's Alcazar palace. Morgan adapted it to enclose the entry to the main building (FIG. 21).[27]

Rarely seen in America's early twentieth-century Spanish Colonial architecture is the use of wood trim ornamentation to complement stone carving and expanses of masonry. As Hearst was consulting his books on the Spanish Renaissance, his searching gaze caught the elaborate carved wooden cornice (also called an *alero*, or eave) of a building in Navarre that he saw illustrated in the *Arte y Decoración en España* series.[28] He decided to add a cornice to the Casa Grande facade, where this element would become a large gable that framed the windows of the Gothic suite (FIG. 20). For continuity, he added flat cornices to run along the longitudinal rooflines of the fourth floor, extending east from the facade—three wooden sections in all. In a stroke of good luck, Morgan found a warehouse of Siamese teakwood apparently abandoned by its purchaser. Jules Suppo (1881—1964), a Swiss artisan in San Francisco, was commissioned to do the wood carving from designs supplied by Morgan.[29]

The rim of the gabled cornice—a repeat band incorporating an undulating line, acanthus leaves, and dentils—accents the overhang. The underside of the cornice is composed of a series of panels featuring relief carvings of animal grotesques. The overhang is supported by corbels (right angle brackets) carved into aquatic or land animals, alternating with pendants (FIG. 21). A varied array of griffins, lions, dragons, sea creatures and bust-length humans were installed on the vertical panels extending below

Left
FIG. 23
Augustus Saint-
Gaudens, *Sherman
Monument*, bronze
with gilt, 1902–03,
Grand Army Plaza,
New York City. Civil
War general William
Tecumseh Sherman is
heralded by Victoria,
the Roman goddess
of victory, especially
military success.

the overhang. Some of the figures were derived from historical motifs; others are contemporary creations. Over the years the teakwood cornices have acquired a pleasing patina of warm sienna.

Hearst continued to work on Casa Grande in the 1930s, hoping to finish the back of the structure. If the west facade suggested a bishop's residence, the main building's rear facing, the east courtyard, with its partially completed Venetian loggia surveying the court below, suggested ducal occupancy. Indeed, this gallery was part of the aptly named doge's suite (FIG. 22). Morgan was charged with creating frontage that evoked a Venetian Gothic mood, apparently drawing on elements of Venice's Palazzo Ducale and the Ca' d'Oro palazzo. Patron and architect may have been inspired by John Ruskin (1819—1900) and the meticulous drawings in his three-volume 1853 masterwork *The Stones of Venice*, which was oft reprinted through the nineteenth and the early twentieth centuries.[30] But the rear courtyard was only partially done when Hearst ran out of money in 1937. He was successful, however, in completing the Neptune pool and the Roman pool before the Depression halted construction.

IMPERIAL DOMESTICITY
The Roman and Neptune Pools

"It is the general opinion that for monumental work, Greece and Rome furnish the styles of architecture best adapted to serve the manifold wants of today, not only as to beauty and dignity, but as to utility."[31]
—JAMES McMILLAN

In turn-of-the-century America, enthusiasm ran high for archaeological discoveries of Greco-Roman ruins. Academic drawings reimagining Rome's massive third century C.E. bath complex of Emperor Caracalla inspired American classicist architects in their design of grand Beaux-Arts passenger rail stations in New York (Pennsylvania Station, 1910, McKim, Mead & White) and Chicago (Union Station, 1925, Daniel Burnham and later, Graham, Anderson, Probst and White).

Academic painters piqued the public's imagination of the classical world with romantic re-creations of antiquity. One such painter was Sir Lawrence Alma-Tadema—popular with Gilded Age collectors—who often painted comely, gauzily clad young women lounging in Roman architectural settings (FIG. 18). In a more serious vein, Augustus Saint-Gaudens

(1848—1907), who trained in a sculpture atelier at the École des Beaux-Arts, memorialized the nation's military heroes through the sober and triumphant classicist imagery of the American Renaissance (FIG. 23).

The grandeur of ancient Greece and Rome—evoking the expansionist empire of Alexander the Great and its successor, the Roman Empire from emperor Octavian (Caesar Augustus) to the Antonines—resonated with the territorial aspirations of America's corporate, industrial, political, and cultural elites. Indeed, between 1876 and 1900, the United States annexed Hawaii, Guam, and Puerto Rico and militarily occupied Cuba and the Philippines. In 1904 Americans seized the unfinished Panama Canal; they annexed the land it traversed and completed the waterway in 1915. On the continent, eight former western territories achieved statehood.

In addition to national expansion abroad, the acquisition and consolidation of open western lands enhanced many personal fortunes, historically corresponding to the growth of aristocratic estates (*latifundia*) and their luxurious villas in the Roman Empire. Correspondingly, the Hearst family owned some seven mansions, including a castle in Wales. According to some estimates, the peak land holdings of Hearst and his mother in the United States and Mexico came to 7.5 million acres.[32] And as a Bay Area booster, Hearst imperially editorialized the awarding of a munitions contract to San Francisco during World War I, evoking ancient imperial glory: [This] "means also money and business and prestige for this glorious city of ours, set here among the hills, as Rome was set when the great builders laid the foundation stones of the Eternal City."[33]

THE ROMAN POOL

As San Simeon was evolving in the 1920s, Hearst desired a large Roman-style indoor pool to be built in a separate structure east of Casa Grande. This effort paralleled the efforts of Rome's emperors, who were the chief benefactors of numerous bathing complexes constructed in and around that city. San Simeon's pool with its heated water would be like the *caldaria* of Roman baths. Hearst signed off on the designs for the reinforced concrete Roman pool in 1927, mandating that all the interior surfaces be covered with mosaic *tesserae*, one-inch glass tiles in gold leaf and shades of blue (FIG. 24). Fittingly, these were produced by

Opposite
FIG. 24
Roman Pool, Casa Grande, various mosaic applications designed by Camille Solon and Julia Morgan

Following spread
FIG. 25
Roman Pool, Casa Grande, view onto the alcove with its extended diving platform

Italian-American artisans in San Francisco. For the pool's ornamentation from basin to rafters, Morgan directed her draftsman Camille Solon (1877–1960) to design a series of large rectilinear panels framed by bands of abstract wave scrolls, arabesques, checkers, and frets (FIG. 25) drawn from ancient classical motifs. Within and along these sections Solon created accent imagery of naturalistic and mythical beings, including seahorses, dolphins, starfish, and mermaids. To assist swimmers entering and exiting the pool, Morgan designed marble ladder pairs in an elegant S-curve design. These were also installed in the outdoor Neptune pool. In the tradition of Roman baths, Morgan placed copies of Greco-Roman statuary around the perimeter of the pool (FIG. 26). Due to the many delays encountered, as well as the sheer quantity of mosaic work, the 80-foot-long plunge was not completed until 1935, but without the originally planned heating.[34]

THE NEPTUNE POOL

Thrice redesigned and constructed, the Neptune pool is the most imperial of the media mogul's San Simeon buildings. The visitor approaches the pool from flanking stairs framed by slender Italian cypress trees, descending from the esplanade between Casa del Monte and Casa del Sol to encounter a stunningly beautiful panorama of classical architecture, sky-blue water, nature, and the Pacific coast below (FIG. 27). A grandiose facility far exceeding domestic recreational needs, the Roman Pool is a residential adaptation of Beaux-Arts display architecture from earlier world fairs (see INTRODUCTION, FIG. 8, the Grand Basin of the 1893 World's Columbian Exposition).

Continuing the descent, the visitor passes walls with insets of marble relief sculpture (female nudes bearing a cornucopia with fruits of the harvest, an imperial iconographic staple signifying abundance) before traversing another stairway to arrive on the marble deck surrounding the pool. Here one comes upon the three-piece sculpture group in the pool's eastern alcove (FIG. 28). Hearst commissioned these from the French sculptor Charles-Georges Cassou (1887–1947), who studied at the École des Beaux-Arts and was awarded the Prix de Rome. Cassou's theme was the birth of Venus, the goddess of love. Held aloft on a gigantic clamshell borne by mermen, she rises from the sea foam while surrounded by putti. On

either side of this group are voluptuous mermaids, cavorting in erotic abandon.

Beyond the alcove at the near and far end of the crosswise section of the pool are four similar sculpture groups by Cassou depicting nymphs and swans. Their bilateral arrangement frames the focal point of Morgan's pool: the Roman temple of the sea god Neptune (FIG. 29).

While Beaux-Arts purists might fault the correctness of the Neptune temple, for Hearst that was beside the point. It functions as a stage set for the leisure of the seigneur and his guests. To that end, Morgan was tasked to create a new structure from ancient Roman fragments integrated with new matching stone work—a classicist collage. The Neptune statue, minus his trident, is squeezed into the center of the tympanum. At his right is a male figure astride a horse; at left a female figure riding a bull illustrates Ovid's poem *The Rape of Europa*.

One would think that the Neptune pool with its grand double stairway descending the upper terrace, elongated basin of brilliant turquoise water, multiple sculpture ensembles, and temple facade would be sufficient. But when building showcase architecture, more calls for still more. To that end, Hearst had Morgan design a pair of monumental colonnades that curved around the Neptune pool, enhancing the theatricality of the space (FIG. 30). This effect is not lost on today's visitors, who throng to the Neptune pool more than any other structure at San Simeon. Colonnades extending from a central feature, however, were not novel in early twentieth-century classicist architecture. As previously noted, Bernard Maybeck's Palace of Fine Arts at the Panama-Pacific International Exposition featured a pair of colonnades extending from a circular temple and reflected in a lagoon (INTRODUCTION, FIG. 22). Similarly, at the San Diego exposition Harrison Albright attached curving colonnades with ornate gazebos to his Spreckels Organ Pavilion (INTRODUCTION, FIG. 27 and FIG. 28). One arrived at the Spreckels colonnades after strolling the length of a narrow pool. It seems water features and colonnades were frequent architectural aspirations in early twentieth-century California.

Beyond decoration, classical colonnades performed a function, inviting processions and participation within and along their corridors. At the Beaux-Arts themed fairs they transitioned attendees

206

Right
FIG. 28
Charles-Georges Cassou, *Birth of Venus* grouping, Neptune Pool, ca. 1929–33

Following spread
FIG. 29
Neptune Temple facade, Neptune Pool, with Cassou sculptures at left and right

from one site to another in mock-imperial dignity. At San Simeon, Hearst and his guests comported themselves against the Roman temple—a stage set—and lounged under the colonnades. At the end of each portico, placed just beneath their friezes, relief-sculpted portrait busts of men in classical attire oversaw the goings-on. If the lords of the Roman Empire were transported from their villas to the Neptune pool, they would feel right at home.

This ancient comparison bears pursuing: the third century C.E. Roman villa at Nennig near the German/French border provides a context for interpreting the Neptune pool. In the nineteenth century, archaeologists excavated a sprawling aristocratic residence paved with pictorial mosaics.[35] They also found a 400-foot-long (!) colonnade extending from the main block to an elaborate bath complex. Moreover, in the mosaics and the minor arts of this period, aristocratic art patrons had themselves depicted in luxurious garb trailed by servants in processions along colonnades and porticos leading to baths.[36] From the Roman Empire to the American Renaissance, in art and in life, it seems that estate holders shared a fondness for using architecture and pools for conspicuous displays of their wealth, power, and pleasure.

One wonders how La Cuesta Encantada would have further evolved if the Depression and World War II hadn't halted progress, and if illness and old age hadn't curtailed Hearst and Morgan's capacities. Would Morgan's design for the domed great hall, a Byzantine-Venetian styled structure that betrays a lineage to the palaces of San Francisco's 1915 exposition, have been built? Would Hearst have continued to act upon his penchant for periodically demolishing and redesigning the complex? We will never know and are left to ponder what Hearst and Morgan's eclectic historicist complex—now called Hearst Castle—might possibly mean for our era.

A way forward was suggested by architect Robert Venturi (1925–2018) who more than fifty years ago in his *Complexity and Contradiction in Architecture* promoted a vitality of form, hybridization of elements, and quotations from historical works as long overdue antidotes to the "purity policing" of modernism.[37] Indeed, all of Venturi's components are present in La

Cuesta Encantada. And while Hearst set out to create a modern equivalent to the Spanish Renaissance he so admired—an idealized hill town that was his fantasy dukedom—the days of his dispensing lordly hospitality to his VIP guests have long passed. So what does Hearst Castle—after celebrating its centennial in 2019—provoke in us today? In my visits to San Simeon I have noticed that many visitors seem inspired to participate in the site, abandoning themselves to an appreciation and curiosity—physically engaging the terraces, courts, gardens, pools, and plazas (while heeding the admonishment of guides not to touch). I have overheard the B word—beauty. Yes, there is an exuberance in the Beaux-Arts assemblage that is San Simeon that connects with visitors in ways the chilled classicism of the Vanderbilt mansions does not. Does our presence among buildings with a rich architectural vocabulary and historic and historicist art fuel a desire to find ourselves in the panorama of history, myth, religion, art, and nature so that we may interrogate the past against the prospects of our present, or vice versa? Wouldn't it be ironic if the eclectic residence of America's first media mogul and his publicity-shy architect had a role in such musings?

CODA

At his death in 1951, William Randolph Hearst was entombed in the family mausoleum in Cypress Park, south of San Francisco. Designed by A. C. Schweinfurth (1863–1900) in 1896 as an homage to the Temple of Athena Nike on the Acropolis citadel above Athens, it witnesses the memorial ideals of the American Renaissance in our age (FIG. 31).[38] Oddly, in her passing Morgan wanted no architectural memorial to indicate her grave. She was interred in the family plot in Oakland's Mountain View Cemetery, marked by an unadorned gray granite headstone. ✿

Previous spread
FIG. 30
Neptune Pool, southwest colonnade with Cassou's nymph and swan sculpture. The *Birth of Venus* grouping is just beyond, at right.

Opposite
FIG. 31
A. C. Schweinfurth, Hearst family mausoleum, 1896, Cypress Lawn, Colma, California

TILING ROUND BASE OF FO

6

TAIN (HOUSE C)

CHAPTER 6

THE CERAMIC TILES OF HEARST CASTLE
CALIFORNIA FAIENCE AND JULIA MORGAN

KIRBY WILLIAM BROWN

magine yourself the owner of a tiny art pottery shop in Berkeley, California, in 1920. You are struggling to keep afloat, when a big-city architect across the bay approaches you with a commission to make decorative tiles for one of the world's wealthiest men. You are honored, exhilarated, and a bit overwhelmed. But it's not really a big job, you are told, just a hundred or so tiles for some friezes on a house or two. You eagerly take the job, and you make such pleasing tiles for the client, that before long the order grows into the thousands as the project's demand increases. As a result, you find that you must move to a larger facility and spend the next ten years producing almost one hundred thousand tiles.[1]

This is what happened to my grandfather William Bragdon and his partner, Chauncey Thomas, at their storefront ceramic studio, The Tile Shop, which in two years would become California Faience (FIG. 1).

ORIGINS

While the story of Hearst Castle is generally well known and covered elsewhere in this book, details about the decorative tiles found throughout the property are not. The tiles and their maker, California Faience, go unmentioned in most studies of Hearst Castle. When I first toured the complex in the 1980s, the guide claimed that the tiles were made in Italy! In fact, there is sparse documentation about this aspect of the design of Hearst Castle. California Faience records from this era are lost. An interview with William Bragdon in the *Berkeley Daily Gazette* in 1958 is the only personal account of the tilework we have.[2] Fortunately, related correspondence between

the designer of the tiles, architect Julia Morgan, and her patron, William Randolph Hearst, has been preserved, along with hundreds of designs by Morgan and her studio. From these sources it is possible to piece together an account of the design of the tiles and their placement at Hearst Castle.

Having traveled with his mother to Europe at age ten, Hearst early on became interested in Spanish Renaissance architecture. This accounts for his later fascination with the Spanish Colonial Revival style at both world's fairs held in California in 1915: the Panama-California Exposition in San Diego and the Panama-Pacific International Exposition (PPIE) in San Francisco. Among other contemporary illustrated books and folios, Hearst's ideas for the design of San Simeon were influenced by Austin Whittlesey's 1917 study *The Minor Ecclesiastical, Domestic, and Garden Architecture of Southern Spain*.[3] When he first visited Spain he may have seen the Church of Santa María la Mayor in Ronda, later illustrated in Whittlesey.[4] This became the inspiration for the main building, or Casa Grande, in the hilltop complex. Referring to Whittlesey, Hearst wrote to Morgan on December 10, 1919: "The immediate thing of value is on page 84. The treatment of the roof beams, the cornice and the tile frieze seems to me to be very interesting and effective, and very characteristically Spanish. . . . I think we could apply it to our cottages."[5] Hearst is referring here to Casa del Monte, Casa del Sol, and Casa del Mar, the three guesthouses (also known respectively as houses B, C, and A) opposite Casa Grande. He further wrote to Morgan on December 27 of that year: "I hope you will see your way to work in those curved

Previous spread
Julia Morgan,
*Tiling Round
Base of Fountain,
House C* (Casa del
Sol), pencil and
watercolor, ca.
1920s

Opposite
FIG. 1
The Tile Shop,
Berkeley,
California,
ca. 1920

Following spread
FIG. 2
California
Faience tile frieze,
ca. 1920s. A band
of these tiles were
installed under the
eaves of Casa del
Sol, house C.

and colored cornices in the Moorish style, and to use some tiling for the frieze and perhaps other places where it will be effective. I think this will take the cottages away from the bungalow look, and give them a character which is perfectly appropriate, as many of the buildings of Southern Spain have this motif in their architecture."

Still contemplating the then in vogue Spanish Colonial Revival style—an American variation of the Spanish Renaissance—Hearst wrote to Morgan four days later on December 31, 1919: "The best things that I have seen are at the [1915–1917] San Diego Exposition." He disliked the elaborate ornamentation of the Mexican Baroque and the stark simplicity of the California Mission style and felt that the revivalist architecture at the San Diego fair struck a good balance between those extremes. The style adopted by Hearst and Morgan for Hearst Castle has been dubbed "Southern Mediterranean Renaissance," although other stylistic terms are also used, due to the eclectic character of its designs.

On January 7, 1920, Hearst wrote to Morgan, "I am sending you some old Spanish tiles, merely as motifs for the frieze under the cornice around the cottages." On February 9, Hearst clarified his directive: "Of course the tiles I sent you are only motifs, and can be enlarged or modified in any way you want when you are having modern tiles made after them." The sample tiles that Hearst sent to Morgan have been lost, but it is possible to identify some of them based on the modern ones that are derived from antique precedents. One notable example is the Moor's head at the center of a three-piece frieze (FIG. 2).

February 1920 saw the groundbreaking for the three guesthouses: Casa del Mar (house A), Casa del Monte (house B), and Casa del Sol (house C). Hearst had hoped that these, and the "big house" (Casa Grande) would be completed in a year or so, but the logistics of the massive project and its complicated evolution determined that Casa Grande would have to wait.

THE TILE SHOP AND CALIFORNIA FAIENCE

With construction at San Simeon underway in early 1920, a tile maker had not yet been found. Hearst continued to be impressed with the tilework used in the San Diego exposition and asked Morgan to seek out the maker, California China Products, in National

City. On March 12, 1920, Morgan wrote to Hearst: "As regards decorative tiles for cornices, the firm who made all the colored tile work for the San Diego Exposition and for the Los Angeles Examiner domes, was forced out of business during the war, which is certainly to be regretted as the director, Mr. Nordhoff, had reached a point where his clear strong color was both beautiful and harmonious. . . . No regular tile or terra cotta company will undertake to deliver any special tile in the time limit, so am having them made by a small concern who have excellent glazes, but where kilns are so small they cannot produce enough to go around each house, but have promised enough of each for the fronts and courts and I will camouflage

the rest until they are ready. I think you will like them. I took the motifs from your tile [historical examples]." The "small concern" Morgan refers to surely is The Tile Shop.

The Tile Shop was founded by Chauncey Rapelje Thomas (1876–1950) in 1913. It was located in a ramshackle store front at 2336 San Pablo Avenue, the main north-south thoroughfare of a burgeoning university town. Thomas had closed his pottery operation in Deerfield, Massachusetts and moved to California for health reasons. He produced hand-cast art pottery and a small number of tiles. In 1915 Thomas had a display of his wares at the PPIE across the bay. During that summer, he invited his old friend and

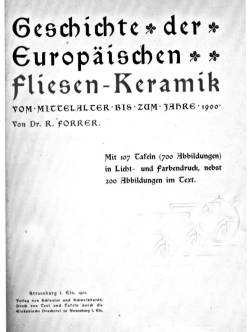

Far left

FIG. 3
California Faience
Co., Berkeley,
California, 1922

Left top

FIG. 4
Title page from
Robert Forrer,
*Geschichte der
Europäischen fliesen-
Keramik*, 1901

Left bottom

FIG. 5
Plate 34 published
in Robert Forrer,
*Geschichte der
Europäischen fliesen-
Keramik*, 1901.
Forrer designated
these motifs as
"Hispano-Moresque."

Alfred University classmate, William Victor Bragdon (1884–1959), to stay with him. Bragdon had been the ceramic chemist at the University City Porcelain Works near St. Louis, but it had just gone bankrupt and Bragdon needed work. Upon his arrival in 1915, he helped Thomas with the PPIE display and taught ceramics at the California School of Arts and Crafts. Bragdon became Thomas's partner the same year and moved his family to Berkeley. As a result of the growing demand for tiles at Hearst Castle, The Tile Shop moved to a new, larger factory under the name California Faience Company in 1922 (FIG. 3).

Fortunately, the list of tiles displayed at the PPIE by The Tile Shop are known—designated separately as "Dragon," "Pelican," "Rabbit," "Lion," "Dog," and "Eagle," and specified as "13th–14th century design." Chauncey Thomas copied these medieval designs directly from Robert Forrer's 1901 study, *Geschichte der Europäischen fliesen-Keramik* (History of European Ceramic Tiles, FIG. 4).[6] Most are pictured on Plate XXXIV (FIG. 5). Hearst Castle visitors will recognize numbers 2, 4, 6, 8, and 9, which are seen throughout the grounds and on the three guesthouses.

How Julia Morgan found The Tile Shop is not known. She likely saw the company's tile display at the PPIE in 1915. The firm later provided the tiles for Morgan's 1919 MacGregor House in Berkeley, prior to her beginning work at San Simeon. But the key

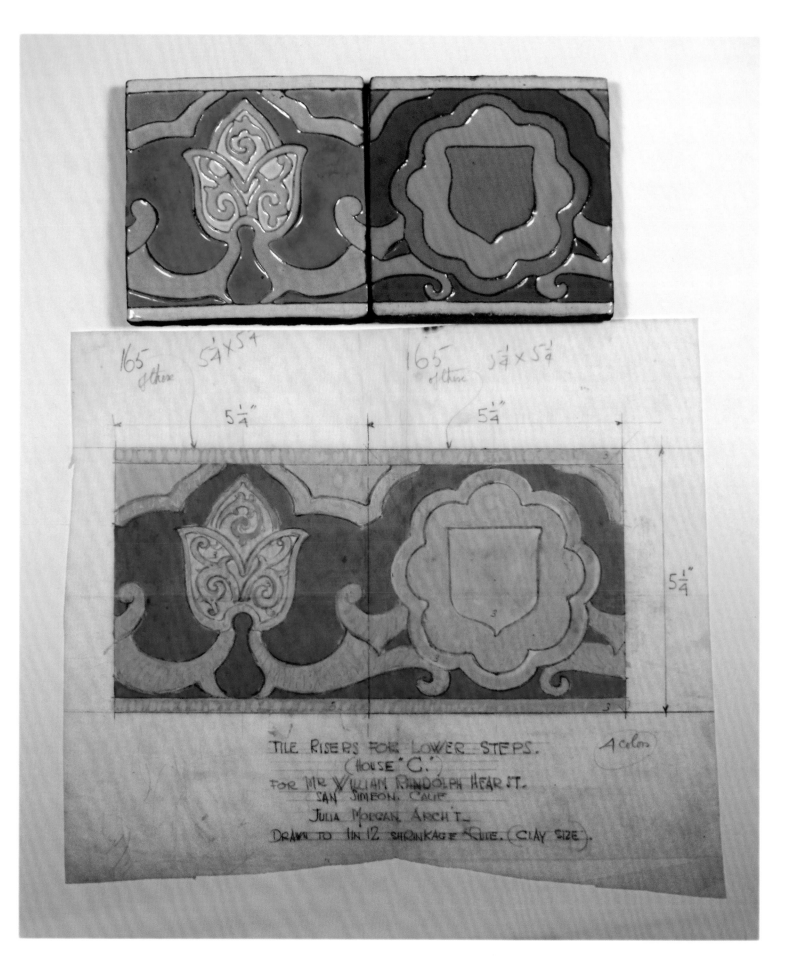

TILE RISERS FOR LOWER STEPS.
(HOUSE "C.")
FOR MR. WILLIAM RANDOLPH HEARST.
SAN SIMEON. CALIF.
JULIA MORGAN ARCH'T.
DRAWN TO 1 IN 12 SHRINKAGE SCALE. (CLAY SIZE).

connection may have been through E. L. Bradley, a "manufacturer's agent" for Thomas and Bragdon. Bradley's association with Julia Morgan is evidenced by the tiles installed in his home that were designed by the architect exclusively for the Hearst commission. These were not available to the general public.

GUESTHOUSES AND GROUNDS

The friezes under the eaves of house B (Casa del Monte) and house C (Casa del Sol) were the first decorative needs at Hearst Castle. (See Gordon Fuglie's essay for a structure-by-structure treatment of the San Simeon complex.) Morgan set to work

designing these tiles (FIG. 6), turning them over to Bragdon and Thomas to execute faithfully. Within two months of Morgan's informing Hearst about The Tile Shop, the first completed sections arrived on site. On May 7, Morgan wrote to Hearst regarding house C: "The frieze is divided by small stone shields separating the polychrome tile panels. . . . The first of the tile is out of the kiln and is brilliant in quality. The plant [shop] is a tiny one and only a small number of panels can be made in a week." Tiles were also made for window surrounds (FIG. 7). The shop framed a nineteenth-century Persian tile panel depicting a group of figures in a garden, bordering it with bright blue sections (FIG. 8). It was installed in the entry court of house C.

FIG. 8

Persian tile panel, nineteenth century, Qajar Period (1794-1925), installed in entry court of house C. It is framed with blue half-round ridge sections from The Tile Shop, ca. 1920-21.

Above

FIG. 9

Rabbit riser tile, from fifteenth-century Spanish motif, ca. 1921-25

Right

FIG. 10

Plate 21, no. 49, published in *Puente del Arzobispo Ware* (or "leaping rabbit"), Spanish, fifteenth century, published in Edwin Attlee Barber, *Spanish Maiolica*, 1915

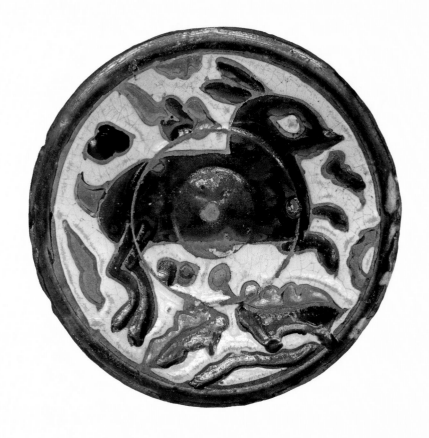

Previous spread

FIG. 11

Rampant lion tiles from a frieze adorning house A. Chauncey Thomas adapted this motif from Robert Forrer's history of European ceramic tiles.

Right top

FIG. 12

Hexagonal tile of a sea nymph riding a dolphin, ca. 1922-23, installed on the bedroom floor, house A

Right bottom

FIG. 13

Trapezoidal tile of an angel paddling a swan boat, ca. 1921-23, installed on the bedroom floor, house A

Opposite

FIG. 14

Trapezoidal tile of three severed heads (*tricephalos*), ca. 1921-23, installed on the bedroom floor, house A

On September 15, 1920, Hearst sent Morgan a copy of Edwin Atlee Barber's *Spanish Maiolica in the Collection of the Hispanic Society of America* and wrote, "I like the tile you had made very much.— There are some fine tile designs in the little book—Spanish Maiolica."[7] Ultimately, several tile designs for San Simeon were derived from Barber's plates. The leaping bunny rabbit riser tile (FIG. 9) is almost an exact copy of the rabbit in Barber's Plate XXI, No. 49 (FIG. 10).

As the volume of tile orders increased, the little shop was hard pressed to keep up. In several letters Morgan expressed her concerns about the slowness of deliveries. She wrote to Hearst on January 5, 1921, "Sample tiles are being burned [fired] for the floor and wall. The Berkeley tile people could not get the desired iridescence, and finally found a new kiln in San Jose where they were willing to make the effort . . . The friezes are complete at last and all other tile on its way, but we cannot get it in quantities but have to take it as the little kilns can deliver it." More than six months later, on June 28, she wrote, "Tile is gradually arriving for steps of various terraces but the output of the kilns is as small as ever and it is coming in spoonfuls, as it did for the friezes. Some of it is lovely in color." And with the arrival of winter, she wrote on December 22, "Now if we can get our tile people to just hurry tile along a bit, Hadley [a construction boss] will have clear sailing for some months." With the continually rising demands from San Simeon, Thomas and Bragdon moved to a larger facility in March of 1922 and changed the name of their business to California Faience Company. There were no further complaints from Morgan about small outputs and slow deliveries.

Left
FIG. 15
Entry walkway
with bar tile
borders, house C,
ca. 1921-23

Work on the larger Casa del Mar (house A) lagged behind that on house B and house C, which were completed in mid-1921. Completed in 1923, Casa del Mar had friezes similar to the other houses. Two of its decorative tiles are opposing lion designs that Thomas adapted from illustrations in Forrer (FIG. 11). While the other two houses did not have California Faience work in their interiors, the floors of the main bedrooms of Casa del Mar were entirely laid in polychrome tiles produced in Berkeley. These were designed by Morgan and featured classical mythological figures. The ancient Greeks were a seafaring people and dolphins, regarded as beneficent creatures, were an important part of their world. In classical art dolphins were sometimes depicted being ridden by humans or demi-gods (FIG. 12). By contrast, an image of an angel paddling a swan boat (FIG. 13) is probably derived from Renaissance iconography. Drawing on pre-Christian Celtic mythology, Morgan reproduced a tricephalos, a composition of three severed heads (FIG. 14). This eclectic use of various decorative sources typifies the design and construction of Hearst Castle.

While construction was progressing on the three guesthouses, design of the adjacent landscape, terraces, and stairways proceeded. This work continued well into the 1930s and eventually incorporated tens of thousands of California Faience tiles. These transformed what would otherwise be ordinary walkways into colorful and rhythmic works of art. Morgan wrote to Hearst on August 14, 1926, that she had "transformed our walks into formal Esplanades and paved them with tiles." Trails of inlaid bar tiles formed intriguing mosaic patterns. The layout ranged from simple, winding borders in alternating colors (FIG. 15) to complex geometric compositions (FIG. 16).

The Hearst Castle site is hilly, mandating differing networks of stairs—narrow, wide, and winding. Most were decorated with bands of California Faience tiles in the stair risers. In a number of cases the motifs varied or alternated in each ascending level (FIG. 17). The castle motif, an image often appearing on late medieval Spanish tiles, was frequently deployed (FIG. 18).

The Sekhmet terrace sits above the South Terrace and offers a view onto the Pacific Ocean; it was one of the last walkways completed at Hearst Castle. Four ancient Egyptian sculptures of the lion-headed goddess Sekhmet were arranged within a Morgan-designed semi-circular fountain at the center of the terrace. The twin stairs with ten risers ascending around the basin are decorated with stylized lotus tiles, an ancient Egyptian motif (FIG. 19). At the base of the fountain, the first riser features a band of tiles with a stepped tree design (FIG. 20). This motif is found in Spanish architecture, though it is derived from an earlier Islamic design.[8] On August 7, 1928, Morgan wrote to Hearst, "Hadley has made fine progress with the terraces and walks—is now putting in the esplanade paving back to the patio entrance on one side and the tennis court line the other. The south terrace and Sekhmet pavements are in[,] but waiting the arrival of the[ir] colored tile inserts."

Tiles decorated not only walkways and stair risers but also wall surfaces in dramatic displays. One such panel that appears in several locations (FIG. 21) combines an eighteenth-century floral design of Mexican origin and an escutcheon derived from a Spanish tile pictured in Barber's *Spanish Maiolica*.[9]

The tilework on the three guesthouses and the grounds was a massive job for California Faience and took at least ten years. Bragdon recalled that ten people eventually were employed in making the tiles, each of which, per the cuenca technique, had to be pressed and glazed by hand. In 1930, construction was still underway on the terraces and stairs. On August 12, 1930, Morgan reported to Hearst, "The north terrace [concrete] work is completely poured." In doing an inventory of California Faience tiles at San Simeon, David Wilson, Hearst Castle restoration work specialist, tallied more than 88,000 pieces (not including Casa Grande and the interiors of the guesthouses).[10] Moreover, one should also consider that in the course of construction, a number of completed tiled terraces and stairways were demolished and remodeled, as ordered by Hearst. Accounting for these losses, the quantity of California Faience tiles produced for Hearst Castle approaches 100,000.

CASA GRANDE

The "castle" of Hearst Castle, also known as the main building, and formally as Casa Grande, had a later start than the guesthouses. Ground was broken in late 1922 and what was dubbed the "big pour" of cement around the building's tall steel frame occupied much of 1923. By this time the guesthouses and terraces around them were mostly finished. Work progressed rapidly, and the main part of Casa Grande was mostly finished by 1926. The first version of the

Opposite

FIG. 16

Patterned bar tile mosaic in four colors framing a Spanish floral tile, south terrace, ca. 1928

Following spread

FIG. 17

Alternating bands of stair riser tiles, east courtyard, house A, ca. 1922-24

Left

FIG. 18

Tile with castle motif repeat pattern, ca. 1921–30

Following spread

FIG. 19

Right bank of stairs with Egyptian lotus and stylized tree riser tiles, Sekhmet terrace, completed ca. 1928

FIG. 20

Stair riser tile
with abstract tree
repeat pattern,
ca. 1921-30

Opposite

FIG. 21

Diamond-pattern
tile panel installed
in the east court-
yard of house A,
ca. 1924

twin bell towers flanking the facade had plain and pointed concrete spires—a medieval look. In 1926, however, Hearst decided to demolish the original bell towers and replace them with more elaborate ones in a Spanish Renaissance style. He wanted these towers to be decorated with polychrome ceramic tiles (FIG. 22). This started a new phase of tile production at California Faience. The replacement towers were poured in 1927, and on February 4 of that year Hearst wrote to Morgan instructing her to "kindly send [your] designs for tile on towers, one tower all tiles, the other part tiles. Please use the design with yellow [and blue] marks . . . . for [the] lower part, and with the light white and blue tile for the narrow upper portions. If we get these [designs] soon we can order tiles." On September 1, 1927, he telegraphed Morgan: "Suggest we get [complete the] designs for tower tiling and start making tiles soon." Several of Morgan's tile designs are dated September 1927.

Morgan's detailed pencil drawings were faithfully reproduced as polychrome compositions by California Faience as this comparison of Morgan's design (for the vertical and arch sections of the belfry arches) to their finished, installed state shows (FIG. 23). The tiling on the new towers and the balcony connecting them was completed late in 1928.

A prominent image repeatedly seen on the tower areas is the visage of a figure known as the Green Man (FIG. 24). Derived from pagan mythology, he was a common character in the iconography of the late Middle Ages and Renaissance and frequently appeared on tiles of the Iberian Peninsula. A spirit of the natural world, he is depicted with leaves growing out of his face to associate him with trees and plant life. More elaborate iconography has him accompanied by clusters of fruits and flowers representing the bounty of nature. Hearst may have felt that the Green Man was a particularly apt symbol of the natural beauty and productivity of his San Simeon lands.

In a variation in ceramic technique, the Italian Renaissance method of flat glazing of tiles is said to have been introduced in Spain in the early sixteenth century by Niculoso Francisco Pisano (1470–1529), a tile artist from Pisa.[11] In flat glazing, coats of pigment are simply painted onto the tile. This contrasts with the Spanish cuenca technique, in which design components are isolated by raised lines molded into the clay. This prevents different colors from mingling during kiln firing. For a while the painterly Italian flat glazing was the rage in Spain, but the indigenous cuenca ultimately prevailed, perhaps because its high

Left

FIG. 22
Remodeled towers of Casa Grande under construction, 1928. California Faience tiles were to be installed on the cupolas, the octagonal belfries beneath them, and the balcony wall between the towers.

Following spread, left

FIG. 23
Two 1927 Julia Morgan studio drawings (left and top) for the tiling of the belfry arches. The photo shows their installation on a double-arch section of one of the Casa Grande bell towers.

Following spread, right

FIG. 24
Face of the Green Man on the tiles installed along the Celestial Bridge, Casa Grande, ca. 1928

contrast appearance was easier to "read" from a distance. Morgan delineated nearly all of her designs in cuenca, which was the preferred production method at California Faience.

For decorating the bell towers, Hearst was partial to the color blue, as seen in his note of July 14, 1928, to one of Morgan's supervising architects, Thaddeus Joy: "Tile field between arches and belt course between [I want the] color of blue to predominate to blend with sky." The angular wall of the Celestial Bridge—the long balcony that bridges the two bell towers—was entirely covered with decorative tiles, with bold use of blue shades (FIG. 25).

What is particularly striking in the ornamentation of the bell towers is the attention to detail in areas that are not visible from the ground level. The interiors of the belfry arches are elaborately tiled (FIG. 26). Even the sills of the arches facing skyward are adorned with decorative tile panels. Because of their remote location, there is some doubt that Hearst himself ever saw them in situ. A complete set of unused tiles for one of these panels is, fortunately, in the Hearst Castle collections. It was assembled by restoration work specialist David Wilson and displayed so that visitors may conveniently appreciate its design and craft (FIG. 27).

The most elaborate and intricate designs were inexplicably saved for the highest and most out-of-sight parts of the bell towers—the cupolas. In 1927 Morgan prepared an extremely detailed diagrammatic drawing of the tiling for the cupolas that topped the bell towers to guide California Faience in their production (FIG. 28 and FIG. 29).

In the areas between the twisting double pillars of the drum beneath the cupola, tile panels of an elaborate candeliere (candlestick) design were installed. This Renaissance ornamental feature was likely brought from Italy to Spain by Niculoso Pisano (FIG. 30).[12]

TILE PANELS
THAT NEVER WERE

To this day Casa Grande remains unfinished. During its construction, Hearst ordered repeated changes to the structure, some of which were not carried out. Eventually, the travails of the Great Depression curtailed its completion. As a result, many California Faience tiles intended to adorn Casa Grande were never installed; they remain in the collection of Hearst Castle.

One of these is a design by Julia Morgan dated January 26, 1927, showing an elaborate window-surround tile treatment that was produced by California Faience but never installed (FIG. 31). Hearst Castle restorationist Wilson located the tiles and assembled them in their intended configuration (FIG. 32). Incorporating more than forty pieces, the surround depicts the Green Man, fruit clusters, and floral blossoms intertwined with drapery swags and ribbons. Inside this composition, Morgan created another motif—a series of fleur-de-lis tiles intended to be placed in the recessed, curved, keyhole-shaped space framing the window itself. This treatment was intended for all of the four octagonal mini-towers that rise from the corners of the building's central block (FIG. 33). They remain bare to this day.

Also in the Hearst Castle collection are an ensemble of tiles for an eight-piece panel with a leafy and floral configuration, framed by a repeat pattern of geometric forms (FIG. 34). Where in the San Simeon complex this panel was intended to be placed is unknown. A similar panel was displayed in the California Faience showroom to demonstrate the firm's artistry (FIG. 35).

HISTORICAL RESTORATION

Much of the brilliant coloration that characterizes California Faience tiles is due to the relatively low temperatures of their kiln firing. As the years passed, the use of these low temperatures inadvertently led to problems of durability at Hearst Castle. Lower fired ceramics do not stand up to wear and weathering as well as higher fired ceramics. If this matter was considered by Hearst when he was deciding on the decoration of his complex, he may have thought that the weather at San Simeon was mild enough that the durability of the tiles would not be an issue. However, almost one hundred years after the tiles were installed—on a site that has received millions of visitors since its 1958 opening, with attendance in excess of 500,000 annually—the wear and tear over time is a major factor in the preservation of the ceramic tilework.

Tile damage takes many forms. Cracking from ground subsidence and heavy foot traffic is common. Colored glazes deteriorate from long exposure to sun and weather. In some fortunate instances, when a tile becomes damaged, an original surplus tile is available to replace it. In most cases, however, the originals are

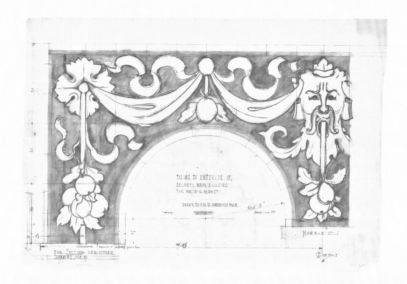

Previous spread

FIG. 25

Tile panels and framing sections adorning the wall of the Celestial Bridge that connects the bell towers of Casa Grande, completed 1928

Left

FIG. 26

Interior tiling of one of the belfry arches, Casa Grande, completed 1928

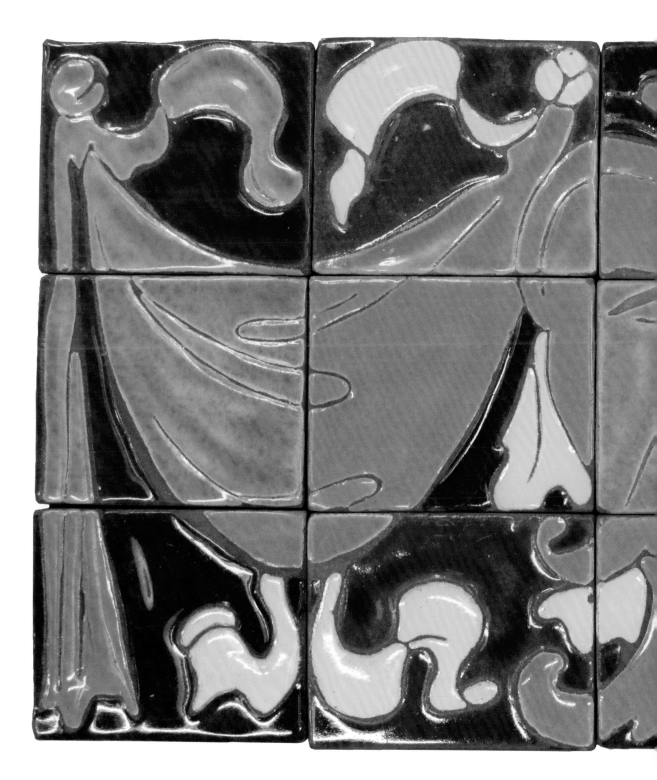

Right

FIG. 27
Fifteen-tile panel
for one of the
sills of the belfry
arches, bell towers,
Casa Grande,
completed 1928.
The composition
depicts the Green
Man with drapery
swag and ribbon
ornamentation.

DEVELOPED ELEV.
OF TILE PANEL
8 PANELS AS THIS

8 PANELS AS THIS

SECTION AA

8 PANELS AS
DRAWING
8 PANELS OPP.
HAND

ONE INCH SCALE

CORNICE

tile
face

tile
face

CUPOLA TO TOWERS OF MAIN BLDG.

FOR MR. W.R. HEARST, SAN SIMEON

JULIA MORGAN, ARCH'T

OCT 3.27.

DRG No 503 M-600
ROLL

Opposite

FIG. 28

Julia Morgan and studio, *Cupola to Towers of Main Building*, graphite, ink, and colored pencil, Oct. 3, 1927. The design shows the cupola plan (below), elevation (above), and section (right).

Above

FIG. 29

Cupola of one of the bell towers, Casa Grande, completed 1928

Right

FIG. 30

Candeliere composition, vertical tile panel adorning the area between the double pillars of the drum of one of the cupolas, Casa Grande, completed 1928

DESIGN·A·

STUDY·FOR·TILING·TO·TOP·
·OF·STAIR·TOWER·

FOR·MR·W·G·HEARST·
Scale 1"=1'0"

Jan 26 27 Julia Morgan Arch't.

506

FIG. 31
Julia Morgan and
studio, *Design A:
Study for Tiling to
Top of Stair Tower*,
ink and colored
pencil, January 26,
1927

FIG. 32
Polychrome tile
window frame
of California
Faience ceramics,
intended for lower
octagonal towers
of Casa Grande

not available. This leads to the classic dilemma facing conservators and art historians: whether to just let the objects deteriorate, attempt to repair damaged items, or replace damaged items with modern reproductions. When the object is a damaged colored tile, repair is not viable. Because of the need to maintain aesthetic appearances for visitors to Hearst Castle, the only option is replacement. The goal of the restorer, then, is to make the replacements as close to the originals as possible. A chipped and faded tile can be replaced by an almost exact duplicate (FIG. 36 and FIG. 37).

Hearst Castle restorationist David Wilson has labored faithfully to reproduce the original California Faience tiles for replacement of damaged originals. In so doing, he also has developed tiles that are fired at higher stoneware temperatures, making them more durable. But this meant Wilson had to experiment to obtain the original bright colors at higher heat levels.

At first this proved an elusive goal, but he eventually succeeded. Among Wilson's successes is a wall panel incorporating a square of antique Spanish tiles so badly weathered it could not be repaired (FIG. 38). His restoration was achieved only with great patience and persistence (FIG. 39).

One problem with reproduction tiles, however, is that they risk being confused with the real thing. Efforts before Wilson's time were occasionally substandard and not marked as reproductions. These inferior imitations escaped into the collector's market, incorrectly offered by sellers as California Faience. Collectors may also confuse unmarked tiles that were produced by Deer Creek Pottery in Grass Valley in the late twentieth century with California Faience.[13] These reproductions were once sold as souvenirs at Hearst Castle. To avoid confusing originals with replicas, Wilson marks the tiles he makes

Opposite

FIG. 33

One of four lower towers, undecorated, Casa Grande. Tiles were to be installed around the central window of the lower tower (near center). One of the two bell towers with its tiled cupola is seen beyond the lower tower.

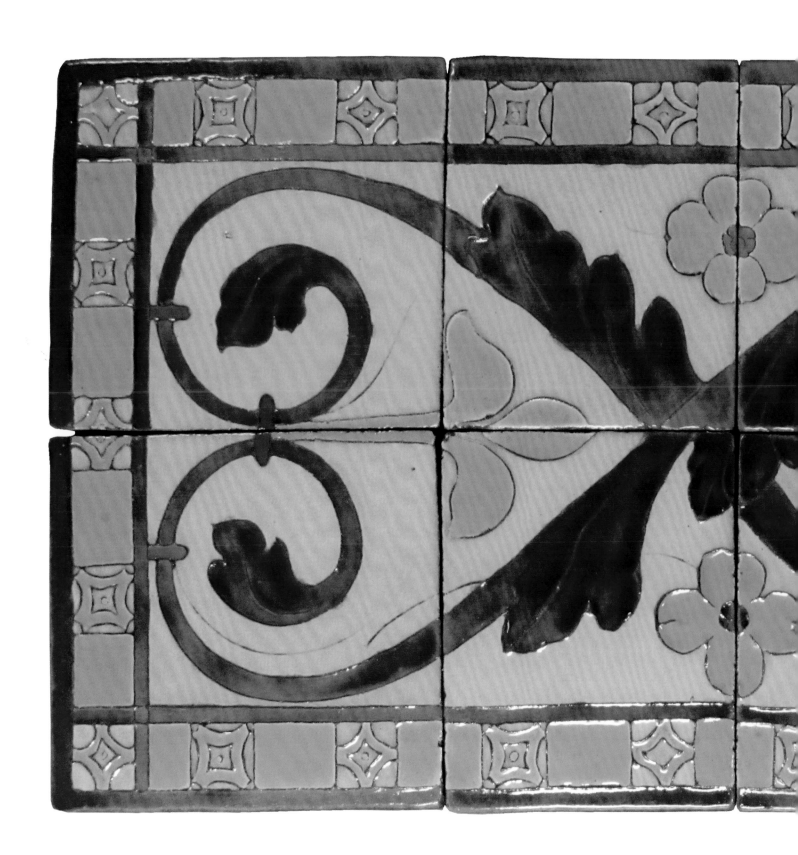

Previous spread, *right*
FIG. 35
Showroom of California Faience Co., Berkeley, ca. 1922-30. The panel with the leafy and floral design is at upper left. Below it is a grouping featuring the so-called "Moor's Head" motif. Both were designed by Julia Morgan for Hearst Castle.

Left
FIG. 34
Polychrome tile panel, ca. 1920s

by stamping them on the underside "Hearst Castle Reproduction." These tiles are sometimes offered in benefit sales and auctions by the Friends of Hearst Castle (since 2019, the Foundation at Hearst Castle).

When Hearst Castle commissions for California Faience dried up in the 1930s, the firm continued to produce a variety of ceramic wares for the commercial market, including some prestigious commissions. In 1938, Chauncey Thomas left the company, leaving William Bragdon as sole proprietor. After World War II, the shop began a decline due to competition from cheap ceramics and figurines imported from Japan. Bragdon sold the firm in 1955; he passed away four years later. ✿

Right top

FIG. 36
Damaged California Faience paver tile from the main terrace in front of Casa Grande depicting a stylized dolphin.

Right bottom

FIG. 37
Contemporary reproduction tile for replacement of damaged tiles

Opposite top

FIG. 38
Damaged insert (square at center) of antique Spanish tiles, 2006. The panel is located on the wall of the entry court of guest house B.

Opposite bottom

FIG. 39
Restored section reproducing the antique Spanish tile insert, 2014

Schmid Édit.

FRAGMENTS DIVERS A POMPÉI

Relevés et restauration de E. PAULIN

CHAPTER 7

PRESENCE OF THE PAST
JULIA MORGAN'S DESIGN INSPIRATIONS FOR SAN SIMEON

VICTORIA KASTNER

Along with her male counterparts studying architecture at the École des Beaux-Arts in the 1890s, Julia Morgan took inspiration from the great buildings of the past. Her situation was unique, however. She was not only the first woman admitted to the school's two-hundred-year-old program; she would also become one of the most prolific American architects ever to study there. In addition to designing hundreds of homes, community structures, schools, hospitals, churches, and commercial projects during her fifty-year career, Morgan spent forty years producing a wide range of buildings for the newspaper publisher and art collector William Randolph Hearst. Conservatively estimating her Hearst commissions alone yields some 500,000 square feet of projects, both built and unbuilt. Few alumni from the École had the opportunity to apply their architectural knowledge on an equivalent scale.[1]

Immediately upon arriving in Paris, Morgan began to prepare for the École's arduous entrance examinations. She studied and sketched from many books in its comprehensive library of historic architectural illustration, to which she had gained access through the advocacy of James Biddle Eustis, American ambassador to France. In spite of his request that she should receive library privileges, Morgan still had difficulty viewing its finest volumes, as she explained to her American cousins in 1898: "Just now I'm filling in very contentedly with lectures, drawing a good deal, the B.A. [Beaux-Arts] library, and the city—I'm getting a fine opinion of my good taste in books for I seldom pick out one but the library guards go look at it and come back with, 'Pas possible, it is too valuable!' The value of the Library [for my study] is much hampered by the amount of red tape—and it seems a pity."[2]

A cornerstone of the École's curriculum was architectural composition, indicated by the skill with which students could distill their complex designs into drawings that illustrated the primary elements of the intended building: plan, section, and elevation. Within the demands of this course, it was crucial for Morgan to gain a deep knowledge of architectural precedent. In *Americans in Paris*, the French-American architect and critic Jean Paul Carlhian explained: "Historic elements, far from being mere illustrations in a book . . . , became his [the architect's] own to use, manipulate, distort, or rearrange. Should he or she one day decide to discard them deliberately, it would be . . . with full knowledge of the tradition—and not through sheer ignorance."[3] Jean Labatut, a former student at the École, summed up the process more succinctly: "The four indispensable steps are: learn, assimilate, forget, and create."[4] In this sequence, the third action—forgetting—was perhaps the most important. Through imitation, repetition, and adaptation, the basic principles of architectural composition became subconsciously ingrained—second nature—and could subsequently be forgotten while the student focused on solving the problems specific to each project.

Nevertheless, the "full knowledge of the tradition" should always be at hand. An article advising architects on assembling reference libraries appeared in 1898 in *The American Architect and Building News*: "It is through our eyes that we take in knowledge of architecture and of architectural construction also. This is best done by seeing buildings, and next best by seeing them or parts of them represented; accordingly, an architect's books are mostly picture books. . . . Obviously it is of great importance to know which these standard books are, and to study them thoroughly."[5]

Previous spread, left and right
Julia Morgan student work, sketch in portfolio, pencil and ink, ca. 1900

Opposite
FIG. 1
Fragments Divers à Pompei, published in Hector d'Espouy, *Fragments d'architecture antique d'après les relevés & restaurations des anciens pensionnaires de l'Académie de France à Rome*, vol. 1 (Paris: Ch Massin, 1897), pl. 27

Above

FIG. 2

View of the winding Pergola (foreground) under construction, ca. late 1920s. Hearst Castle can be seen in the distance. The hilltop access road is at right.

Opposite

FIG. 3

Santa Maria la Mayor, published in Austin Whittlesey, *The Minor Ecclesiastical, Domestic, and Garden Architecture of Southern Spain* (New York: Architectural Book Publishing Company, 1917), p. 15

Following spread

FIG. 4

Julia Morgan, facade of Casa Grande, Hearst Castle. The bell towers are derived from *Santa Maria la Mayor,* Ronda, Andalusia, Spain, as seen in fig. 3.

PLATE XLII

SCALE OF ⁻² ᵕ ⁰ 1 ² 3 4 5 6 7 8 FEET

SCALE DRAWING OF A WINDOW OF THE AYUNTAMIENTO, SEVILLE.
Diego de Riaño, Architect, 1527–35.

✿ ✿ ✿

Founded in 1876, *The American Architect and Building News* was one among many journals that dispensed advice, analyzed historic buildings, and featured the current work of leading architects, as the discipline professionalized in the late nineteenth century. Morgan consulted several of these trade periodicals, thanks to the generosity of her cousin Lucy Latimer LeBrun and her husband, Pierre LeBrun (1846–1924), a New York architect who may have been a motivating force behind Morgan's choice to become a master builder. LeBrun was the son of the well-known French-American architect Napoleon LeBrun (1821–1901), who moved his firm to New York in 1864, then welcomed Pierre into the business in 1870 and made him a partner in 1880. In 1892, Pierre's younger brother, Michel, was also brought into the firm, from then on known as Napoleon LeBrun & Sons. One of the most notable buildings Pierre and Michel designed after their father's death was the Metropolitan Life Insurance Company Tower (known as the Met Life Tower), a skyscraper built in 1909 and crowned with a historicist Venetian campanile. Morgan's family recalled the long talks she had with both Pierre and Napoleon LeBrun prior to her departure for Paris in 1896. Morgan's lengthy correspondence with Pierre and Lucy LeBrun provides the most detailed account of her experiences at the École. Among their gifts to her were copies of *Architectural Record*, *The American Architect*, and *Architect and Builder*. Morgan wrote: "I was very much pleased to receive the 'Architect and Builder' in Monday's mail—the pictures seemed like old friends [I was] very glad to meet with. . . . I took the magazine to the atelier where it created much interest."[6]

In 1897, Julia Morgan began to build her personal library of fine illustrated volumes. Many of these were folios in formats 20 inches high or more. In this, too, she looked to Pierre LeBrun for advice: "I am very proud, having bought my first expensive book, *Fragments d'Architecture, Antique, et—de le Renaissance* [sic], edited by M. d'Espouy. . . . Cousin Pierre, would you make me a little list of the books, or kind of books, you think most useful and suggestive? I am fairly lost at the choice. . . . I have about $250 funds—and if that meant 6 books as full as the d'Espouy's, it would be enough to take a long while for this [book] worm to digest thoroughly"[7] (FIG. 1). She was definitely

asking the right person, since Pierre LeBrun's library was his great pride. Morgan's eldest brother, Parmelee, confessed to her after visiting the LeBruns, "I usually bring up some question [about architecture] . . . when I go around there because I know he likes to show his books, but then I am really interested as well."[8] LeBrun himself proudly explained to Julia Morgan, "I have more than doubled my collection since you were here & the problem will be where to store those I must keep adding—It forms now quite a respectable array such as I know you would enjoy dipping into—Indeed when I think of my books I do not envy anyone and feel so contented! Vanderbilt cannot be more so."[9]

When Morgan's San Francisco office was destroyed in the cataclysmic 1906 earthquake and fire, the loss of her books was of great concern to LeBrun, who wrote, "Were many of your books in your office? I hope not—Yet some of those destroyed must have been essential to your work and must be difficult to replace in San Francisco at this juncture. Won't you give me the great pleasure of sending me a list of such structural handbooks, manuals, or other office material as you would find useful at this juncture. I would be so pleased to send them to you. [sic] I do not see how, in the face of such wholesale destruction, Architects will manage their initial [rebuilding] work."[10] Seven years later, LeBrun presented Morgan with many volumes from his own library, writing, "In dismantling the office in preparation for our retirement I put aside about forty volumes and had Dutton & Co box & ship them to your address in San Francisco."[11] Throughout her career, Morgan's reference library served as her auxiliary office. Typically, she met with clients at a large table in the center of the room, where they could consult her books for ideas and inspiration.[12]

In the 1960s and 1970s, modernist critics belittled the Beaux-Arts method as passé. They claimed that relying on historic precedent limited creativity. Architectural historian Mark Alan Hewitt refuted this charge in *The Architect and the American Country House*: "To an eclectic architect the choice of a source was itself a creative act. . . . Historical sources were foils, not ends in themselves. . . . . The eclectic [architect's] library was adjunct and fodder to his imagination. His creativity was measured not in the degree of originality, but in what he added to tradition."[13]

While other architects who trained at the École typically used modern materials to create historically

Opposite
FIG. 5
"Scale drawing of a window of the Ayuntamienta, Seville," published in Arthur Byne and Mildred Stapley, *Spanish Architecture of the Sixteenth Century* (New York & London: G. P. Putnam's Sons, 1917), pl. 42, p. 219. Byne's drawing inspired the ground floor ornamental window frames and metal grille work on Casa Grande.

inspired ornament for their buildings, Morgan's projects for William Randolph Hearst required her to perform a far more difficult task: integrating preexisting antique objects—of varying material, condition, origin, and scale—into her designs. Many of these were purchased in Europe, shipped to warehouses in New York, and transported to San Simeon (FIG. 2). Considering this daunting task, Hewitt observed: "It is tempting to view . . . pastiche or assemblage of architectural fragments from actual buildings, as a method requiring no skill or originality whatsoever. Julia Morgan . . . would not have seen it that way, however. Though much of the material in [San Simeon's] vast historical pile was salvaged or removed from [various] European buildings, Morgan was required to act as artist, scholar, scene designer, and decorator in her synthesis of architectural elements. . . .Working within the restrictions imposed by the preexisting elements created an artistic challenge."[14]

Many of Hearst and Morgan's early discussions about San Simeon's architectural style centered on one illustrated book: *The Minor Ecclesiastical, Domestic, and Garden Architecture of Southern Spain*. Hearst sent Morgan a copy of this volume, with which she was already familiar. Its author, the young architect Austin Whittlesey, had dedicated his book to "Pierre LeBrun, Founder of the LeBrun Travelling Scholarship, with the grateful regards of the Author."[15] LeBrun's award had allowed Whittlesey to journey through Spain and photograph the buildings featured in his book. The New Yorker's beneficence to the twenty-two-year-old Californian must have pleased Morgan herself, who had benefited from the support of her cousin early in her career. Hearst wrote to her in 1919 on his acquisition of Whittlesey's survey: "I am mailing you . . . a book on architecture in Spain which I picked up. The suggestion [of a Gothic doorway] would certainly go very well with the bell towers, if we made them after the style of the church at Ronda (FIG. 3). The Gothic and Renaissance of Spain are so very much more interesting than the Baroc [sic]. . . . On the whole I do not think it will be bad to have . . . the Gothic pinnacle towers of the Ronda church of Santa Maria . . . . Of course, all these things are just thoughts, and if you do not like them, we will not try to follow them. In any case we would not follow them exactly but more approximately. My purpose in citing Whittlesey is simply to convey to you a general idea of the decoration I think would be fitting, so that when you are

working you will be working somewhat along those lines."[16] Morgan's reply was enthusiastic: "I believe we could get something really very beautiful by using the combination of the Ronda Towers and the Sevilla doorway, with [statues of] your Virgin over it and San Simeon and San Christophe on either side. This would allow for great delicacy and at the same time, brilliance in the decoration, and I see how it could be executed without running into very great expense"[17] (FIG. 4). From the beginning, their eclectic plan was not only to create modern structures that blended architectural references to several historic Spanish buildings, but also to incorporate genuine objects—in this case, a fifteenth-century statue of the Virgin Mary and two carved medallions of saints—into the fabric of the building itself.

Many of the architectural elements and historic objects that became part of San Simeon were supplied by one Philadelphia couple: architect and artist Arthur Byne (1883–1935) and his wife, art historian Mildred Stapley Byne (1875–1941), whose shared interest in historic Spanish art and architecture was kindled on their honeymoon in Spain in 1910. They moved there permanently in 1916, and the earliest scholarly publication, *Spanish Architecture of the Sixteenth Century*, was completed the following year (FIG. 5).[18] Mildred Stapley Byne and Julia Morgan were old friends, and in the course of designing San Simeon Morgan became friends with Arthur as well, which resulted in the architect freely sharing information with the couple about her work on the project Starting in 1914 she began purchasing historical architectural photographs from the Bynes while they were still in New York, working as curators at the Hispanic Society of America. Subsequently they published a series of illustrated scholarly texts on Spanish architecture, gardens, ironwork, textiles, ceilings, and furniture, and these volumes served Morgan and Hearst as resources in their designs for San Simeo.. Morgan confided to the Bynes, "Your books are as a gospel to him."[19]

In a typical transaction, two years into San Simeon's construction, Morgan wrote requesting detailed photographs of a ceiling in Granada that she and Hearst had admired in a photograph from the Bynes' folio volume *Decorated Wooden Ceilings in Spain*: "As usual, I jump into it breathlessly, to know [sic] if you have any more photographs of the 'Hero' [sic] ceiling at Granada . . . Mr. Hearst is very much interested in it and would like to get a full set

Opposite

FIG. 6

"Ceiling of the Principal Salon, Casa de los Tiros, Granada," published in Arthur Byne and Mildred Stapley, *Decorated Wooden Ceilings in Spain* (New York & London: G. P. Putnam's Sons, 1920), pl. 6

PLATE VI

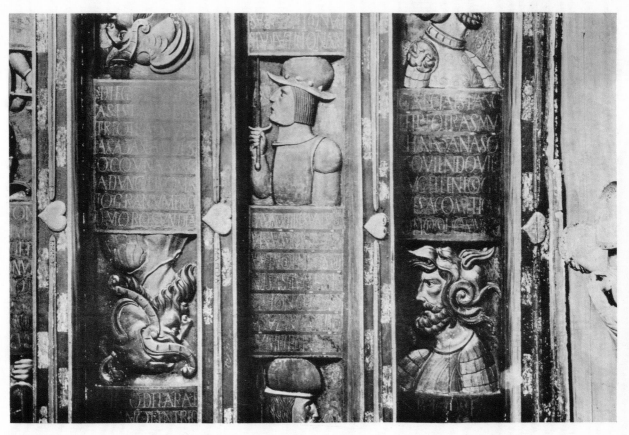

CEILING OF THE PRINCIPAL SALON, CASA DE LOS TIROS, GRANADA

of photos and [explanatory] text [FIG. 6]. We are building for him a sort of village on a mountain-top overlooking the sea and ranges and ranges of mountains, miles from any railway, and housing incidentally his collections as well as his family. Having different buildings allows the use of very varied treatments; as does the fact that all garden work is on steep hillsides, requiring endless steps and terracing. If you have any specially interesting garden plates, I would much like it if you would send me what you think would be helpful—say to the extent of $100 to $200."

In what was surely no coincidence, the Bynes announced one month later that they had become art dealers. Mildred Byne wrote to Morgan, "Knowing as we now do, the charm of the traditional Spanish house, we envy you architects of California your opportunity to create something fine in this line. . . . Meanwhile, if we can't build Spanish residences, we can furnish them. Our opportunities for disposing of good old private collections were so numerous that it seemed a pity not to take advantage of them, so we have become antiquaries. . . . Should you know anyone in S.F. who wants genuine old Spanish articles sent direct, anything from a bride's chest of old linens to the contents of a whole Castillo [castle], will you be good enough to mention us?"[20]

Over the next fifteen years, Arthur Byne sold Hearst more than three dozen antique Spanish ceilings, even as he and his wife were documenting them in their scholarly research (FIG. 7). Byne located, purchased, and removed them from historic buildings, replacing their original frameworks with modern reproductions. These fragile, centuries-old panels were then shipped in numbered crates to San Simeon, where Morgan had the challenge of putting them back together, cropping or extending them where necessary, and then attaching the reconstituted antique panels onto new structurally supportive ceilings hidden above them.

Byne also sold Hearst two twelfth-century Cistercian monasteries—St. Bernard of Clairvaux and Santa Maria de Óvila—which his dealer referred to by the respective code names Sacramenia and Mountoliv. These ancient edifices were dismantled in Spain and shipped to America in vast numbers of crates (using buying methods which—though relatively common in the 1920s—would be regarded much more critically today). In the 1940s Hearst commissioned Morgan to design a large medieval museum for San Francisco's

Golden Gate Park, constructed from reinforced concrete to which they planned to attach the architectural fragments of the Mountolive compound. It would have been similar to the Cloisters medieval museum in New York, which had opened in 1938. Morgan completed the design, but the project ran into trouble and the museum was never built.[21]

Hearst had exhausted his funds by the late 1930s, as a result of collecting on a massive scale while ignoring the economic consequences of the Great Depression. He was more than eighty million dollars in debt, which required him to sell several properties and thousands of art objects that had been stored in his warehouses, awaiting future use. His liquidations and the booming post–World War II economy restored him to wealth in 1946, but by then Morgan's health had begun to fail. She suffered from increasingly severe inner ear infections and her family despaired of her ever taking the time to eat properly or get sufficient rest. Her health challenges became catastrophic with the onset of dementia, and therefore architect and patron built no more projects together. Hearst died at age eighty-eight in 1951, and Morgan succumbed in 1957 at age eighty-five.[22]

But during their final active years, the two continued to plan and dream. In 1944, Morgan sent Hearst a volume that delighted him: *Old Architecture of Southern Mexico*.[23] It was not a random selection. Over the previous three years, she and Hearst had been struggling to complete Babicora, a vast hacienda located on his 900,000-acre cattle ranch in the mountains of northern Mexico. The project was beset with problems—damaged adobe bricks, frequent labor shortages, and scarce building materials—caused by the scarcities of the war years. Morgan (herself in her early seventies) had paid three lengthy visits to the site in hopes of getting construction going again, but to no avail. Perhaps by presenting Hearst with an illustrated volume on Spanish Colonial architecture, Morgan was letting him know that there were still exciting architectural prospects ahead. It also may have reminded him of what she already knew: the best way for them to plan their future projects was to become inspired by great architecture from the past. ✿

Opposite

FIG. 7

Watercolor of chapel ceiling and trusses, Roca Verde Castle, Perelada, Spain, published in Arthur Byne and Mildred Stapley, *Decorated Wooden Ceilings in Spain* (New York & London: G. P. Putnam's Sons, 1920), pl. 17

PLATE XVII

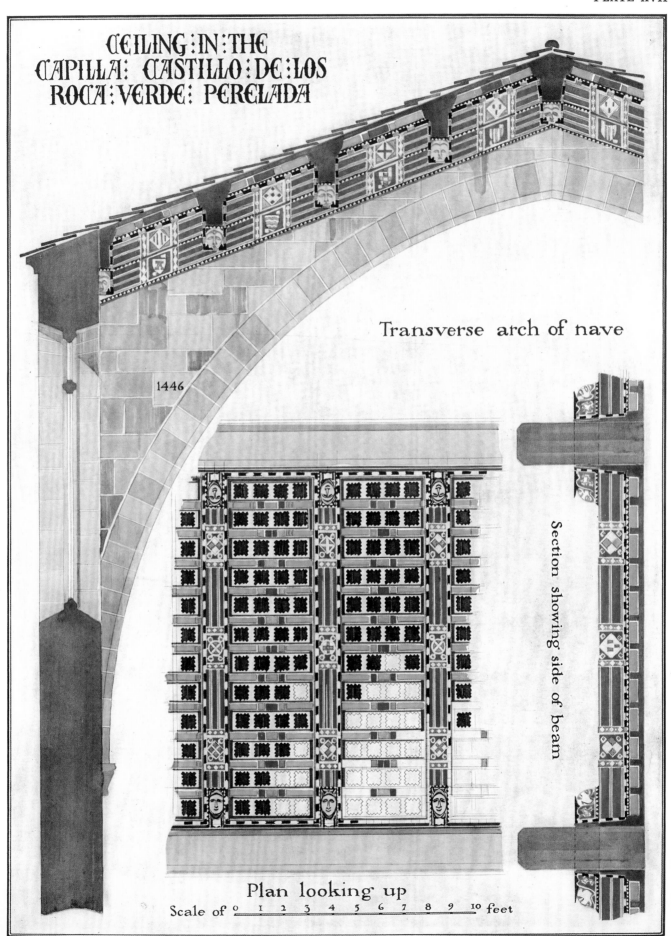

CEILING : IN : THE
CAPILLA : CASTILLO : DE : LOS
ROCA : VERDE : PERELADA

1446

Transverse arch of nave

Section showing side of beam

Plan looking up

Scale of 0 1 2 3 4 5 6 7 8 9 10 feet

NOTES

PREFACE

1   The villa was sporadically explored during the nineteenth century, with the first systematic archaeological campaign getting underway in 1929. Its ruins—including its dazzling mosaic pavements—have since been largely excavated and restored. "Villa Romana del Casale," UNESCO, accessed May 26, 2020, https://whc.unesco.org/en/list/832. R. J. A. Wilson, *Piazza Armerina* (Austin: University of Texas Press, 1983).

2   The Getty Villa is modeled after the Villa dei Papiri in Herculaneum that was—until excavation—buried in volcanic ash from the eruption of Mount Vesuvius in 79 C.E.

INTRODUCTION
BEAUX-ARTS ARCHITECTURE AND THE AMERICAN RENAISSANCE IN CALIFORNIA

1   Viollet-le-Duc chose not to be educated at the École des Beaux-Arts in Paris and challenged the school's approach to architecture. Despite initial resistance from his École colleagues, Viollet-le-Duc's comprehensive understanding of the architecture of the past; his convictions about architectural education; his philosophy of method and principles of design; and his guidelines for historical restoration won him a wide audience, not only in France, but throughout Europe and the United States. His two major publications, *Entretiens sur l'architecture* and the multi-volume *Dictionnaire raisonné de l'architecture française du XIe au XVIe siècle* were translated into English in whole or in part. M. F. Hearn, ed., *The Architectural Theory of Viollet-le-Duc: Readings and Commentaries* (Cambridge: MIT Press, 1990) provides a solid sampling and interpretation of this once highly influential theorist.

2   Julien Guadet, *Elements et theorie de l'architecture: cours professé à l' École nationale et speciale des beaux-arts*, 4 vols. (Paris: Librairie de la Construction Moderne, 1902). Professor John F. Harbeson, an American advocate of Beaux-Arts theory who taught architecture at the University of Pennsylvania, called *Elements* "the Bible of Architecture." He adapted many of its principles for his *The Study of Architectural Design* from 1927. It is currently available as a reprint edition (New York: Norton, 2008).

3   Andrea Palladio, *The Four Books on Architecture*, trans. Richard Schofield and Robert Tavenor (Cambridge: MIT Press, 2002). The elaborately illustrated and descriptive *Quattro Libri* has undergone numerous editions and translations since the seventeenth century and was available to architects practicing during the American Renaissance.

4   Richard Longstreth, *On the Edge of the World: Four Architects in San Francisco at the Turn of the Century* (Cambridge: MIT Press, 1983), 78, 368–69. Peixotto's critique appeared in the *Overland Monthly*, May 1893. His sister, Jessica Peixotto, traveled with Julia Morgan to Paris when the latter sought admission to the École des Beaux-Arts. Jessica was the second woman in the history of the University of California, Berkeley to be awarded a Ph.D. She later taught at the university and became the first woman to attain the rank of full professor and serve as a department head.

5   Although a growing number of Americans went to Paris to study at the École, they were not eligible to earn the *diplôme* until the late 1880s. Pissis's paternal heritage, trilingual fluency, and strong performance sped his progress through the curriculum. Therese Poletti, "The Bank and the Man Who Lead San Francisco Out of Architectural Chaos," *The Argonaut* 22, no. 1 (Spring 2011), provides a solid introduction to Pissis, who deserves a monograph.

6   VerPlanck quoted in Poletti, 58.

7   By 1900, the United States had acquired or controlled the overseas territories of the Hawaiian Islands, the Philippines, Guam, parts of Samoa, and in the Caribbean, Cuba and Puerto Rico.

8   Norman Bolotin and Christine Lang, *The World's Columbian Exposition: The Chicago World's Fair of 1893* (Champaign: University of Illinois Press, 2002), provides a broad pictorial survey of the fair, in addition to its architecture.

9   Brown learned Beaux-Arts theory and practice in the New York offices of McKim, Mead & White. This fired his interest in traveling to Europe to study historical architecture on site from 1883 to 1884. He opened an office in San Francisco in 1889 and is credited with shifting the city towards Beaux-

Previous spread
Julia Morgan, library with relief-patterned wood ceiling, Casa Grande, Hearst Castle

Arts planning and academic classicism.

10 Gray Brechin, *Imperial San Francisco: Urban Power, Earthly Ruin* (Berkeley: University of California Press, 1999), 180–81. In contrast to the Chicago Exposition, the architecture of the midwinter fair was reshaped along more exotic lines, including Orientalist fantasies of Ottoman palaces and grand mosques and even a pharaonic facade from the trending Egyptian Revival.

11 Longstreth, 223–25. Polk later served as the West Coast representative for Chicago architect Daniel Burnham.

12 Morgan's fellow attendees included John Bakewell, Arthur Brown, Jr., Edward H. Bennett, Lewis Hobart, and G. Albert Lansburgh. All pursued further architectural studies at the École des Beaux-Arts.

13 Brechin, 284–86. Sally B. Woodbridge, *Bernard Maybeck: Visionary Architect* (New York: Abbeville Press, 1992), 75–77; and Alexandra M. Nickliss, *Phoebe Apperson Hearst: A Life of Power and Politics* (Lincoln: University of Nebraska Press, 2018), 187–97. At the time Maybeck and Phoebe Hearst devised the competition, he was the first and only instructor of architecture at the University of California, Berkeley.

14 Kevin Starr, *Americans and the California Dream: 1850–1915* (New York: Oxford University Press, 1973), 299.

15 Starr, 291.

16 Mansel G. Blackford, *Businessmen and City Planning on the Pacific Coast, 1890–1920* (Columbus: Ohio State University Press, 1993), 38–41.

17 Renée Dreyfus, "The Classical Ideal in the New Athens," in *Jewel City: Art From San Francisco's Panama-Pacific International Exposition*, ed. James A. Ganz (Oakland/San Francisco: University of California Press, 2015), 66 (footnote 20) and 68, citing six sources expressing a civic desire to "crown" the hill with "the ruins of the Acropolis."

18 Starr, 292.

19 Joan E. Draper, "The École des Beaux-Arts and the Architectural Profession in the United States: The Case of John Galen Howard," in *The Architect: Chapters in the History of the Profession*, ed. Spiro Kostof (New York: Oxford University Press, 1977), 209–237. For an updated study of American architects—particularly those of Howard and Julia Morgan's generation—and their training at the École, see Jeffrey Tilman's chapter in this volume.

20 Sally B. Woodbridge, *John Galen Howard and the University of California: The Design of a Great Public University Campus* (Berkeley: University of California Press, 2002), 50 and 52. Both Carrère and Thomas S. Hastings studied at the École des Beaux-Arts. One of their early works was the Hotel Ponce de Leon in St. Augustine, Florida (1887). An example of academic eclecticism, the hotel is styled in the Spanish Renaissance mode. Julia Morgan would utilize a similar style for her design of Hearst Castle.

21 Woodbridge, *John Galen Howard*, 22–57, treats the history of the international competition for the Hearst Architectural Plan leading to Howard's appointment. A different emphasis on the University of California, Berkeley competition and the role of Howard is found in Renaissance art historian Loren W. Partridge's *John Galen Howard and the Berkeley Campus: Beaux-Arts Architecture in the "Athens of the West"* (Berkeley: Berkeley Architectural Heritage Association, 1988).

22 The following year Howard purchased a scenic lot and designed a house for his family in the eclectic style of a Beaux-Arts trained architect: craftsman + shingle style + a dominant stuccoed tower evoking a Spanish colonial mission.

23 Sara Holmes Boutelle, *Julia Morgan, Architect*, rev. ed. (New York: Abbeville Press, 1995), 39.

24 Studying historical architecture and archaeological discoveries from antiquity was an important part of École des Beaux-Arts instruction. During his professorship at the University of California, Berkeley, Howard taught the history of ancient and classic architecture, along with planning and architectural theory.

25 Morgan later designed life-size baroque deco gilt and polychrome caryatids to accent the red damask walls of the interior of the theater at Hearst Castle.

26 Morgan's undergraduate degree was earned at Berkeley in 1894 in the College of Engineering. Ferroconcrete is a building material produced from a cement of finely ground powder made by heating and pulverizing limestone and clay that is applied over a matrix of steel bars or thick wire mesh to increase its tensile strength. In the popular imagination, the École is thought to have resisted modern building methods. This is untrue. During Morgan's study, courses were offered in iron framing, stone cladding, and ferroconcrete construction—all then-recent building technologies.

27 Stylized circular garlands and horizontal rows of small blocks (dentils) on slanting cornices were standard Beaux-Arts decorative details.

28 Herbert Croly, "The New University of California," *Architectural Record* 23 (April 4, 1908), 271–93, quoted in Woodbridge, *John Galen Howard*, 79. Croly was one of the leading advocates for progressive causes in the early twentieth century.

29 Labrouste is acclaimed for his synthesis of French rationalism, light, and classical influences, devising his own architectural language in the mid-nineteenth century. Immigrants from Catalonia, the Guastavino family of engineers produced vaulting systems for numerous American Beaux-Arts buildings, most notably the Boston Public Library (1895), designed by McKim, Mead & White.

30 Partridge, 22.

31 Woodbridge, *John Galen Howard*, 83.

32 In 1925, Morgan would revisit UC Berkeley to collaborate with Bernard Maybeck to design the Phoebe Apperson Hearst Memorial Gymnasium for Women. Conceived in an austere Beaux-Arts style, it was commissioned by William Randolph Hearst as a monument to his mother's memory. Phoebe Hearst died in 1919. See Boutelle, 53–55; and the September 2005 report by Architectural Conservation, Inc., PGA Design, Michael Corbett (architectural historian), *Hearst Memorial Gymnasium: Historic Structure Report*. https://capitalstrategies.berkeley.edu/sites/default/files/hsr_hearst_gymnasium_sept2005.pdf.

33 The fourteenth-century St. Mark's campanile was restored and rebuilt with Renaissance additions in the sixteenth century. Occasionally, Beaux-Arts architects sought inspiration from medieval monuments. A. Page Brown, among the first wave of Beaux-Arts architects working in San Francisco, drew upon the twelfth-century campanile (with its Renaissance additions) of the Cathedral of Seville, Spain, for his clock tower for the 1898 Ferry Building on the Embarcadero. In the first half of the twentieth century, historicist bell towers at colleges and universities enjoyed a vogue in the United States and were erected at the University of Northern Iowa, Cedar Falls; the University of Texas, Austin; Ball State University, Muncie, Indiana; and South Dakota State University, Brookings, to name a few.

34 After the completion of Sather Tower, Howard continued as supervising architect for another seven years. Eventually, friction developed between him and the regents and they cancelled his contract in 1924. He retired from the directorship of the school of architecture in 1927.

35 Boutelle, 55–58. The ten bronze bells were donated before the tower was conceived. They were in storage when Morgan was commissioned to integrate them into a tower design.

36 Maryanne Stevens, "The Exposition Universelle: 'This Vast Competition of Effort, Realization and Victories,'" in Robert Rosenblum, et al., *1900: Art at the Crossroads* (London: Abrams, 2000), 54–71. This scholarly catalogue of an exhibition (Royal Academy of Arts, London, and the Solomon R. Guggenheim Museum, New York) of art shown at the Paris exposition reassesses a historical moment when modern and traditional cultural mandates were in competition.

37 Quoted in Laura A. Ackley, *San Francisco's Jewel City: The Panama-Pacific International Exposition of 1915* (Berkeley: University of California Press, 2015), 15. See also footnotes numbers 1 through 4 for chapter 2, "Envisioning the Imperial City," 352.

38 Like Julia Morgan, Bennett was supported in his studies at the École des Beaux-Arts with a stipend from Phoebe Apperson Hearst. He earned the *diplôme* in 1902, the year Morgan received the *certificat*.

39 The original PPIE Architectural Advisory Council included École alumni Albert Pissis and John Galen Howard, both of whom later resigned.

40 Jeffrey T. Tilman, *Arthur Brown, Jr: Progressive Classicist* (New York: Norton, 2006), 50–53. Brown and Morgan attended the École at the same time and were lifelong friends. Similar to the YWCA Building at the PPIE, the Palace of Horticulture featured caryatids sculpted by John Bateman. Jean Louis Bourgeois was responsible for most of the classical ornament decorating the building.

41 Ackley, 104–106. Sherry Edmundson Fry's neoclassical sculpture was placed around Festival Hall. He was a graduate of the sculpture division at the École des Beaux-Arts.

42 Maybeck's "palace" was actually an architectural prologue. Fairgoers strolled along its paths with towering colonnades to reach the actual building housing a display of recent art from around the world, a pavilion configured as a wide arc. Woodbridge, *Bernard Maybeck*, 101–105; Kenneth H. Cardwell, *Bernard Maybeck: Artisan, Architect, Artist* (Salt Lake City: Peregrine Smith, 1977), 135–50.

43 Nickliss, 353–54.

44 Champney previously served as one of the architects for the Alaska-Yukon-Pacific Exposition held in Seattle in 1909.

45 The sculpting of the YWCA caryatids was done by John Bateman. Departing from the classical model, he portrayed his maidens decked out in floral garlands. They appear similar to the ones used for Brown's Palace of Horticulture.

46 Boutelle, 101–105. Whatever the actual division of design labor for the PPIE YWCA Building, it is worth noting that shortly before Morgan had designed William Randolph Hearst's Los Angeles Examiner Building (dedicated New Year's Day, 1915) with flanking domed towers that are similar in concept to the domed pavilions of the woman's building. In addition, her prior work with Howard on the UC Berkeley Hearst Memorial Mining Building with its high foyer from 1902 to about 1905 would have given her firsthand experience with translucent domes made of sectioned glass like those produced for the YWCA Building. Further still, the YWCA shares with the Mining Building a Mediterranean red tile roof and hanging eaves supported by protruding ornamental brackets.

47 Ackley, 127–39. The large glass dome of Arthur Brown, Jr.'s horticultural hall had colored lights projected onto it from inside the building. These were put in motion, creating an aurora effect, and were observable outside as fairgoers strolled the Avenue of the Palms and South Gardens. This light show anticipated the dynamic color projections that would accompany San Francisco rock concerts in the 1960s.

48 Ackley, 101, lists Guérin's precisely calculated palette: "French Green, Yellow-Golden-Orange, Pinkish-Red-Gold, Cerulean Blue, Mud Pink, Oxidized Copper-Green, Wall Red and Oriental Blue."

49 Christian Brinton, "The San Diego and San Francisco Expositions, Part II: San Francisco," *International Studio Magazine* (July 1915), 56. Brinton's praising of San Francisco, however, came at the expense of the San Diego fair, which he wrongly characterized as in the style of a "concise . . . local tradition." Bertram Goodhue's design actually was a Latin amalgam of Spanish Colonial Mexican and Mediterranean influences.

50 Richard W. Amero, "The Making of the Panama-California Exposition, 1909–1915," *The Journal of San Diego History* 36, no. 1 (Winter 1990): https://sandiegohistory.org/journal/1990/january/expo/

51 Richard Oliver, *Bertram Grosvenor Goodhue* (Cambridge: MIT Press, 1983). Goodhue's extensive drawings from his Mexican travels illustrated volumes 2 to 12 in Sylvester Baxter, *Spanish-Colonial Architecture in Mexico* (Boston: J. B. Millet, 1901). His enthusiasm for "Latin culture" radiates warmly from his travel memoir, *Mexican Memories: The Record of a Slight Sojourn Below the*

Yellow Rio Grande (New York: G. M. Allen Company, 1892).

52 Oliver, 112–13.

53 Winslow supplemented his early education with coursework at the École des Beaux-Arts and is equally credited with Goodhue for advancing the Spanish Colonial style in Southern California. For his account of the PCE, see Carleton Monroe Winslow, *The Architecture and the Gardens of the San Diego Exposition* (San Francisco: Paul Elder and Company, 1916).

CHAPTER 1
THE ÉCOLE DES BEAUX-ARTS AT THE FIN DE SIÈCLE

1 Donald Drew Egbert, *The Beaux-Arts Tradition in French Architecture Illustrated by the Grands Prix de Rome*, (Princeton: Princeton University Press, 1980), 25.

2 Richard Chafee, "The Teaching of Architecture at the École des Beaux-Arts," in *The Architecture of the École des Beaux-Arts*, ed. Arthur Drexler (New York: The Metropolitan Museum of Art, 1977), 65.

3 Chafee, 66–72.

4 Chafee, 79–82.

5 The four years' pension was reduced to two years with a series of reforms to the Grand Prix in the late nineteenth century.

6 The admissions process is described in great detail in Henry Guédy, *L'Enseignement à l'École Nationale et Spéciale des Beaux-Arts, Section Architecture* (Paris: EBA, 1899), 111–12. Copy located in the library of the École des Beaux-Arts, Paris.

7 Charles Collens, "The Beaux-Arts in 1900," *AIA Journal* XXXV, no. 2 (February 1947): 84–85.

8 Edmond Augustin Delaire, *Les Architectes Élèves des École des Beaux-Arts*, 1908, 227–28, 344. McKim was the foremost classical revival architect in the United States at the turn of the twentieth century. His firm, McKim, Mead & White, was the nation's first large corporate firm, producing significant buildings across the nation for nearly fifty years.

9 Chafee, 105–106.

10 This project and many studies are published in Sara Holmes Boutelle, *Julia Morgan, Architect*, rev. ed. (New York: Abbeville Press, 1995), 36–37.

11 J. L. Pascal, "Préface," in *Concours Rougevin & Godeboeuf* (Paris: École Nationale des Beaux-Arts, 1910), iii–iv.

12 Victoria Runyon Brown to Arthur Brown, Sr., February 15, 1901.

13 Egbert, 11–15.

14 Delaire, 374. "Albert Pissis Is a Victim of Pneumonia," *Pacific Coast Architect* VIII, no. 2 (August 1914).

15 For example, one such apartment at 13 Rue Bonaparte, directly across from the École buildings, was occupied thusly: 1897–1899, by Jack Humphries and Harvey Wiley Corbett; 1899–1900, by Harvey Wiley Corbett, Arthur Brown, Jr., and Victoria Runyon Brown; 1900, by Harvey Wiley Corbett and Mrs. John Corbett; 1901–1902, by William Adams Delano and Walter Dodge.

16 This is described as the "Minstrel Show" in several of Victoria Runyon Brown's letters.

17 Brown subsequently disappeared and was later presumed to be dead; she died of consumption in 1896. J. Godefroy, "Origine des Bal des Quat'-z'-Arts," in *Hommage à Laloux*, 1925. (A pamphlet dedicated to Victor Laloux on the occasion of his retirement from the École des Beaux-Arts.)

18 "École des Beaux-Arts: Concours d'Admission en 2e Classe," *La Construction Moderne*, December 3, 1898. The text of the article reads: "Pour la première fois depuis le vote de la loi autorisant l'admission des femmes à l'École nationale des Beaux-Arts, nous apprenons l'admission d'une femme à la section d'architecture (2° classe): M"" Morgan, de nationalité américaine, a, comme on a vu ci-dessus, été admise sous le n" 13, sur 40 admis. C'est d'un bon exemple pour nos gracieuses et jeunes compatriotes."

19 "Pour les Élèves Architectes Femmes," *La Construction Moderne*, December 24, 1898, 152. Original text: "Nous ne savons si l'égalité, inscrite entre deux points sur tous nos édifices publics et sur nos monnaies, exigeait l'entrée des femmes à l'École des Beaux-Arts ; mais, répétons-le, la décence exige que les femmes admises à l'École y soient traitées en femmes ayant des habitudes de bonne éducation, et non en vachères."

20 Victoria Runyon Brown to Arthur Brown, Sr., April 7, 1899. Letter is in the possession of Brown's great-granddaughter.

21 Victoria Runyon Brown to Arthur Brown, Sr., November 7, 1899. "Miss Morgan is all ready to go on with her Construction now [that] she has got through with everything else so she can do the Projets in the 1st Classe as soon as she does her Construction. I took a long walk with her on Sunday to try and cheer her up. She is very nervous. I think she has overtaxed her strength and then she was disappointed at her brother's failure."

22 Victoria Runyon Brown to Arthur Brown, Sr., January 5, 1901. "I am sorry to say that Miss Morgan did not finish her *Projet* on Saturday. She was not well and had worked too hard and was too worn out to finish although she worked as hard as she could until the very last moment. Arthur [Brown, Jr.] did her coupe and thought she would finish. I went down on Saturday and put the plan and coupe on the frames and it looked fine, but she could not get through with her façade. She felt so badly about it, and quite discouraged and gives up all hope of doing her *Diplôme*. I do not like her Patron and wish she would change and have Redon. She heard that he said he would take her, and I am sure he would be much better for her. It would be better to have a Patron who has an atelier. She is very self-reliant and will do her own way. She has gone *en loge* today and will go on for the Rougevin and if she gets good *esquisses* she will do the Projets. [Roger] Gilman has promised to help her on the Rougevin if it should be anything that two can work on. It will be hard for her because it is done *en loge* and mounted there, and of course she will not have any *nouveaux* as the men have. I do not know how she will manage. Please do not say anything of all this I have written to the Morgan family. I do not know what she will write to them."

23 Arthur Drexler, ed., *The Architecture of the École des Beaux-Arts* (New York: Museum of Modern Art, 1977).

1   Sara Holmes Boutelle, *Julia Morgan, Architect*, rev. ed. (New York: Abbeville Press, 1995), 23; E. Richey, *The Ultimate Victorians of the Continental Side of San Francisco Bay* (Berkeley: Howell-North, 1970), 83; Julia Morgan Architectural History Project (JMAHP), vol. 2 (Berkeley, 1976), 195–96; "Roxie's Column," *Saturday Weekly*, March 28, 1896, and May 30, 1896, JMAHP.

2   The École des Beaux-Arts offered instruction in four disciplines: painting, sculpture, engraving (the graphic arts), and architecture. See Annie Jacques, ed., *Les Beaux-Arts, de l'Académie aux Quat'z'arts* (Paris: École Nationale Supérieure des Beaux-Arts, 2001).

3   Though grounded in a moralistic crusade to protect the virtue of American women abroad, the American Girls' Club also fostered women's success in the art world. French feminists marveled at the institution, citing it as a model to replicate in their quest to empower women. See Mariea Caudill Dennison, "The American Girls' Club in Paris: The Propriety and Imprudence of Art Students, 1890–1914," *Woman's Art Journal* 26, no. 1 (Spring–Summer 2005): 32–37; Emily C. Burns, "Revising Bohemia: The American Artist Colony in Paris, 1890–1914," in Karen L. Carter and Susan Waller, eds., *Foreign Artists and Communities in Modern Paris, 1870–1914: Strangers in Paradise* (New York: Routledge, 2016), 97–110; *La Fronde*, July 28, 1898; Claire de Pratz, "Les Boarding-Clubs de Femmes en Amérique," *La Fronde*, September 26–29, 1898; Paule Vigneron, "Carnet Artistique," *La Fronde*, December 18, 1897; and Haryett Fontanges, "Les Club de Femmes à Paris," *Le Figaro*, September 4, 1896.

4   Correspondence from Julia Morgan to Pierre LeBrun between June 1896 and May 1898, Box 17, folders 10–12, Julia Morgan Papers (JMP), Special Collections, California Polytechnic State University, San Luis Obispo, Kennedy Library; "Bartol Wants a Divorce," New York *Sun*, August 12, 1885; "The Bartol Divorce Suit," *New York Times*, February 8, 1887; "Blame Your Mother, Bartol Wrote Son After Making Will," *Philadelphia Inquirer*, March 26, 1919; Katherine de Montclos [*sic*], United States Petition for Naturalization; Marie-Laure Crossnier Leconte, "Pérouse de Monclos, Marcel," AGHORA, Bases de données de l'Institut national de l'histoire de l'art, accessed January 5, 2019, https://agorha.inha.fr.

5   Julia Morgan to Pierre LeBrun, June 8, 1896, Box 17, folder 10, JMP.

6   The atelier of Victor Laloux, most famous for designing the Paris railroad station Gare d'Orsay (1900), and the patron of Morgan's eventual mentor, François-Benjamin Chaussemiche, was the most popular among American architects. He mentored ninety-seven Americans over the course of his career. Jean-Louis Pascal was the second most popular with forty-eight American students. Arthur Drexler, ed., *The Architecture of the École des Beaux-Arts* (New York: Museum of Modern Art, 1977), 459; Morgan to LeBrun, August 15, 1897, December 12, 1897, and May 30, 1898, Box 17, folders 11–12, JMP.

7   Katherine Cotheal Budd (1860–1951) practiced and published about architecture and landscape architecture in New York City. She, along with Julia Morgan and Fay Kellogg (see note 26), was exclusively appointed by the YWCA to design hostess houses at military bases during World War I. See Cynthia Brandimarte, "Women on the Home Front: Hostess Houses during World War I," *Winterthur Portfolio*, Winter 2008, 201–222.

8   Morgan to LeBrun, July 5, 1896, Box 17, folder 10, JMP.

9   Morgan to LeBrun, April 29, 1897, Box 17, folder 11, JMP.

10 For anecdotes and further context about the fraternal culture of the architecture ateliers, see Jacques, *Les Beaux-Arts*, 18–20; Alexis Lemaistre, *L'École des Beaux-Arts, Dessinée et Racontée par en Élève* (Paris: Firmin-Didot, 1889), 23–24, 67–78; John M. Howells, "An Architect at the Gates of the Beaux-Arts," *Harper's Weekly*, December 22, 1894, 1222; Richard Chafee, "The Teaching of Architecture at the École des Beaux-Arts," in *The Architecture of the Ecole des Beaux-Arts*, ed. Arthur Drexler (New York: The Metropolitan Museum of Art, 1977), 89–95; Susan Waller, "*Académie* and *fraternité* : constructing masculinities in the education of French artists," in *Artistic Brotherhoods in the Nineteenth Century*, ed. Laura Morowitz and William Vaughan (Hants, England, 2000), 137–53.

11 Morgan to LeBrun, June 8, 1896 and February 11, 1899, Box 17, folders 10 and 13, JMP.

12 François-Benjamin Chaussemiche was born in Tours to a manufacturer. Chaussemiche traveled to Paris and enrolled in the École, where he studied architecture under Jules André and Victor Laloux. In 1891, Chaussemiche earned his *diplôme* and placed second in the Grand Prix de Rome competition; two years later, he won the Grand Prix de Rome. Between 1893 and 1898, Chaussemiche resided at the Académie de France in Rome and spent his time drawing and writing about his tours of Italy and Greece. Chaussemiche was appointed principal project inspector for the Gare d'Orsay, which was designed by his mentor Victor Laloux, and became chief advisor for public buildings in 1900, then chief architect for public buildings of the national palaces in 1904. M. Prevost and Roman D'Amat, eds., *Dictionnaire de Biographie Française* Vol. 8 (Paris: Letouzey et Ané, 1959), 884; Morgan to LeBrun, May 30, 1898, Box 17, folder 12, JMP; François-Benjamin Chaussemiche to Morgan, June 8, 1919, Box 17, folder 5, JMP.

13 Victoria Runyon Brown to Arthur Brown, Sr., December 25, 1900, and Arthur Brown, Jr., to Victoria Runyon Brown, December 2, 1901, Brown Family Papers, Private Collection; Chafee, "The Teaching of Architecture," 89–94.

14 Morgan to LeBrun, May 30, 1898.

15 See correspondence from Morgan to LeBrun at JMP and Brown Family Papers.

16 Morgan to LeBrun, June 8, 1896.

17 Morgan to LeBrun, July 5, 1896.

18 Morgan actually stated to Pierre and

Lucy LeBrun that she had "covered thoroughly only map IV of Baedeker, and left half of map V," which comprise the sites listed above. Morgan to LeBrun, October 4, 1896, Box 17, folder 10, JMP; Karl Baedeker, *Paris and Environs with Routes From London to Paris: Handbook for Travelers*, 14th ed. (London: Karl Baedeker, 1900), maps IV and V.

19 Morgan to LeBrun, March 1, 1897, Box 17, folder 11, JMP.

20 For Morgan's commentary on the architecture of the Exposition Universelle of 1900, see especially Morgan to LeBrun, February 11, 1899, May 7, 1899, and November 21, 1899, Box 17, folder 13, JMP.

21 Morgan to LeBrun, October 4, 1896.

22 Morgan to Chaussemiche, January 27, 1936, Box 17, folder 9, JMP.

23 For a history of the UFPS as well as the context of women and the arts, spectacle, and feminism, see Tamar Garb, *Sisters of the Brush* (New Haven: Yale University Press, 1994), 4–18, 42–104; Jo Burr Margadant, ed., *The New Biography: Performing Femininity in Nineteenth-Century France* (Berkeley: University of California Press, 2000); David M. Pomfret, "'A Muse for the Masses': Gender, Age, and Nation in France, Fin de Siècle," *The American Historical Review* 109 (December 2004): 1439–74; Mary Louise Roberts, *Disruptive Acts: The New Woman in Fin-de-Siècle France* (Chicago: University of Chicago Press, 2002); Jennifer Waelti-Walters and Steven C. Hause, eds., *Feminisms of the Belle Époque: A Historical and Literary Anthology* (Lincoln: University of Nebraska Press, 1994); Mathew Truesdell, *Spectacular Politics: Louis-Napoleon Bonaparte and the Fête Impériale, 1849–1870* (New York: Oxford University Press, 1997); Vanessa Schwartz, *Spectacular Realities: Early Mass Culture in Fin-de-Siècle Paris* (Berkeley: University of California Press, 1999).

24 Garb, *Sisters of the Brush*, 70–104; Marina Sauer, *L'Entrée des femmes à l'École des Beaux-Arts, 1880–1923* (Paris: École Nationale Supérieure des Beaux-Arts, 1990), 7–13.

25 Author's translation of "Partout les universités commencent à ouvrir leurs portes aux femmes; et je ne crois pas que votre École, le plus fort École des Beaux-Arts du monde voudra toujours empêcher les femmes d'y étudier." Found in Sauer, *L'Entrée des femmes*, Appendix 6.

26 Fay Kellogg (1871–1918) returned to New York in 1896 and found work in the office of John R. Thomas. After his death, she went into business for herself and landed a contract with the American News Company, which kept her busy designing new buildings and updating existing buildings throughout the country. Along with Julia Morgan and Katherine Budd (see note 7), Kellogg was exclusively appointed by the YWCA to design hostess houses at military bases during World War I. "Woman Invades Field of Modern Architecture," *New York Times*, November 17, 1907; "Miss Fay Kellogg, Architect, Dies," *New York Times*, July 12, 1918; Morgan to LeBrun, July 5, 1896; Brandimarte, "Women on the Home Front."

27 "L'École des Beaux-Arts s'est toujours montrée si complaisant envers les étrangers que nous avons été encouragés à vous demander cette nouvelle faveur et nous sentons la conviction que vous ferez en notre faveur, tout ce qui depend [sic] de vous." Bernard Maybeck to Conseil de l'École des Beaux-Arts, April 29, 1897, AJ52 409 Archives nationales de France (ANF).

28 Morgan to LeBrun, July 3, 1898, Box 17, folder 12, JMP.

29 Garb, *Sisters of the Brush*, 102.

30 "La décision Ministérielle qui a ouvert l'École des Beaux-Arts aux femmes ne crée pour celles-ci aucun privilège. Melle [sic] Morghan [sic] aura donc à subir les examens reglementaires si, comme c'est son droit indéniable, elle veut être admise au seconde classe et prendre part aux concours." Séance du mercredi 5 mai 1897, Procès verbaux des séances du Conseil Supérieur d'enseignement de l'École des Beaux-Arts. 1863–1924, AJ52 20, ANF; Conseil des Professeurs, le 22 janvier 1898, Assemblée des Professeurs, AJ52 973, ANF; Avery Morgan to Julia Morgan, March 7, 1897, Box 1, folder 13, Morgan-Boutelle Collection, Special Collections, California Polytechnic State University, San Luis Obispo.

31 Director of the École des Beaux-Arts to Bernard Maybeck, May 7, 1897, AJ52 409, ANF; "Ordre d'Inscription des femmes (à partir du 1er avril 1897) pour suivre les cours oraux et étudier das la galleries," in Appendix 7 of Sauer, *L'Entrée des femmes*; Morgan to LeBrun, July 19, 1897, Box 17, folder 11, JMP.

32 Morgan to LeBrun, July 19, 1897; Lemaistre, *L'École des Beaux-Arts*, 226–27.

33 Howells, "Architect at the Gates," 1222.

34 Morgan to LeBrun, July 19, 1897.

35 Howells, "Architect at the Gates," 1222; Lemaistre, *L'École des Beaux-Arts*, 160–176, 193–211; Jacques, *Les Beaux-Arts*, 18; Morgan to LeBrun, July 19, 1897.

36 John Howells's observations verify those of Morgan regarding failed aspirants. According to him, French students had become so accustomed to failing at least once that they leveraged these low expectations to avoid tedious work assigned to nouveaux in the ateliers. "What do you want me to do?" they would say. "I don't have a chance." Morgan to LeBrun, July 19, 1897; Howells, "Architect at the Gates," 1222.

37 Morgan to LeBrun, December 12, 1897, Box 17, folder 11, JMP.

38 Morgan to LeBrun, December 12, 1897.

39 Victoria Brown wrote to her husband that Bernard Maybeck and a person named Godefrere also thought the jury had marked down Julia Morgan's scores because of her gender. Morgan to LeBrun, December 12, 1897; Victoria Runyon Brown to Arthur Brown, Sr., November 17, 1897, Brown Family Papers.

40 Victoria Runyon Brown to Arthur Brown, Jr., May 21, 1898, Brown Family Papers.

41 Virtually every publication that mentions Julia Morgan's efforts to gain entrance to the École des Beaux-Arts states that she succeeded on her third attempt. In part, this error derives from Morgan's personal dossier of the École, which leaves out the first attempt in June/July 1897; the dossier lists October 1897, April 1898, and October 1898. As documented above, correspondence between Morgan, Pierre LeBrun, Charles and Eliza

Morgan, and Victoria Brown, Arthur Brown, Jr., and Arthur Brown, Sr. all document four examination attempts. Around the same time Morgan was taking the entrance exams in June 1897, the École changed the annual entrance examination schedule from February and June to October and April. She refers to this change in the École's examination schedule in her July 19, 1897 letter to Pierre LeBrun. "Had I known they had changed [the examination schedule] and would have another in October," she stated, "think I might have waited." In addition to correspondence already cited above, see Melle [sic] Morgan, dossiers individuels des élèves, AJ52 409, ANF.

42 Anonymous to M. le D[irecteu]r des B[eaux] A[rts], November 24, 1898, AJ52 909, ANF.

43 Morgan to LeBrun, Nov. 14, 1898, Box 17, folder 12, JMP.

44 Julia Morgan's individual dossier; Brown Family Papers. For more on Arthur Brown, Jr.'s experience, see Jeffrey T. Tilman, *Arthur Brown, Jr.: Progressive Classicist* (New York: Norton, 2006).

45 In their study of American students in Paris, Isabelle Gournay and Marie-Laure Crosnier Leconte make the point that at least as many students studied casually at the École for different lengths of time, without necessarily attempting the entrance examinations and without the pressure of earning a degree of any kind. Morgan did not have this same luxury of casual, anonymous study for studying's sake. Isabelle Gournay and Marie-Laure Crosnier Leconte, "American Architecture Students in Belle Époque Paris: Scholastic Strategies and Achievements at the École des Beaux-Arts," *Journal of the Gilded Age and Progressive Era* 12, no. 2 (April 2013): 154–198; Julia Morgan's individual dossier; Morgan to Pierre and Lucy LeBrun, November 21, 1899, Box 17, folder 13, JMP.

46 AJ52 909 and AJ52 73bis, ANF; "Cette élève architecte, la première femme sans doute qu'ai jamais séduite cette branche de l'art, un nouveau debouche n'avait été indiqué aux progrès feministe," 1899? EA Dos

707, Bibliothèque Marguerite Durand (hereafter BMD); "Jusqu'à ce jour, une seule femme de nationalité américaine, s'est présentée à diverses reprises au concours d'admission dans la section d'architecture." *La Fronde*, May 22, 1898, 3.

47 "California Girl Wins High Honor," *San Francisco Examiner*, December 6, 1898; "Fame Comes to Julia Morgan," *Oakland Tribune*, December 6, 1898.

48 *American Architect and Architecture*, June 15, 1901, p. 82; "The First Lady Architect," *Pall Mall Gazette*, October 28, 1901, later reprinted in the *New York Times*, November 12, 1901.

49 *Saturday Weekly*, March 28, 1896; *La Fronde*, May 22, 1898; "She Qualifies in Paris as Architect," *SF Bulletin*, December 8, 1901; newspaper clippings, BEA Dossier 707, BMD; "Points about People," *Brooklyn Eagle*, November 27, 1901; notices in *Gil Blas*, October 21, 1901, 1; Eliza Parmelee Morgan to Julia Morgan, November 4, 13, 22, and December 6, 15, 29, 1901, Box 4, folder 6, JMP; Emma Morgan North to Julia Morgan, December 7, 1901, Box 4, folder 7, JMP; Gardner Morgan to Julia Morgan, September 29, 1901, Box 4, folder 8, JMP; and Parmelee Morgan to Julia Morgan, November 5 and December 16, 1901, Box 4, folder 6, JMP.

50 Eliza Parmelee Morgan to Julia Morgan, October 26, 1901, Box 4, folder 6, JMP.

51 Julia Morgan's individual dossier; Victoria Runyon Brown to Arthur Brown, Sr., December 28, 1900, May 17, 21, 28, 1901, June 1 and 4, 1901; Victoria Brown to Arthur Brown, Jr., December 25 and 28, 1901, January 12 and 19, 1902, February 20, 1902; Arthur Brown, Sr., to Victoria Brown, March 30, 1901, October 26, 1901, November 2, 1901; Arthur Brown, Sr., to Arthur Brown, Jr., November 28, 1901; Arthur Brown, Jr., to Victoria Brown, February 7, 1902; Brown Family Papers.

52 "Women Doctors in Paris," *Daily Herald* (Biloxi, Mississippi), February 14, 1902, 7. The article likely appeared in dozens of newspapers; it was published internationally, too, including in the New Zealand publication *The Fielding Star*, February 11, 1902, 4.

53 Meredith Clausen, "The École des Beaux-Arts: Toward a Gendered History," *Journal of the Society of Architectural Historians* 69, no. 2 (2010): 153–161; "Statistiques de candidats inscrits et réçus aux concours d'admissions à l'École Nationale et Supérieure des Beaux-Arts et nombre de diplômes descernes pour les années 1900 – 1910 – 1916 – 1920 – 1925 – 1930 – 1931 – 1932," AJ52 909, ANF.

54 Morgan to LeBrun, April 29, 1897, Box 17, folder 11, JMP.

55 For a comprehensive history of the bell tower at Mills College see, Karen McNeill, "Julia Morgan: Gender, Architecture, and Professional Style," *Pacific Historical Review* 76, no. 2 (May 2007), 229–67 and McNeill, "'Women Who Build': Julia Morgan and Women's Institutions," *California History* 89, no. 3 (Summer 2012), 41–74. See also "The Work of Walter Steilberg and Julia Morgan," interview by Suzanne B. Riess in JMAHP, vol. 1.

56 Julia Morgan to Aurelia Reinhardt, September 10, 1917, folder 44, Group 2, Papers of Aurelia Reinhardt, Mills College.

CHAPTER 3
A TWENTIETH-CENTURY REVIVAL:
JULIA MORGAN'S RENAISSANCE
PALAZZO IN OAKLAND

1 The first printed edition of Vitruvius's *De Architectura* (On Architecture) was published in 1486, and the first illustrated edition was printed in 1511. It was translated into English in 1914 as *The Ten Books on Architecture*. The earliest printed edition of Palladio's *I Quattro libri dell'architettura* (The Four Books of Architecture) was published in 1570 and illustrated by Palladio himself.

2 From the Latin *ingenium* meaning ability or cleverness. The English word *engineer* and its modern connotations derive from this root. This term aptly describes Filippo Brunelleschi and the huge dome he designed and engineered for the Florence cathedral.

3 Leland M. Roth, *McKim, Mead & White, Architects* (New York: Harper & Row, 1983), 84.

4 Leland M. Roth, *A Concise History of American Architecture* (Boulder, CO: Westview, 1979). See Chapter 3, "The

Lure of the Past, The Promise of the Future: 1820–1865," 85–125.

5 Charles H. Reilly, "The Modern Renaissance in American Architecture," *Journal of the Royal Institute of British Architects* 17 (June 25, 1910): 634, 630; James J. G. Blumenson, *Identifying American Architecture: A Pictorial Guide to Styles and Terms, 1600–1945* (New York: Norton, 1981), 39.

6 The American Renaissance has been written about extensively by Richard Guy Wilson, professor emeritus of architectural history at the University of Virginia. See Richard Guy Wilson, "Architecture and the Reinterpretation of the Past in the American Renaissance," in *American Architectural History: A Contemporary Reader*, ed. Keith L. Eggener (New York: Routledge, 2004), 231; and *The American Renaissance: 1876–1917* (New York: Brooklyn Museum, 1979).

7 Quoted in *The American Renaissance: 1876–1917*, 13.

8 This includes texts by Leon Battista Alberti, Antonio di Pietro Averlino (known as Filarete), Giacomo Barozzi da Vignola, Sebastiano Serlio, Andrea Palladio, and Francesco di Giorgio.

9 Michael G. Warning, "The Promotion and Construction of the Oakland Young Women's Christian Association Center" (master's thesis, State University of New York College at Oneonta, 1976), 82.

10 Richard Chafee, "The Teaching of Architecture at the École des Beaux-Arts," in *The Architecture of the École des Beaux-Arts*, ed. Arthur Drexler. (New York: Museum of Modern Art, 1977), 62.

11 For a description of the École's environment around the turn of the twentieth century, see Karen McNeill, "Building the California Women's Movement: Architecture, Space, and Gender in the Life and Work of Julia Morgan" (Ph.D. dissertation, University of California, Berkeley, 2006), 58–59.

12 The first American to study architecture at the École des Beaux-Arts was Richard Morris Hunt (1827–1895). Marcus Whiffen and Frederick Koeper, *American Architecture 1607–1976* (Cambridge: MIT Press, 1981), 267. Women were first permitted to attend evening courses at the École in 1896.

13 Karen McNeill, "Building the California Women's Movement," 83–84. The 1900 Exposition Universelle attempted to exceed the 1893 World's Columbian Exposition in Chicago. Morgan saw an extravagant and overwhelming array of Beaux-Arts, historicist, Orientalist, and fantasy pavilions; see Richard D. Mandell, *Paris 1900: The Great World's Fair* (Toronto: University of Toronto, 1967).

14 Suzanne B. Riess, ed., *The Julia Morgan Architectural History Project*, vol. 1 (Berkeley: Regents of the University of California, 1976), 197.

15 Quoted in Riess, 107. Wormser Coblentz was a graduate of UC Berkeley's nascent architecture program when it was overseen by John Galen Howard.

16 Sara Holmes Boutelle, *Julia Morgan, Architect*, rev. ed. (New York: Abbeville Press, 1995) 14–15.

17 "Seaport Logistics Complex History and Timeline," Oakland Seaport, accessed August 12 2021, https://www.oaklandseaport.com/development-programs/seaport-logistics-complex/seaport-logistics-complex-history-and-timeline/

18 John Heinitz, "The Early Development of Lake Merritt, Oakland, California: 1852–1907" (master's thesis, California State University, East Bay, 1992).

19 After 1906, a new shopping and financial neighborhood became the primary commercial center of the city. The "new" downtown is located northeast of Old Oakland. For a detailed history of Lake Merritt, see Linda Watanabe McFerrin, "A Natural History of Oakland's Lake Merritt," *Bay Nature*, January 1, 2001, , accessed August 12, 2021, https://baynature.org/article/loving-lake-merritt/

20 Elizabeth Wilson, *Fifty Years of Association Work Among Young Women: 1866–1916* (New York: Garland, 1987), 265.

21 E. Wilson, 281–82.

22 The problem of attributing the commission of the Oakland YWCA is addressed in Warning, 9–26.

23 Warning, 25–26. Morgan designed Asilomar as a West Coast variant of the Arts and Crafts movement, a popular tendency of the time. She was involved with the Pacific Grove commission from 1913 to 1937.

24 *The Architect and Engineer of California*, January 1913, 113. Grace Fisher made a similar tour in April 1908 to visit YWCAs in a number of cities including Portland, Seattle, Los Angeles, Omaha, Kansas City, and St. Paul. Michael Warning believes that Morgan visited each of these association buildings. See Warning, 11, 17, 46–47.

25 Warning, 49–55, 57.

26 *The Architect and Engineer of California*, March 1913, 112.

27 "Y.W.C.A. Home to Be Built Soon," *Oakland Tribune*, January 21, 1913.

28 Katharine T. Corbett, *In Her Place: A Guide to St. Louis Women's History* (St. Louis: Missouri Historical Society Press, 1999), 185.

29 When compared to the earlier conceptual design for the Oakland YWCA (fig. 5), which more closely resembles the Palais des Études (fig. 4), Morgan's executed design for the building (fig. 7) clearly illustrates the evolution of the design from a more heavily Beaux-Arts-influenced schema to a more historicist Renaissance Revival conception closer in appearance to the St. Louis YWCA. Key differences between the conceptual and executed designs are 1) the increase in overall height from four to five stories; 2) the enlargement of the first-floor entrance from one to three bays in width; 3) the removal of a colonnaded porch at the second floor measuring five bays in width and replacement with three arched windows with decorative railings; and 4) a reduction in the application of overtly classical details and moldings.

30 The former St. Louis YWCA (extant) is located at 1411 Locust Street. The YWCA occupied the building from 1912 until 1975.

31 Ludwig H. Heydenreich, *Architecture in Italy, 1400–1500*, rev. Paul Davies (New Haven: Yale University Press, 1996), 27–29.

32 For more on Vitruvius, see Vitruvius Pollio, *The Ten Books on Architecture*, trans. Morris Hicky Morgan (New York: Dover, 1960).

33 Heydenreich, 27.

34 Despite this economy, Leon Battista Alberti, whose 1453 design for the Palazzo Rucellai in Florence was modeled after the Palazzo Medici, was moved to remark on the general architectural embellishment of Italian cities: "How many cities, which as children we saw all built of wood, have now been turned into marble?" Quoted in Leon Battista Alberti, *On the Art of Building in Ten Books*, trans. Joseph Rykwert, Neil Leach, and Robert Tavernor (Cambridge: MIT Press, 1988), 257. The homes of some of the wealthiest patrons, however, featured selective detailing with precious stones or metals.

35 Walter Steilberg, "Some Examples of the Work of Julia Morgan," *The Architect and Engineer of California*, November 1918, 84.

36 Sanborn fire insurance map, "Oakland 1912–Nov. 1951, vol. 2, 1911–Nov. 1950, Sheet 153."

37 Advertisement for N. Clark & Sons, *The Architect* 12, no. 6 (December 1916): 350. See also Dan Mosier, "N. Clark & Sons," *California Bricks*, 2005, accessed August 12, 2021, http://calbricks. netfirms.com/brick.clark.html.

38 At some point after 1919, Fifteenth Street was extended through this garden. See Wendy Allison Hart, "Dedicated Toward Nobler Womanhood" (master's thesis, Cornell University, 1991), 80.

39 Steilberg, 84. The pilasters with Ionic capitals are overlain on larger Tuscan columns in the Bramante cloister. This was repeated in Morgan's design for the YWCA court, although she chose to use Corinthian capitals.

40 The inscription in the courtyard of Santa Maria della Pace reads, "OLIVERIVS CARRAPHA EPS HOSTIENSIS CARD NEAPOLITAN / PIE A FVNDAMENTIS EREXIT ANNO SALVTIS CRISTIANE MDIIII / DEO OPT MAX ET DIVE MARIE VIRGINI GLORIOSE DEIPARE / CANONICIS QZ REGVLARIBVS CONGREGATIONIS LATERANENSIS." See Paul Marie Letarouilly, *Édifices de Rome Moderne* (Liege, Belgium: D. Avanzo, 1849), 204. For an informed reading of this inscription, see Wolfgang Lotz, "Bramante and the Quattrocento Cloister," *Gesta* 12, nos. 1–2 (1973), 111–21. On Bramante's career and his absorbing of *all'antica*, see Arnaldo Bruschi, *Bramante* (London: Thames & Hudson, 1977).

41 Psalm 19:1–2, American Standard Version. The four lines of this passage represent the manner in which it is inscribed on the four walls of the courtyard. It is most likely that the psalm was chosen by the executive board of the Oakland YWCA.

42 According to Letarouilly, the expanse of the courtyard is approximately 14.4 meters (47 feet and 3 inches). According to the first floorplan of the YWCA, the expanse of the courtyard is 29 feet 6 inches. The courtyard of the YWCA is therefore about 63 percent the size of Bramante's courtyard. Morgan's adaptation of the cloister model entailed her removal of Bramante's pedestals from the ground-level pilasters and employing fewer architectural orders than those found in the Roman design, which were used for their religious symbolism, e.g., the "maternal" Ionic order referred to Santa Maria della Pace, Mary the Mother of Peace. Bramante's combination of four different orders throughout the cloister was an ambiguous application of classical detail rather than an adherence to the traditional (i.e., correct) use of the orders. Avoiding religious symbolism that might elude the average YWCA occupant, Morgan's choice of architectural orders was strictly aesthetic.

43 Hart, 68.

44 Walter Steilberg quoted in Suzanne B. Riess, ed., *The Julia Morgan Architectural History Project*, vol. 1 (Berkeley: Regents of the University of California, 1976), 83.

45 Hart, 67.

46 Hart, 81.

CHAPTER 4
JULIA MORGAN'S LOS ANGELES EXAMINER BUILDING: A BEAUX-ARTS VISION OF SPANISH COLONIAL ARCHITECTURE

1 Dates for the various revivals are based on date blocks I learned from my mentors David Gebhard and Robert Winter and adapted from their many revised and updated architectural guides to Los Angeles architecture (beginning in 1977). This was followed by a Southern California study of building and planning history for an ethnic diversity course I taught at the University of Southern California (from 1998 to 2000) and published in 2002 in *California Colonial: The Spanish and Rancho Revival Styles* (Schiffer Publishing). I addressed the Mission Revival and Spanish Colonial Revival movements and the variety of Spanish, Gothic, Moorish, Andalusian, Mexican, Native American, New England/Early American, and local California vernacular sources related to them. The historical Spanish styles follow period designations from Sir Bannister Fletcher's 1896 (and subsequent editions) *A History of Architecture*. In place of Fletcher's French adaptations, I am using their proper Spanish names: platateresco, Churrigueresco, and desornamentado. Regarding the Examiner Building, Walter Steilberg, a Morgan associate, dated its completion to 1915; see note 7.

2 Elizabeth McMillian, *California Colonial: The Spanish and Rancho Revival Styles* (Atglen, PA: Schiffer Publishing, 2002), 31.

3 Richard Guy Wilson, et al. *The American Renaissance: 1876—1917* (New York: Pantheon, 1979), 75–109. For the impact of the American Renaissance on California, see Gordon Fuglie's Introduction in this volume.

4 Alexandra M. Nickliss, *Phoebe Apperson Hearst: A Life of Power and Politics* (Lincoln: University of Nebraska Press, 2018), 177–180. Schweinfurth was an early enthusiast of Mission and Southwestern-derived architecture in California.

5 Sara Holmes Boutelle, *Julia Morgan, Architect*, rev. ed. (New York: Abbeville Press, 1995), 184. Also see references to the Bynes in McMillian, *California Colonial*, 36, 37, 51, 54, 74, 87, 167, 179, and in Victoria Kastner's chapter in this volume, "Presence of the Past."

6 David Nasaw, *The Chief: The Life of William Randolph Hearst* (New York: Houghton Mifflin, 2000).

7 Walter Steilberg, *Architect and Engineer*,

November 1918, quoted in Boutelle, 174–75. For other Trinkkeller metalwork from the same period, see McMillian, *California Colonial*, 64, 131, and 137.

8   William Randolph Hearst, undated, unidentified period newspaper clipping, in Sara Holmes Boutelle's collection, now housed in Julia Morgan Papers (JMP), Special Collections, California Polytechnic State University, San Luis Obispo, Kennedy Library, and quoted in Boutelle, 174 and 246, footnote 5.

9   Email from Melanie McArtor, Gensler Associates, to McMillian, citing structural engineer Ryan Wilkerson, August 22, 2019.

10   William Randolph Hearst, undated, unidentified period newspaper clipping, in Sara Holmes Boutelle's collection, JMP.

11   "A competition was held and the Mission Style was favored, finally preferring A. Page Brown's eclectic assemblage of Mission elements, including a dome and old mission belfry. Brown's design relied heavily on the ideas of others and caused resentment among the architects [working for him, including Willis Polk, John Galen Howard, Bernard Maybeck, Samuel Newsom, and Ernest A. Coxhead]. It incorporated Samuel Newsom's proposal of 1891 using superimposed Mission Order gable facades for all entrances. Bernard Maybeck designed the dominant center dome and went to Chicago for Brown's office to supervise construction. Brown's only original idea seemed to be the Mission arcade as the linear core of the building," McMillian, *California Colonial*, 29.

12   Richard W. Amero, "The Making of the Panama-California Exposition, 1909–1915," *Journal of San Diego History* 36, no. 1 (Winter 1990): 1–47.

13   Nomination Form, National Register of Historic Places Inventory, July 19, 1977. U.S. Department of the Interior, National Park Service. https://npgallery.nps.gov/NRHP/GetAsset/NHLS/77000331_text. Pitts described the sculpture of the Churrigueresco facade as "represent[ing] the history of California and its Spanish origins."

14   Kevin Starr, *Americans and the California Dream: 1850-1915* (New York: Oxford University Press, 1973), 399 and 401–406. In the 1890s, among those advocating Californians' embrace of the "Spanish metaphor" as the young state was undergoing rapid development was the journalist Charles Fletcher Lummis. Within an aesthetic context, he urged Californians to become adoptive heirs to Spanish civilization as they built their society.

15   Starr, 403–405.

16   McMillian, *California Colonial*, 50–51.

17   David Gebhard, foreword, in McMillian, *Casa California*, 9.

18   William Randolph Hearst to Julia Morgan, December 31, 1919, Boutelle collection, Julia Morgan Papers (JMP), Special Collections, California Polytechnic State University, San Luis Obispo, Kennedy Library, and Boutelle, *Julia Morgan, Architect*, 177. Here is the quote in full: "The San Diego Exposition is the best source for Spanish in California. The alternative is to build this group of buildings in the Renaissance style of southern Spain. We picked out the towers of the Church at Ronda. I suppose they are Renaissance or else transitional, and they have some Gothic feelings; but a Renaissance decoration, particularly that of the very southern part of Spain, could harmonize well with them. I would very much like to have your views on what we should do in regard to this group of buildings, what style of architecture we should select . . . But after all, would it not be better to do something a little different than other people are doing out in California as long as we do not do anything incongruous? I do not want you to do anything you do not like."

CHAPTER 5
HEARST CASTLE: A BEAUX-ARTS
SPANISH VILLAGE OF
THE AMERICAN RENAISSANCE

1   Thorstein Veblen, *The Theory of the Leisure Class* (originally published in 1899), http://moglen.law.columbia.edu/LCS/theoryleisureclass.pdf, pp. 35 – 36 (accessed September 15, 2021).

2   To the north awaits one of the most spectacular drives on the West Coast—Highway 1 and a string of surf-pounded, forested state parks. If traveling south, nearby Cambria ("where adventure meets relaxation, where fun meets flavor, where the pines meet the sea") offers some ninety lodgings. Sojourning further east on Highway 46 takes the motorist through rolling hills and ocean views to the Paso Robles wine region and gastronomic enjoyments.

3   Sara Holmes Boutelle, *Julia Morgan, Architect* rev. ed. (New York: Abbeville Press, 1995).

4   Nancy E. Loe, *Hearst Castle: An Interpretive History of W. R. Hearst's San Simeon Estate* (Santa Barbara: Companion Press, 1994), and Victoria Kastner, *Hearst Castle: The Biography of a Country House* (New York: Abrams, 2000).

5   "Overlooked No More: Julia Morgan, Pioneering Female Architect," *New York Times*, March 6, 2019. The *Times* neglected to post an obituary when Morgan died in 1957.

6   As I write in early 2020, former Hearst Castle historian Victoria Kastner is writing the tentatively titled *Julia Morgan: An Intimate Biography of the Trailblazing Architect*, scheduled for publication by Chronicle Books in January, 2022.

7   Richard Guy Wilson, et al., *The American Renaissance: 1876–1917* (New York: Pantheon, 1979). This catalogue accompanied an exhibition organized by the Brooklyn Museum, October 13 to December 30, 1979. It remains a solid overview of this cultural epoch. We need a new study! Throughout this essay I will use American Renaissance instead of Gilded Age, as the former had a broader cultural impact.

8   In 1895, Hearst contracted with architect A. C. Schweinfurth to design a Spanish-California "mission style" home for his mother, Phoebe Hearst, on the family's Pleasanton acreage. However, Phoebe soon took over the design of what became the sprawling Hacienda del Pozo de Verona. After Schweinfurth's death, she engaged Julia Morgan to expand on the estate following the architect's return from France in 1902. See Alexandra M. Nickliss, *Phoebe Apperson Hearst: A Life of Power and Politics* (Lincoln:

University of Nebraska Press 2018), 177–180. Wyntoon, Phoebe Hearst's Bavarian Gothic castle south of the hamlet of McCloud, was designed by trusted Hearst family architect Bernard Maybeck, Nickliss, 268–271. It was rebuilt by her son after a catastrophic fire in 1929. In New York, Hearst found that his collecting passions had overwhelmed his four-story Lexington Avenue townhouse. In 1905 he leased a "grand new apartment" at the spacious Clarendon building on Eighty-Sixth Street and Riverside Drive, with spectacular views of the Hudson River, to house his collection of stained glass, tapestries, sculpture, antique furniture, suits of armor, and an array of decorative art objects he had been acquiring since the late 1880s. Once Hearst was in his larger lodgings, his acquisitions continued unabated and he eventually purchased the Clarendon for himself in 1913, expanding his residence to five floors and doing heavy remodeling throughout, a practice similar to the evolving stages of San Simeon. See David Nasaw, *The Chief: The Life of William Randolph Hearst* (New York: Houghton Mifflin, 2000), 193–194, 231.

9   Carey McWilliams, *California: The Great Exception*, reprint ed. (Santa Barbara and Salt Lake City: Peregrine Smith, 1976).

10 Gordon Fuglie, "Triumph and Good Living: Aspects of Self-Representation in the Art Programs of the Villas of the Senatorial Aristocracy in Late Antiquity" (master's thesis, UCLA, 1991).

11 Mary L. Levkoff, ed., *Hearst the Collector* (New York: Abrams, 2008).

12 Based in Washington, D.C., Hornblower & Marshall designed a number of federal buildings in an official classicist Beaux-Arts style, including the National Museum of Natural History. Standing on the Washington side of the Columbia River, the Maryhill mansion houses an eclectic collection of art and objets d'art. It opened to the public as the Maryhill Museum of Art in 1940.

13 Peterson was something of a Renaissance man. A thrice-published poet and translator, he collected Chinese paintings.

14 See my Introduction in this volume, where I discuss Hearst's early interest in organizing a fair in San Francisco.

15 Robert Cherny, "Burnham Plan 1905," FoundSF.org, http://www.foundsf.org/index.php?title=Burnham_Plan_1905 (accessed May 29, 2020). Many of the drawings for the Burnham plan were drafted by Julia Morgan's fellow École des Beaux-Arts alumnus and San Franciscan Arthur Brown, Jr.

16 Hearst Castle, http://hearstcastle.org/history-behind-hearst-castle/facts-and-stats/ (accessed May 29, 2020).

17 Prentice's study was first published in Great Britain in 1893; it went through numerous reprints in the United States into the pre-World War I years.

18 Austin Whittlesey, *The Minor Ecclesiastical, Domestic, and Garden Architecture of Southern Spain* (New York: Architectural Book Publishing Company, 1917), 149, and Kastner, 37.

19 Loe, p. 40. The date of acquisition was well after the guest houses were completed. Walker enjoyed a successful career of official commissions for commemorative and memorial works in Britain, and also in the US.

20 See Christopher Wood, *Olympian Dreamers: Victorian Classical Painters* (London: Constable, 1983), 106–130 for examples of paintings staging scenes from Greek and Roman antiquity.

21 Nickliss, xxvi–xxvii, 69–70.

22 Boutelle, 68 – 75.

23 Mark Anthony Wilson, *Julia Morgan: Architect of Beauty* (Layton, UT: Gibbs Smith, 2012), 78–84. This study has numerous color photographs of the exceptional columbarium which was built from 1926 to 1930.

24 The sculptures in the vestibule were by the Beaux-Arts trained American Frederick MacMonnies (1863–1937), *Bacchante*, 1914, and *Pygmalion and Galatea* by Jean-Léon Gérôme (1824–1904), a renowned French academician.

25 Whittlesey, *The Minor Ecclesiastical, Domestic, and Garden Architecture of Southern Spain.*

26 Kastner, 36–37, reproduces the Whittlesey photograph and an early drawing by Morgan, working up the single tower into the final facade of Casa Grande. She also cites Hearst's comment that Ronda was "composite," and "hardly in any style."

27 Kastner, 36.

28 *Arte y Decoración en España: Arquitectura – Arte – Decorativo*, 2 vols. (Barcelona: Casellas Moncanut, 1918). An American edition was produced in the same year by Architectural Book Publishing, New York, and this may have been Hearst's source. The cornice is illustrated in plates 39 and 40.

29 Johanna Kahn, "A Twentieth-Century Revival: The Italian Renaissance and the Architecture of Julia Morgan" (master's thesis, University of Virginia, Charlottesville, 2010), 42–51, treats Suppo and his work for and relationship with Morgan. He was trained at the École des Beaux-Arts in the early 1900s.

30 John Ruskin, *The Stones of Venice*, 3 vols., *The Foundations, The Sea-Stories, The Fall* (London: Smith, Elder & Co., 1851–1853). This work was enormously popular during the American Renaissance and available from British and American publishers.

31 James McMillan, "The American Academy in Rome," *The North American Review* 174 (May 1902), 627.

32 Gray Brechin, *Imperial San Francisco: Imperial Power, Earthly Ruin* (Berkeley: University of California Press, 1999), 220.

33 Quoted in Brechin, 237.

34 I am indebted to the information found in Nancy E. Loe's *Hearst Castle: An Interpretive History*, 26–28. In addition to the Roman pool at San Simeon, large swimming complexes were being built in Northern California at this time: Maybeck and Morgan's Beaux-Arts Phoebe Apperson Hearst Memorial Gymnasium for Women at UC Berkeley, completed in 1927; and the Richmond Plunge (a public pool) during the 1920s. These were preceded in the 1890s by San Francisco's enormous Sutro Baths.

35 Fuglie, 39–88.

36 Fuglie, Ibid.

37 Robert Venturi, *Complexity and Contradiction in Architecture,* 2nd ed. (New York: Museum of Modern Art, 1977). I recommend this specific edition for its supplemental commentary: foreword by Arthur

Drexler, an authority on Beaux-Arts architecture, and introduction by Yale art and architectural historian Vincent Scully.

38 The original was created by Kallikrates in 420 B.C.E. during the High Classical Period of Greek art—another golden age.

CHAPTER 6
THE CERAMIC TILES OF HEARST CASTLE: CALIFORNIA FAIENCE AND JULIA MORGAN

1 This essay is adapted from and an expansion upon Chapter 5, "Of Castles: Julia Morgan and William Randolph Hearst," in Kirby William Brown, *California Faience: Ceramics for Cottages and Castles* (San Francisco: Norfolk Press, 2015), 123–150.

2 Bruce Duncan. "Berkeley Firm Sought out for Hearst Tile Work," *Berkeley Daily Gazette*, May 17, 1958.

3 Austin Whittlesey, *The Minor Ecclesiastical, Domestic, and Garden Architecture of Southern Spain.* (New York: Architectural Book Publishing Company, 1917).

4 William Randolph Hearst, Jr., with Jack Casserly, *The Hearsts: Father and Son.* (Niwot, CO: Roberts Rinehart, 1991), 10.

5 The correspondence between William Randolph Hearst and Julia Morgan and their associates quoted in this chapter is held in the Julia Morgan Papers (JMP), Special Collections, California Polytechnic State University, San Luis Obispo, Kennedy Library.

6 Robert Forrer, *Geschichte der Europäischen fliesen-Keramik vom Mittelalter bis zum Jahre 1900.* (Strasbourg: Schlesier and Schweikhardt, 1901).

7 Edwin Atlee Barber, *Spanish Maiolica in the Collection of the Hispanic Society of America* (New York: The Hispanic Society of America, 1915). This illustrated text was one of many such late nineteenth-century and pre-1920 illustrated publications of historical European art, architecture, and decorative arts consulted by Morgan and Hearst for the design of Hearst Castle. See Victoria Kastner's chapter on the historical sources that Morgan assembled for her professional library.

8 Rexford Newcomb, *The Ceramics of Saracenic Syria, Turkey and Egypt* (Beaver Falls, PA: Associated Tile Manufacturers, 1926), 34.

9 Robin Farwell Gavin, Donna Pierce, and Alfonso Pleguezuelo, eds., *Cerámica y Cultura: The Story of Spanish and Mexican Mayólica* (Albuquerque: University of New Mexico Press, 2003), 214, fig. 9.5, illustrates the Mexican tile. For the escutcheon tile, see Barber, plate 4, XXXV, no. 85. The Latin inscription on this tile, "Ave Maria, Plena Gracia," is a traditional Roman Catholic intercessory prayer to the Virgin Mary.

10 David Wilson, "Hearst Castle Tile Survey," (unpublished manuscript, 2001). Hearst San Simeon State Historical Monument.

11 Anthony Ray, *Spanish Pottery 1245–1898 with a Catalogue of the Collection in the Victoria and Albert Museum* (London: V&A Publications, 2000), 357.

12 Like the belfry arches below the cupola, the interiors of these arches are flamboyantly embellished in Spanish Renaissance motifs, colored in deep blue, lemon yellow, and white glazes.

13 In 1982, Rob Kellenbeck of Deer Creek Pottery discovered a large collection of original California Faience molds. He created transfer molds from the originals and produced a line of tiles called the Julia Morgan Collection. Production of these copies ceased in 2009. Although Kellenbeck's tiles are unmarked, they are easily distinguished because of their notable thinness when compared to California Faience originals.

CHAPTER 7
PRESENCE OF THE PAST: JULIA MORGAN'S DESIGN INSPIRATIONS FOR SAN SIMEON

1 William Randolph Hearst's 165-room compound at San Simeon, which he formally christened La Cuesta Encantada (the Enchanted Hill), is listed in Julia Morgan's office records as Job 503, among an overall estimate of seven hundred buildings. Her additional designs for Hearst include Wyntoon (an almost equally large estate in the Northern California forest near Mount Shasta), as well as two unbuilt medieval museums, a sprawling hacienda for his near million-acre ranch in northern Mexico, and office buildings and residences located in San Francisco, Hillsborough, Los Angeles, Beverly Hills, Santa Monica, and Great Britain. Very few Beaux-Arts trained American architects equaled Julia Morgan in the variety and scale of their projects. Richard Morris Hunt (1827–1895), who entered the École in 1846 as its first American student, had an equivalent output—especially in grand mansions, including his designs for The Breakers and Marble House in Newport, Rhode Island, as well as the Biltmore Estate in Asheville, North Carolina. Stanford White (1853–1906) also created many magnificent houses, notably in Long Island, New York,; New York City; and Newport, Rhode Island.

2 Letters from Julia Morgan to Lucy and Pierre LeBrun, circa July 6, 1896 and May 30, 1898. Julia Morgan Papers (JMP), Special Collections, California Polytechnic State University, San Luis Obispo, Kennedy Library. Women painters and sculptors were finally admitted into the École des Beaux-Arts in 1897, the preparations for which gave Morgan and her California mentor Bernard Maybeck reason to hope that she, too, might be allowed to enter the architecture division of the École, where she was the sole female applicant. Prior to 1897, women artists in France formed their own art societies, including the Union des Femmes Peintres et Sculpteurs. See Laurence Madeleine, et al., *Women Artists in Paris 1850–1900* (New Haven: Yale University Press, 2017), 14–15, 18–19.

3 Jean Paul Carlhian and Margot M. Ellis, *Americans in Paris: Foundations of America's Architectural Gilded Age, Architecture Students at the École des Beaux-Arts, 1846–1946.* (New York: Rizzoli, 2014), 25, 230. Carlhian graduated from the École in 1948.

4 Carlhian and Ellis, 231. École alumnus Labatut (1899–1986) emigrated from France to the United States in 1928. Appointed to a position at Princeton, he is credited with developing the Princeton University School of

Architecture into one of the foremost graduate programs in the United States by the mid-twentieth century.

5   "Setting up an Architect's Library," *The American Architect and Building News* 42 (November 25, 1893): 100–103.

6   Julia Morgan to Lucy and Pierre LeBrun, April 29, 1897 and March 30, 1898, JMP; "Julia Morgan, Her Office, and a House," in Suzanne B. Riess, ed., *The Julia Morgan Architectural History Project*, vol. 2 (Berkeley: Regents of the University of California, 1976), 161, 194, 197.

7   Julia Morgan to Lucy and Pierre LeBrun, October 12, 1897, JMP. *Fragments d'Architecture Antique* by École professor Hector-Jean-Baptiste d'Espouy (1854–1929) became an essential visual reference for architects utilizing the Beaux-Arts method. It was published in 1905 as an eight-volume set. The first four volumes featured detailed drawings from Greece, Rome, and the Italian Renaissance; the succeeding four presented meticulously intricate compositions of ancient architecture, as monumentally reimagined by École graduates whose work earned them residencies at the Académie de France in Rome. Their original drawings were reproduced for *Fragments* in heliogravure, a photographic etching process. The publication was issued as a folio; its oversized pages were not bound. This allowed architects and their clients to use *Fragments* by selecting a number of images and moving them around for inspiration and comparison. This may account for compositions like plate 27 being produced as collages, combining classical capitals, columns, bases, moldings, mosaic floorings, sculpted masks, and acroteria (pediment ornaments) in a single image.

8   Parmelee Morgan to Julia Morgan, November 5, 1901, JMP.

9   Pierre LeBrun to Julia Morgan, May 9, 1906, JMP. The education-minded Lebrun was committed to developing resources for a new generation of American architects. He formed the Willard Collection of architectural casts in the Metropolitan Museum of Art, and later gave to the museum what came to be known as the Pierre L. LeBrun Library—described with

pride in his letter to Julia Morgan. Accumulating a vast fortune from shipping and railroads, the Vanderbilts were the quintessential Gilded Age family. Lebrun may be referring to Cornelius Vanderbilt II (1843–1899), who commissioned Richard Morris Hunt to design The Breakers, a neoclassical Beaux-Arts oceanfront mansion in Newport, Rhode Island.

10 Pierre LeBrun to Julia Morgan, May 9, 1906.

11 Pierre LeBrun to Julia Morgan, October 4, 1913, JMP.

12 "Julia Morgan, Her Office, and a House," 236.

13 Mark Alan Hewitt, *The Architect and the American Country House, 1890–1940.* (New Haven: Yale University Press, 1990), 40.

14 Hewitt, 40.

15 Austin Whittlesey, *The Minor Ecclesiastical, Domestic, and Garden Architecture of Southern Spain* (New York: Architectural Book Publishing Company, 1917). The preface was written by Whittlesey's mentor, Bertram Grosvenor Goodhue, fresh from his design triumph at the 1915 San Diego Panama-California Exposition. Goodhue's buildings were a reworking of the ornate Spanish Baroque and its colonial Mexican Churrigueresco derivations. While in Spain, Whittlesey photographed the single bell towered Church of Santa María la Mayor, Ronda, 15. It became the model for the twin belfries of San Simeon's Casa Grande.

16 Hearst's early discussion with Julia Morgan about San Simeon was overheard by her employee Walter Steilberg, who recalled Hearst walking into her office carrying R. Randall Phillips's 1920 survey, *The Book of Bungalows* (London: Country Life, 1920), and turning to the page marked "Jappo-Swiss bungalow," an odd phrase that made them both laugh. Hearst said, "I was browsing around in the bookstore, as I am wont to do, and I came across this book, and—though it isn't exactly what I had in mind, it will give you the general idea of what I'm thinking about for San Simeon." For a complete account, see "The Work

of Steilberg and Morgan," in *The Julia Morgan Architectural History Project*, vol. 1, ed. Suzanne B. Riess (Berkeley: Regents of the University of California, 1976), 56–57. The term "Jappo-Swiss bungalow" may refer to the Asian stylistic influences evident in elegant homes like the Gamble House in Pasadena, designed in 1908 by Charles Sumner Greene and Henry Mather Greene. Hearst also initially considered imitating the Spanish Colonial Revival style of Goodhue's buildings for San Diego's 1915 Panama-California Exposition. But he and Morgan soon decided they were "heavy and clumsy" in appearance, and turned instead to the Spanish Renaissance for inspiration. W. R. Hearst to Julia Morgan, December 19, 1919 and December 27, 1919, JMP.

17 Julia Morgan to W. R. Hearst, January 8, 1920, JMP. Morgan referred to "San Simeon and San Christophe." The fifteenth-century stone medallions that were mounted on both sides of Casa Grande's front entrance are, in fact, carvings depicting Saint Peter and Saint Paul.

18 Arthur Byne and Mildred Stapley, *Spanish Architecture of the Sixteenth Century: General View of the Plateresque and Herrera Styles* (New York and London: G. P. Putnam's Sons, 1917). A graduate of the University of Pennsylvania's architectural program when it taught Beaux-Arts theory and practice, Byne produced the drawings for *Spanish Architecture of the Sixteenth Century*. Mildred often published under her maiden name.

19 Julia Morgan to Arthur Byne and Mildred Stapley Byne, November 1, 1921, JMP. Arthur Byne and Mildred Stapley, *Decorated Wooden Ceilings in Spain: A Collection of Photographs and Measured Drawings with Descriptive Text* (New York and London: G. P. Putnam's Sons, 1920). Byne produced the drawings and watercolors for the folio.

20 Mildred Stapley Byne to Julia Morgan, October 1, 1921, JMP.

21 "Julia Morgan, Her Office, and a House," 201–202, 210–211. The Hearst-Morgan-Byne correspondence—housed as part of the Kennedy Librarys Julia Morgan collection—includes a detailed

account of Hearst's many purchases: not only ceilings and monasteries, but also gates, grilles, doors, choir stalls, balconies, staircases, and fountains, as well as a chronicle of the legal and logistical complexities inherent in acquiring such pieces. The two monasteries were subsequently sold, and portions were reassembled elsewhere. Sacramenia was rebuilt as the St. Bernard de Clairvaux church, located on the Dixie Highway in Miami, Florida; stones from Mountolive's Chapter House have been incorporated into Our Lady of New Clairvaux's monastery near Stockton, California.

22   At Morgan's death, an unfortunate fate befell her architectural library. Her relatives initially were unable to find her will and assumed she had died intestate. Her nephew, Morgan North, was appointed executor. He saw that Julia's library was extensive and the family had nowhere to store it, so he invited Bay Area booksellers to examine the collection. "We sold them to the highest bidder," North recalled. He later regretted his decision, especially after the family found Julia's will and learned that she had wanted her books to go to the University of California. The family tried to retrieve the collection, but by then portions had already been sold. For a further account, see "Julia Morgan, Her Office, and a House," 192–93. The consequence of this dispersal was that it cast to the winds Morgan's carefully assembled library of architectural references, without which it is difficult to fully comprehend her work.

23   Garrett Van Pelt, Jr. *Old Architecture of Southern Mexico*. (Cleveland: J. H. Jansen, 1926). A contemporary of Morgan, Van Pelt (1879—1972) was a Southern California architect with interests in Mexican culture.

SELECT BIBLIOGRAPHY

GENERAL INTEREST, ART, AND CULTURAL HISTORY

Allaback, Sarah. *The First American Women Architects.* Champaign: University of Illinois Press, 2008.

Barron, Stephanie, Sheri Bernstein and Ilene Susan Fort. *Made in California: Art, Image, and Identity, 1900–2000.* Los Angeles, Los Angeles County Museum of Art; Berkeley, University of California Press, 2000.

Brechin, Gray. *Imperial San Francisco: Urban Power, Earthly Ruin.* Berkeley and Los Angeles: University of California Press, 1999 and 2006. Separate chapters treat the Hearst and the de Young families.

Hewitt, Mark Alan. *The Architect and the American Country House, 1890–1940.* New Haven: Yale University Press, 1990.

Jones, Howard Mumford. *The Age of Energy: Varieties of American Experience, 1865–1915.* New York: Viking Press, 1971.

McMillian, Elizabeth. David Gebhard, Foreword. *Casa California: Spanish Style Houses from Santa Barbara to San Clemente.* New York: Rizzoli International Publications, 1996. McMillian surveys the historicist Spanish architecture that was built in Southern California while Hearst Castle was under construction.

Wilson, Richard Guy. *The American Renaissance: 1876–1917.* New York: The Brooklyn Museum, 1979. Since Wilson's seminal study, scholars have noted that architecture and art influenced by American Renaissance aesthetics persisted through the 1920s.

Woods, Mary N. *From Craft to Profession: The Practice of Architecture in Nineteenth-Century America.* Berkeley and Los Angeles: University of California Press, 1999. Woods delivers the first comprehensive study of the American architectural profession, encompassing architectural organizations, schools, workshops, offices, ateliers, drafting rooms, building yards, and construction sites. By the 1890s, the American architectural profession had expanded and consolidated in the East and Midwest, and along with the spread of Beaux-Arts training nationwide, set the stage for ambitious building programs in booming California.

Beaux-Arts Theory and American Architecture

Carlhian, Jean-Paul and Margot M. Ellis. *Americans in Paris: Foundations of America's Architectural Gilded Age. Architecture Students at the École des Beaux-Arts 1846–1946.* New York: Rizzoli International Publications, 2014.

Chafee, Richard. "The Teaching of Architecture at the École des Beaux-Arts." Arthur Drexler, ed. *The Architecture of the École des Beaux-Arts*, ed. Arthur Drexler. New York: The Museum of Modern Art, 1977.

Egbert, Donald Drew, David van Zanten, ed. *The Beaux-Arts Tradition in French Architecture: Illustrated by the Grands Prix de Rome.* Princeton, NJ: Princeton University Press, 1980.

Harbeson, John F. *The Study of Architectural Design, With Special Reference to the Program of the Beaux-Arts Institute of Design.* New York: W. W. Norton, 2008. This is a re-issue of the 1926 edition with a contemporary introduction by John Blatteau and Sandra L. Tatman. Architect Harbeson (1888–1986) trained American students during his long tenure at the University of Pennsylvania.

Ware, William R. *The American Vignola: A Guide to the Making of Classical Architecture.* New York: W. W. Norton, 1977, and New York: Dover Publications and Classical America, 1994. Ware (1832–1915) was among the earliest advocates of of the "Beaux-Arts method" in the United States. He taught architecture at MIT and Columbia University. *The American Vignola* was originally published in two installments: 1903 and 1905.

INTERNATIONAL EXPOSITIONS IN CALIFORNIA AND CHICAGO

Ackley, Laura A. *San Francisco's Jewel City: The Panama–Pacific International Exposition of 1915.* Berkeley, CA: Heyday Books, 2015.

Bokovoy, Matthew F. *The San Diego World's Fairs and Southwestern Memory, 1880-1940.* Alburquerque: University of New Mexico Press, 2005. See the Preface, Prologue, Part One, and the following four chapters on the 1915 exposition.

Bolotin, Norman and Christine Lang. *The World's Columbian Exposition: The Chicago World's Fair of 1893.* Champaign, IL: University of Illinois, 2002.

Benedict, Burton, ed. *The Anthropology of World's Fairs: San Francisco's Panama Pacific International Exposition of 1915.* Berkeley, CA, and London: Scolar Press, 1983.

Burg, David F. *Chicago's White City of 1893.* Lexington: University Press of Kentucky, 1976 and 2009.

Ganz, James A. ed. *Jewel City: Art from San Francisco's Panama-Pacific Exposition.* San Francisco: Fine Art Museums of San Francisco and University of California Press, 2015.

Starr, Kevin. *Americans and the California Dream: 1890–1915.* New York: Oxford University Press, 1973. See chapter IX, "The City Beautiful and the San Francisco Fair."

HEARST FAMILY AND HEARST CASTLE STUDIES

Brown, Kirby William. Chapter 5, "Of Castles: Julia Morgan and William Randolph Hearst." *California Faience: Ceramics for Cottages and Castles.* San Francisco: Norfolk Press, 2015.

Brown, Thomas. *The Illustrated History of Hearst Castle.* Rev. ed. Atascadero: Nouveaux Press, 2019.

Coffman, Taylor. *Building for Hearst and Morgan: Voices from the George Loorz Papers.* Berkeley, CA: Berkeley Hills Books, 2003.

Kastner, Victoria. *Hearst Castle: Biography of a Country House.* New York: Harry N. Abrams, 2000.

Loe, Nancy E. *Hearst Castle: An Interpretive History of W. R. Hearst's San Simeon Estate.* Santa Barbara, CA: Aramark, 1994.

Nasaw, David. *The Chief: The Life of William Randolph Hearst.* New York: Houghton Mifflin, 2000.

Nicklass, Alexandra M. *Phoebe Apperson Hearst: A Life of Power and Politics.* Lincoln: University of Nebraska Press, 2018.

Steele, Carole MacRobert. *Phoebe's House: A Hearst Legacy.* Eugene, OR: Luminare Press, 2016. A basic introduction to Hacienda del Pozo de Verona in Pleasanton, California. It was designed by A. C. Schweinfurth and Julia Morgan for Phoebe Apperson Hearst.

CALIFORNIA AND BAY AREA ARCHITECTURE AND ARCHITECTS

Draper, Joan. "The École des Beaux-Arts and the Architectural Profession in the United States: The Case of John Galen Howard." Spiro Kostoff, ed. *The Architect: Chapters in the History of the Profession.* New York: Oxford University Press, 1977 and 2000.

Longstreth, Richard. *On the Edge of the World: Four Architects in San Francisco at the Turn of the Century.* Cambridge, MA: The MIT Press, 1983, and 1998 (University of California Press). The architects studied are Bernard Maybeck, A. C. Schweinfurth, Ernest Coxhead, and Willis Polk.

McCoy, Esther, and Randall L. Makinson. *Five California Architects.* Los Angeles: Hennessey + Ingalls, 1975. In addition to the eclecticism of the Beaux-Arts trained Maybeck, FCA surveys the work of Irving Gill, Charles and Henry Greene, and R. M. Schindler who each developed different styles between 1895 and 1935.

Starr, Kevin. *Inventing the Dream: California Through the Progressive Era.* New York: Oxford University Press, 1985. See chapter 7, "Arthur Page Brown and the Dream of San Francisco."

Tilman, Jeffrey T. *Arthur Brown, Jr.: Progressive Classicist.* New York: W. W. Norton, 2006.

Woodbridge, Sally B. *Bernard Maybeck: Visionary Architect.* Rev. ed. New York: Abbeville, 1992.

Woodbridge, Sally B. *John Galen Howard and the University of California: The Design of a Great Public University Campus.* Berkeley and Los Angeles: University of California Press, 2002.

JULIA MORGAN

Boutelle, Sarah Holmes. *Julia Morgan, Architect.* Rev. ed. New York: Abbeville, 1995.

Kastner, Victoria. *Julia Morgan: An Intimate Biography of the Trailblazing Architect.* San Francisco: Chronicle Books, 2021.

Wilson, Mark Anthony. *Julia Morgan, Architect of Beauty.* Layton, UT: Gibbs Smith, 2007 and 2012.

Citations to historical texts (in English and French), personal correspondence, newspaper and magazine articles, as well as scholarly essays from journals, are found in the Notes section starting on page 280.

PHOTO CREDITS

PAGE 1: Julia Morgan Papers, Special Collections and Archives, California Polytechnic State University, San Luis Obispo

PAGE 2: Photo by Lawrence Anderson, Los Angeles, CA

PAGES 4-5: ©Kitleong/123RF.com

PAGES 6-7: Wikimedia Commons https://commons.wikimedia.org/w/index.php?title=File:Gilded_fountain_statue_-_Hearst_Castle_-_DSC06441.JPG&oldid=457234644

PAGES 10-11: Palace of Fine Arts, Bernard Maybeck Collection, Environmental Design Archives, UC Berkeley

PAGE 12: Image courtesy of Jeffrey Tilman from his collection

PAGE 13: Julia Morgan Papers, Special Collections and Archives, California Polytechnic State University, San Luis Obispo

PAGES 14-15: Wikimedia Commons https://commons.wikimedia.org/wiki/File:Atascadero_City_Hall_-_Atascadero,_CA_-_DSC05365.jpg

PAGE 16: Photograph courtesy of Tim Griffith, Tim Griffith Photographer FAIPP, San Francisco

PAGES 18-19: Sergei Lemtal/Shutterstock

PAGES 20-21: Postcard, Colortype, Cardinell-Vincent Co. Collection of Gordon Fuglie

PAGE 22: Courtesy of 1 Jones, San Francisco

PAGE 25: Boston Public Library

PAGES 26-27: California History Section, Picture Catalog, California State Library, Sacramento

PAGES 28-29: Courtesy of Jeffrey Tilman

PAGES 30-32: John Galen Howard Collection, UC: Hearst Competition, Environmental Design Archives, UC Berkeley

PAGE 33: Reproduced in Sally Byrne Woodbridge, *John Galen Howard and the University of California: The Design of a*

Great Public University Campus (Berkeley: University of California Press, 2002): 82. Photo Courtesy of Chuck Byrne

PAGE 34: Courtesy of William A. Porter

PAGE 35: Courtesy of Chuck Byrne

PAGE 36: Special Collections, F. W. Olin Library, Mills College

PAGE 37: Vintage Postcard, Edward H. Mitchell, Publisher, San Francisco, No. 1202. Courtesy of Gordon Fuglie

PAGE 39: Courtesy of the Phoebe A. Hearst Museum of Anthropology and the Regents of the University of California

PAGE 40: Image Courtesy Laura A. Ackley Collection

PAGES 42-43: Image courtesy of Jeffrey Tilman

PAGES 44-45: Joel Puliatti, Puliatti Photographic

PAGES 46-47: Sepia-toned postcard, Cardinell-Vincent Co., E99. Collection of Laguna Art Museum

PAGE 48 (ABOVE): Julia Morgan Papers, Special Collections and Archives, California Polytechnic State University, San Luis Obispo

PAGE 48 (BELOW): Image Courtesy Laura A. Ackley Collection

PAGE 51: San Diego History Center

PAGES 52-53: ©Malgorzata Litkowska/123RF.com

PAGES 54-55: ©Mikhail Pogosov/Shutterstock

PAGES 56-57: Series I. Personal Papers, 1884–1931. Student Drawings, ca. 1891–1892. John Galen Howard Collection, Environmental Design Archives, UC Berkeley

PAGES 58, 61-67, 69-70, 72, 75: Image courtesy of Jeffrey Tilman from his collection

PAGE 60: Graphic by Jeffrey Tilman

PAGES 76-78: Julia Morgan Papers, Special Collections and Archives, California Polytechnic State University, San Luis Obispo

PAGES 80-81: Collection of Karen McNeill

PAGES 82-83: Musée des Beaux-Arts, Tours. Image courtesy of Karen McNeill.

PAGES 85-87: Julia Morgan Papers, Special Collections and Archives, California Polytechnic State University, San Luis Obispo

PAGE 88: Albert Chevojon, Le Grand Palais en construction, photo de 1899, Archives Moisant-Savey, Domaine Public, Wikimedia Commons https://commons.wikipedia.org/wiki/File:Le_Grand_Palais_(en_construction).jpg

PAGES 90: Brown Digital Repository. Brown University Library. https://repository.library.brown.edu/studio/item/bdr:87112/

PAGE 93: Library of Congress, https://lccn.loc.gov/2001698514

PAGES 94-95: From the collection of Karen McNeill

PAGE 97: Dnipropetrovsk State Art Museum, Dnipropetrovsk, Ukraine/Bridgeman Images

PAGES 98-99: Environmental Design Archives, UC Berkeley. Published in *Les Medailles des Concours d'Architecture de l'École National des Beaux-Arts: 4e Année Scolaire 1901–1902* (Paris: A. Guérinet, 1902), PL 76

PAGES 100-104: Julia Morgan Papers, Special Collections and Archives, California Polytechnic State University, San Luis Obispo

PAGE 106-07: Julia Morgan Collection, 1893–1980, Environmental Design Archives, UC Berkeley

PAGE 108: Wikimedia Commons, Library of Congress, Prints & Photographs Division, PA-1389-1

PAGES 110-111: Boston Pictorial Archive, Boston Public Library

PAGE 112: Wikimedia Commons, Library of Congress, Prints & Photographs Division, NY, 31-NEYO, 120-1

PAGES 114-115: Wikimedia Commons, File:Paris-6-arrdt-Palais-des-Études-de-l'École-Nationale-Supérieure-des-Beaux-Arts-DSC0023.jpg

PAGES 116-117: Julia Morgan Papers, Special Collections and Archives, California Polytechnic State University, San Luis Obispo

PAGE 119: Superior Quality Postcard, P-25083. Collection of Gordon Fuglie

PAGE 120: Photograph by Alvis E. Hendley

PAGE 121: Florence Choral, https://www.florencechoral.com/venues/palaces/palazzo-medici-riccardi/

PAGE 122: *The Architect* vol. 12, no. 6 (December 1916): 350

PAGE 123: Photograph by Johanna M. Kahn

PAGE 124: *The Architect and Engineer of California* vol. 55, no. 2 (November 1918): 91

PAGE 125: Burckhardt, Jacob. *Geschichte der Renaissance in Italien.* Stuttgart: Verlag Von Ebner & Seubert, 1878, pg. 169

PAGES 126-27: Julia Morgan Collection, Environmental Design Archives, UC Berkeley

PAGE 128: Sailko/Wikimedia Commons; Santa maria della pace, chiostro del bramante 02.JPG 2011

PAGE 129: Joel Puliatti, Puliatti Photographic

PAGE 130: Julia Morgan Papers, Special Collections and Archives, California Polytechnic State University, San Luis Obispo

PAGE 131: *The Architect and Engineer of California* vol. 55, no. 2 (November 1918): 92

PAGES 132-133: Patrick Isogood 2019/ Shutterstock

PAGES 134-35: Julia Morgan Papers, Special Collections and Archives, California Polytechnic State University, San Luis Obispo

PAGES 136, 138-39: Photograph by Tavo Olmos

PAGE 140: mssLatta Skyfarming, Box 117, Folder 33, Item 1, The Huntington Library, San Marino, California

PAGES 142-43: Museum on Main, Pleasanton, California

PAGE 144: Museum on Main, Pleasanton, California

PAGE 145: Edward Trinkkeller Papers, Special Collections and Archives, California Polytechnic State University, San Luis Obispo

PAGES 146-47: Photography by Tavo Olmos

PAGES 148-49: Photography by Tavo Olmos

PAGES 150-51: Photography by Tavo Olmos

PAGE 152: ©sainaniritu/123RF.com

PAGE 155: ©Steven Heap/123RF.com

PAGE 156: Tichnor Brothers, Publisher, Boston Public Library, Tichnor Brothers collection #60142, Wikimedia Commons

PAGES 158-59: Julia Morgan Papers, Special Collections and Archives, California Polytechnic State University, San Luis Obispo

PAGE 160: Special Collections and Archives, California Polytechnic State University, San Luis Obispo, David F. Stevens, photographer

PAGES 162-63: Collection of Maryhill Museum of Art, Goldendale, WA

PAGE 164: *Yearbook of the Architectural League of New York and Catalogue of the Thirtieth Annual Exhibition* (New York: Owen Brainard, Secretary of the Architectural League of New York, 1915), 196

PAGES 166-67: Julia Morgan Papers, Special Collections and Archives, California Polytechnic State University, San Luis Obispo

PAGE 169: Kirby William Brown, reproduced in *California Faience: Ceramics for Cottages and Castles* (San Francisco: Norfolk Press, 2015), 125

PAGES 170-71: Kim Petersen/Alamy Stock Photo

PAGES 172-73: Wikimedia Commons https://commons.wikimedia.org/wiki/File:Lower_entrance,_Casa_del_Monte_-_Hearst_Castle_-_DSC06651.jpg

PAGES 174-75: mauritius images GmbH/ Alamy Stock Photo

PAGES 176-77: Iv-olga/Shutterstock

PAGES 178-79: ©mkopka/123RF.com

PAGE 180: len shigemoto/Shutterstock

PAGES 182-83: setchfield/Alamy Stock Photo

PAGES 184-85: Iv-olga/Shutterstock

PAGE 186: unitysphere/123RF.com

PAGE 187: Iv-olga/Shutterstock

PAGES 188-89: Abbie Warnock-Matthews/ Shutterstock

PAGE 190: Paul R. Jones/Shutterstock

PAGE 191: Manchester Art Gallery, Manchester, England

PAGES 192-93: Shutterstock

PAGES 194-95: Shutterstock

PAGES 196: Paul R. Jones/Shutterstock

PAGE 197: Wikimedia Commons https://commons.wikimedia.org/wiki/File:Closed_%26_Fractured_Rear_Vestibule_from_Unlikely_Scenario_of_Dante%27esq_and_Frigid_Temperatures_due_to_Zeus_%CF%9CAnax.jpg

PAGES 198-99: Peter Horree/Alamy Stock Photo

PAGE 201: ©americanspirit/123RF.com

PAGES 202-03: Joel Puliatti, Puliatti Photographic

PAGES 204-05: Sundry Photography/ Shutterstock

PAGES 206-07: jejim120/Alamy Stock Photo

PAGES 208-09: ©quasargal/123RF.com

PAGES 210-11: Wikimedia Commons https://commons.wikimedia.org/wiki/Category:Neptune_Pool_(Hearst_Castle)#/media/File:Neptune_Pool_(Hearst_Castle)_-_DSC06490.jpg)

PAGES 212-13: Wikimedia Commons https://commons.wikimedia.org/wiki/Category:Neptune_Pool_(Hearst_Castle)#/media/File:Hearst_castle_Neptune_pool.jpg)

PAGE 214: Photograph by Terry Hamburg, Courtesy of Cypress Lawn, Colma, California

PAGES 216-17: Julia Morgan Papers, Special Collections and Archives, California Polytechnic State University, San Luis Obispo

PAGES 218-24, 226-35, 238-43, 246-53, 255-63: Kirby William Brown, PhD, from his book *California Faience: Ceramics for Cottages and Castles* (San Francisco: Norfolk Press and Kirby William Brown, 2015)

PAGE 225: ©Brenda Kean/123RF.com

PAGES 236-37: melissamn/Shutterstock

PAGE 244: Courtesy of the History Center of San Luis Opispo County

PAGE 254 (LEFT): Julia Morgan Papers, Special Collections and Archives, California Polytechnic State University, San Luis Obispo

PAGES 264-65: Julia Morgan Papers, Special Collections and Archives, California Polytechnic State University, San Luis Obispo

PAGE 266: Special Collections and Archives, California Polytechnic State University, San Luis Obispo

PAGE 268: Courtesy of the History Center of San Luis Obispo County

PAGE 269: Julia Morgan Papers, Special Collections and Archives, California Polytechnic State University, San Luis Obispo

PAGE 270-71: 1000Photography/Shutterstock

PAGE 272, 275, 277: Julia Morgan Papers, Special Collections and Archives, California Polytechnic State University, San Luis Obispo

PAGE 278-79: ADLC/Shutterstock

INDEX

ACKNOWLEDGMENTS

In the ambitious endeavor of creating this comprehensive survey, I have immensely enjoyed collaborating with Jeffrey Tilman, Karen McNeill, Johanna Kahn, Elizabeth McMillian, Victoria Kastner, and the late Kirby Brown in producing this unprecedented study about Julia Morgan, her times, and California architecture as the state was coming into its own. At Rizzoli Electa, a division of Rizzoli International Publications, I am grateful to Charles Miers, publisher; Margaret Rennolds Chace, associate publisher; Andrea Danese, senior editor; Natalie Danford, copyeditor; and Sarah Gifford, book designer extraordinaire. Douglas Curran, senior editor, also worked on the project in its early stages of development.

I am indebted to the support of the Laguna Art Museum throughout this project's development, as well as its former executive director Malcolm Warner, and his successor Julie Perlin Lee. Emeritus Curator of Historical Art, Janet Blake, gave me valuable assistance, as did her colleagues Tim Campbell, collections manager and registrar, and Tim Schwab, director of design and installation. Valuable contributions from the museum also came from Bernadette Clemens, Dawn Minegar, and Joelle Warlick.

In addition, my research benefited from access to these archives: The Department of Special Collections and Archives, Robert E. Kennedy Library, California Polytechnic University, San Luis Obispo, and its director Jessica Holada and reference specialist Laura Sorvetti; the History Center of San Luis Obispo County, and its executive director Thomas Kessler and Kaylee Scoggins Herring, collections manager; the Environmental Design Archives, College of Environmental Design, University of California Berkeley, and its emeritus and acting curator Waverly B. Lowell and Katie Riddle, reference archivist; and the UCLA Arts Library and its preservationist Hannah Moshier (now at Stanford). All were gracious and most helpful hosts, and I thank them for their labors, collegiality, and professionalism.

Early in this project, I appreciated my conversations with Mary L. Levkoff, former museum director at Hearst Castle. On behalf of my project colleagues and all scholars of California art history, I hope *Julia Morgan, the Road to San Simeon* will encourage California State Parks to finally open up Hearst Castle to the research and the publication of its art, architecture, and remarkable history.

GORDON L. FUGLIE

First published in the United States of America in 2022 by
Rizzoli Electa, A Division of
Rizzoli International Publications, Inc.
300 Park Avenue South
New York, NY 10010
www.rizzoliusa.com

Preface, Introduction, and Chapter 5 by Gordon L. Fuglie
Additional essays by Jeffrey Tilman, Karen McNeill,
Johanna Kahn, Elizabeth McMillian, Kirby William Brown

Publisher: Charles Miers
Associate publisher: Margaret Rennolds Chace
Senior editor: Andrea Danese
Designer: Sarah Gifford
Copyeditor: Natalie Danford
Production manager: Kaija Markoe

Printed in China

2022 2023 2024 2025 / 10 9 8 7 6 5 4 3 2 1

ISBN: 978-0-8478-6955-8

Library of Congress Control Number: 2021952489

Visit us online:
Facebook.com/RizzoliNewYork
Twitter: @Rizzoli_Books
Instagram.com/RizzoliBooks
Pinterest.com/RizzoliBooks
Youtube.com/user/RizzoliNY
Issuu.com/Rizzoli

Page 1
Julia Morgan at
Notre-Dame de
Paris, 1901

Page 2
Lobby, Los Angeles
Examiner building,
1915

Pages 4–5
John Bakewell Jr.
and Arthur Brown
Jr. (Bakewell and
Brown), Pasadena
City Hall, Pasadena,
California,
1925-27

Page 6–7
Gustav Adolf
Daumiller, *The
Frog Prince,*
fountain sculpture
at Hearst Castle,
southwestern view
from guest house A